The New East End

The East End of London has always been the door to Great Britain: it was a haven for Huguenots fleeing persecution in France and Irish escaping from famine, and has welcomed Jewish refugees from Central and Eastern Europe. And in the second half of the twentieth century their descendants have been joined in Tower Hamlets by Bangladeshi immigrants – who now represent the largest concentration of a single minority group in any borough in Britain.

The place of newcomers did not play a large part in Michael Young and Peter Willmott's hugely influential sociological study of 1957, *Family and Kinship in East London*. But it became fundamental to the research when Young and new colleagues returned to the area four decades later. Here they present their findings, which explore the changes in the interim and the way that real Eastenders live now.

They analyze the roots of white hostility towards Bangladeshis, explain where blame lies for policy failures and question the 'culture of entitlement' brought about by the development of the welfare state. Hundreds of interviews give detailed insights in to ordinary lives and reveal the ways in which – after the arrival of a young white middle-class – tension exists along class as well as ethnic lines.

Bringing together the history of immigration and contemporary politics, family networks and the end of Empire, social policy and the impact of the Second World War, *The New East End* is a wide-ranging analysis of life in one of the most diverse places in Britain. And with many towns and cities home to large minority ethnic and poor white communities, its implications stretch beyond the

Geoff Dench is a Professor of Sociology at Middlesex University and a fellow at the Young Foundation. He trained as a social anthropologist at Cambridge and the LSE and his books include *Maltese in London* and *Minorities in the Open Society*, both originally published for the Institute of Community Studies. **Kate Gavron** is a fellow at the Young Foundation and a vice-chair of the Runnymede Trust. She studied the British Bangladeshi community in Tower Hamlets for her PhD at the LSE. The late **Michael Young** (Lord Young of Dartington) was co-author of *Family and Kinship in East London* and the founder of many great institutions, including the Consumers' Association and the Open University, and has been described by Harvard Business School as 'the most successful social entrepreneur in the world'.

The New East End

Kinship, Race and Conflict

Geoff Dench, Kate Gavron, Michael Young

P
PROFILE BOOKS

First published in Great Britain in 2006 by
Profile Books Ltd
3A Exmouth House
Pine Street
Exmouth Market
London EC1R 0JH
www.profilebooks.com

Typeset in Stone by MacGuru Ltd
info@macguru.org.uk

Printed and bound in Great Britain by
Clays, Bungay, Suffolk

A CIP catalogue record for this book is available from the British Library.

ISBN-10: 1 86197 928 2
ISBN-13: 978 1 86197 928 5

Contents

This book is dedicated with admiration and affection
to the memory of
Michael Young
1915–2002
and
Peter Willmott
1923–2000

Authors' Note and Acknowledgements

This is neither an academic text book nor a government report, but a fairly general study of how life has changed over the last half century in London's East End. Our sources were varied, and included a random sample of residents in the area, a number of other local contacts and officials, local and national newspapers and a wide range of books and journals. We have quoted extensively from interviews, because of our wish to explain opinions and attitudes in the words of those expressing them. In this way we have tried to retain the accessibility of the earlier Institute of Community Studies books and which Michael Young himself used in all his own work. We have quoted from local and national newspapers, as they are one of the main sources of information for our own interviewees and must be influential in forming – and reflecting – changing attitudes.

In the period covered by this book, the land which is now Bangladesh was part of India until the partition in 1947, then it was East Pakistan from 1947 until the 1971 war of liberation, which saw the birth of Bangladesh as an independent nation. The British Bangladeshi population has therefore described itself in several different ways during that last sixty years: Indian, Pakistani, Bengali, Bangladeshi. Nowadays the last two terms are used interchangeably. In addition, many use the term 'Sylheti' to describe themselves, this being the part of Bangladesh from which most British Bangladeshi families originate. However, because 'Bengali' strictly speaking also describes the Indians of West Bengal, for the sake of clarity we describe British Bangladeshis as 'Bangladeshi' throughout, even in some places where we are discussing events prior to 1971.

Our main thanks must go to all those local people who have talked to us over the years about the issues raised in this book. Above all, we are grateful to the 799 anonymous informants who contributed to the 1992 Institute of Community Studies survey of residents of the old borough of Bethnal Green. The names of all informants have been changed throughout and any resemblance to other individuals outside the survey pool is entirely accidental. Many of them, together with additional informants we found by other methods, gave a considerable amount of time to answering our questions, whether in the initial rather long survey questionnaire or in subsequent in-depth informal interviews and follow-up discussions. We are grateful to them all.

We have had a great deal of contact with local Bangladeshi residents, all of whom remain anonymous. This would have been much more difficult to do without the help of a grant from the Commission for Racial Equality, which enabled us to employ two

Bangladeshi researchers, Shariful Islam and Sultana Begum, who did a lot of interviewing both in English and Bengali. We are grateful for this and for all the additional help and information they gave us.

More generally, this project was supported by a generous grant from the Leverhulme Trust, and also in its early stages from the Nuffield Foundation.

A number of our colleagues at ICS worked on the original survey and also helped Michael Young at later stages of research. These include David Robins, James Smith, Sarah Benton, Tessa Dugmore, Lipika Afroze, Peter Willmott, Jim Ogg and Rushanara Ali. Sue Chisholm (who sadly died just before publication) was tireless in typing endless drafts of the manuscript and Wyn Tucker kept the show on the road.

The following have given us valuable help by reading and commenting on various drafts of the book: Tony Flower, Paul Barker, Vickie Macnair, James Cornford, Peter Hall, Sean Carey, Chris Phillipson, Tariq Modood, Michelynn Lafleche and Geoff Mulgan.

We are very grateful for the maps which were produced by Lucy Peck. The cover photograph is by Benedict Hilliard. Photographs in the text are by Benedict Hilliard, Marek Stacharski, Lucy Peck and the authors (see credits below).

Our grateful thanks go to the following at Profile Books: Andrew Franklin, Daniel Crewe, Penny Daniel and Ruth Killick, and to Trevor Horwood, copy-editor.

Finally, we know that we would not have been able to carry out this work, over the years, without the interest and support of Bob, Rush, Fan and Belinda.

Geoff Dench
Kate Gavron
Bethnal Green, 2005

Photograph credits

The borough of Tower Hamlets

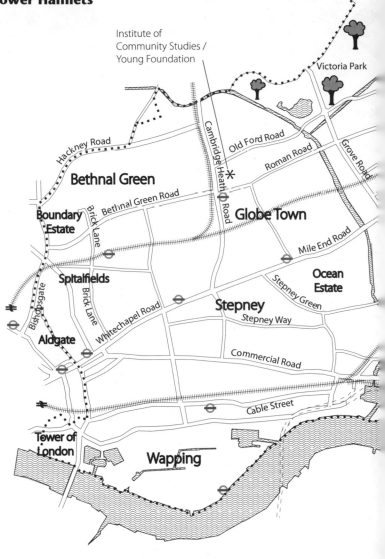

Institute of
Community Studies /
Young Foundation

Victoria Park

Hackney Road

Cambridge Heath Road

Old Ford Road

Roman Road

Grove Road

Bethnal Green

Bethnal Green Road

Globe Town

Boundary
Estate

Brick Lane

Mile End Road

Spitalfields

Ocean
Estate

Bishopsgate

Brick Lane

Whitechapel Road

Stepney Green

Stepney

Aldgate

Stepney Way

Commercial Road

Cable Street

Tower of
London

Wapping

...... Borough boundary
⊖ Underground station
⣿⣿⣿ Railway lines

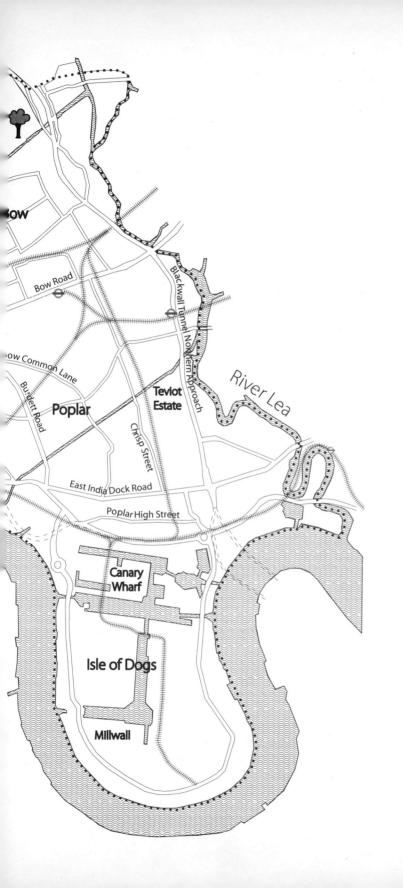

Introduction: Outside the City Gates

The East End of London is the backside of the City. As the City of London evolved over six centuries into the centre of global capitalism, the areas on its eastern fringe evolved too in symbiotic differentiation. At first they supplied food for the emerging urban community, then as the City concentrated increasingly on the pursuit of profit it gradually exported its less valuable and more polluting trades to just outside the City walls – where the benefits accrued without offending the dignity of the City itself. Leather trades, clothing, furniture, shipping and distribution were expelled in turn, and established to the east. As the City became wealthier and more important, the contrast between it and the East End grew sharper. Together they became the hub of the British imperial trading system. In the heyday of this system, until it was disrupted by the Second World War, the City bought and sold commodities and controlled finance, while the docks and warehouses of east London moved the actual goods around.

By the middle of the nineteenth century this unequal partnership had created in east London the largest impoverished urban enclave in the world, 'abandoned entirely', as Peter Sanders put it, 'to the working class'.[1] Confined to low-status occupations, and virtually cut off from the rest of the country, the East End was almost wholly dependent on the London docks and on work and income from the City. This included charity dispensed by numerous City foundations – which itself ensured that the area was a magnet for destitute people from elsewhere in Britain and, via the docks, other countries too. As social reformers from the 1850s on started to grapple with issues of poverty, the East End developed a new role as breeding ground for social policy ideas and visionary thinking. Much of the background work for the post-war welfare state grew from analysis of East End conditions, and the Labour government which put this into legislation was firmly rooted in the locality.

It was in this context that Michael Young set up the Institute of Community Studies (ICS) in Bethnal Green in 1954. As head of Labour Party research, Michael had written (with Herbert Morrison) the 1945 Labour election manifesto, 'Let us Face the Future', on which much of the welfare state was based. But he was unhappy with the centralism of the Attlee administration and wanted to see what lessons might be learned from the local family and community life which had enabled East Enders to survive without the welfare state. His founding ICS study (with Peter Willmott), *Family and Kinship in East London*, published in 1957, drew attention to the central part played in local working-class life by extended families, and cautioned against state policies which might damage them.

This new book – the final offering from the Institute of Community Studies, and the first report from its successor the Young Foundation – is based on the last piece of research directed by Michael. It originated as a sequel to *Family and Kinship*, with the commissioning in 1992 of a new survey in Bethnal Green to see how the area had changed. Although Michael did not survive to see the final draft he was fully involved in it up to the day of his death in January 2002, and contributed fully to earlier drafts.

This second study, begun in 1992 and continuing throughout the 1990s and into the new century, has ended up with a different focus from the 1957 book. The questionnaire used in the 1992 survey replicated that used in 1953 and concentrated on family life and neighbourhood. However, a few open questions were added regarding perceived change in the locality, and it was the answers to these that alerted us to the importance of community relations as matters occupying people's attention and concern. The problem of ethnic conflict could not be avoided. Dealing with it, however, entailed broadening the research project to include the rest of Tower Hamlets. The heartland of the largest new community of the post-war population, the Bangladeshis, is in Spitalfields, straddling the boundary between the former boroughs of Stepney and Bethnal Green, and the area of communal conflict coincided with the present borough of Tower Hamlets. To reflect this, our enquiries during the decade following the initial survey in Bethnal Green were conducted in this larger arena.

There had been some conflict between white and Bangladeshi* residents in the borough for the previous twenty years and it was an issue which badly needed proper attention. Most local researchers either studiously avoided it or simply put everything down to white racism. We felt that dismissing white behaviour as merely irrational constituted a failure of analysis. As one of us has described, at the time Michael himself was both attracted to the strong family support structures he saw in the East End's Bangladeshi community and defensive of the local white working class, who were vilified nationally as intolerant racists following the election of a BNP councillor in Tower Hamlets in 1993.[2] By moving community relations to the centre of our study, we committed ourselves to probing very carefully – and in the event extensively – in order to discover the roots of hostility. Anything less than that did not seem to be worth doing. As we analysed the results of our research and considered how to report it, we realised that it was important, where possible, to balance the views of each group against the other. In this book we have some chapters looking almost exclusively at the lives of one or other community, but in the book as a whole we have tried to give the people of each community an equal voice.

A basic reason to focus on ethnic division and competition is that this is, of course, a recurring feature of East End life. East London has seen the arrival of many immigrant groups and has been witness to many previous conflicts. *Family and Kinship* ignored this because it was, unusually, not relevant in the 1950s. But the situation had changed

---

*For the use of 'Bangladeshi' as a description see Authors' Note, page ix.

entirely by the 1990s, and this offered us an important opportunity. The Bangladeshis represent the first major settlement of a new minority ethnic community in the East End for the best part of a century, and certainly since the creation of the welfare state. Their arrival gives us a chance to explore whether the process of incorporation of new-comers has altered and, if so, why.

Although these questions are where our investigation really began, simple compari-son with earlier arrivals was ruled out by the sheer scale and complexity of recent local change, which meant that key influences on migration (and their consequences) would be hard to untangle. The pace of change in the area had always been slow. The docks suffered ruinous bomb damage during the war, but the subsequent decision to move all dock activity downstream to Tilbury guaranteed several more decades of stagnation and further economic decline before the City, fired up by Margaret Thatcher's policy of deregulation, expanded vigorously into the void. Hence Docklands, and much new building lining the Thames. Grimy warehouses have been refurbished as flats and offices or replaced by shiny skyscrapers. The average income of workers in Tower Hamlets (though not yet of its residents) has soared from lowest to second highest po-sition among London boroughs, behind only the City itself. In the last couple of decades the character of the area has been thoroughly updated and diversified.

But while this massive economic decline and regeneration clearly had an effect on the process of migration and settlement, it did not seem to us to provide a sufficient explanation for the pattern of relationships emerging in our study between the two main communities. The economy hardly figured in the accounts that people living in the area – whether white or Bangladeshi, and in Bethnal Green or Tower Hamlets more generally – gave us about their lives and how they interacted with other local people. We followed up the initial survey with several waves of close personal interviewing – using the traditional ICS technique of attempting to understand things through the eyes of people involved in them.

We therefore carried out extensive interviewing among both white and Bangla-deshi residents, some newly arrived in Tower Hamlets (in both categories) and some (again in both categories) whose families had been resident in the area for genera-tions, and in the case of a few white residents for many generations. We built up a picture of the Bangladeshi settlement and of their present-day family life, set out here in chapters 2, 3 and 4. Bangladeshi families today have lives that evoke, in some ways, those of the post-war Bethnal Greeners described by Young and Willmott. As argued later, this is principally due to the importance in many, if not most, Bangla-deshi families of the practical and emotional support given within extended families, including members still living in Bangladesh. In many respects these families still have something which binds them together, exactly as pre-war Bethnal Green fami-lies were bound together by economic insecurity, ill-health and mutual dependence. The safety net of the welfare state is not yet thought of as reliable enough to replace the supports of kinship, and we argue later in chapter 5 that it is to the detriment of some white families that, in their case, kinship support has been largely superseded by impersonal welfare provisions.

We found that the personal accounts pointed towards effective sources of change rooted more in politics and the *moral* economy than in material circumstances, despite almost everybody's considerable material prosperity by 1950s standards. The reason for this seemed to lie in the forms of modern citizenship created by the post-war welfare state. In the past, conflict between existing residents and newcomers had been framed by competition in the economy. Competition for work, discussed in chapter 6, is still a factor, but increasingly we felt that this had been replaced by competition between communities for access to welfare support and public services, including education and, crucially, housing, dealt with respectively in chapters 7 and 8.

This interpretation certainly fitted the great majority of responses elicited in the 1992 survey. Among white respondents, the open questions about change in the area resulted in an overwhelmingly bitter cataloguing of complaints about Bangladeshis draining the welfare state in one way or another, as we describe in chapter 9. But this did not seem wholly attributable to simple competition, and there were aspects of these complaints which seemed to us to require additional explanation. This is when we began to realise the importance of the Second World War. Many white respondents of all ages linked their complaints about draining the welfare state with remarks to the effect that Bangladeshis had not been here during the war, in a way that suggested this reduced their entitlement. The modern welfare state was consolidated at the end of the war, and is commonly seen as being an outcome of it – and even a reward to ordinary citizens for the efforts which they made during it. As explained in chapter 10, a search through local historical records revealed special circumstances which made this view particularly telling in the East End.

Most people in Britain are aware of the importance of London's docks in the war, and the massive bomb damage inflicted on the East End as a result. Less well known outside the area is the extent to which politicians trod the local streets during the war, drumming up morale by promising that, after victory, the new welfare state would rebuild the devastated neighbourhood for its heroic community. After the war had been won some gestures were made in this direction and the results were analysed in *Family and Kinship in East London*. In fact, as that book showed, those changes tended to involve not so much rebuilding existing communities as dispersing people outside Inner London. Back in Tower Hamlets, little beyond grand planning was achieved in the first couple of decades other than the building of some of the dismal blocks described in this book. Not until the 1980s was there more extensive reconstruction, and then much of the new housing was privately built and sold to the middle classes who were newly arriving in the area. Some of the better new social housing was also allocated to the most needy Bangladeshi families, although less than local opinion suggested. However, it is understandable that many old Bethnal Greeners felt cheated out of the promised rewards for war service, and unsurprising that some blamed migration for it.

This explained not only the frequent references to the war, but also another aspect of white complaints against Bangladeshis: the dismay at, or incomprehension of, the bases on which benefits were granted. There was clearly a lack of sympathy with current welfare principles. When we delved into this we were able to see how white feelings of betrayal had also been aggravated by the way in which the administration of welfare has developed since the 1950s. The welfare state provisions put in place at the end of the war were designed to back up conventional family units. They could be regarded as an extension of working-class mutual insurance, following the principle that not all faced problems at the same time. But from the mid-1960s onwards the administration of supports and benefits became increasingly freed from reciprocity and oriented instead towards the needs of individuals.

This shift of principles has arguably weakened the fabric of working-class communities, and may be a factor in the decline of trust in the state. More to the point, though, the new principle appears to serve the interests of recent migrants as effectively as those of longer-standing residents. Indeed, as recent migrants to Bethnal Green have tended to be more needy, their needs have taken priority. We argue in chapter 11 that the indigenous working class understand this all too easily, and this feeds their hostility towards migrants. They see the(ir) welfare state as having been adapted to suit migrants and morally undermined in the process.

When looking again at our original survey data, we identified another significant finding which took us right back to the importance of family and kinship networks in people's everyday lives. It has been suggested that having strong family and friendship networks is likely to correlate with a tolerant and anti-racist attitude to life. However, our own findings were that, on the contrary, the more bound into a family network our white informants were, the more hostile their attitudes were likely to be towards the Bangladeshi community. The likely reasons for this are discussed in greater detail in chapter 9, but it seems to us that this is a finding which could helpfully be adapted to study similar situations in other parts of the country.

This brings us to the final element of the white complaints which required additional attention: the suggestion put to us frequently that 'middle-class do-gooders' are stoking the flames of communal tension by favouring newcomers against 'local' people – a charge which is now, significantly, made also by earlier waves of post-war immigrants as well as longer-established groups of 'indigenous' whites. At the time of the 1950s study there was some class tension in Britain, as the classlessness engendered by the war had by then waned. However, working-class people were still positive towards the state and servants of the state, whom they saw as on their side. This no longer seems to be the case; again this seems partly traceable to the arrival of immigrants from the late 1950s onwards. Since then the middle classes have been regarded as favouring newcomers, changing the welfare state to suit their needs and then labelling as racist any members of the white working class who do not accept the new regime. One of our informants referred to such people as 'those big-hearted ones who've got their own big houses and make these rules'. The gulf between middle and working classes has deepened and widened as a result, and the movement of many working-class people over this period into the expanding middle class may have aggravated rather than mollified the feelings of those left behind. This is all germane to the vexed issue of declining social mobility out of the white working class.

Putting all this together, and stepping back from the study to take a broader view, what seems to have happened in post-war Britain is that the compact between classes which made the late 1940s and early 1950s a golden age of aspirations and expectations has been undermined by the consequences of the unravelling of Britain's imperial history. When the welfare state was codified at the end of the Second World War, metropolitan Britain was still sealed off politically from the rest of the empire. So the extension of social democracy was a limited exercise, and gave rights to ordinary British people which they felt both to have been earned and to be valuable. With the subsequent dismantling of the empire, and the granting of residence and citizenship rights in Britain to a tiny proportion of the millions of former imperial subjects, this national legacy became shared out among a much larger group. In the eyes of some, the original post-war compact has been devalued as a result.

Immigration of these new British citizens into the metropolis has subsequently created a situation in which the nation has become divided vertically into culturally distinctive segments, as well as horizontally between these segments and a new ruling class. The potential for tension is high. Descendants of members of former dependencies now compete for opportunities and national welfare resources on equal terms with white Britons who see themselves as indigenous to the area; needy pensioners find themselves having to share what they had considered to be their reward for heroic effort with newcomers who are even *more* needy – and who do not appear to them to have earned their rights.

These ethnic divisions increase the moral authority of the British administrative elite, as policy resulting from this new class system revolves partly around finding ways to contain conflict between its constituent parts. Most middle-class liberals have been drawn by their sympathy for poor migrants into supporting them – as the long-term underdogs in day-to-day disputes – against white working-class hostility. They have promoted a swathe of political measures and institutions which consolidate the rights of minorities while multiplying the sanctions against indigenous whites who object to this. Meanwhile, working-class whites who refuse to accept the new social order feel progressively disenfranchised. This analysis would no doubt be disputed by black and Asian groups, who see little evidence in their own day-to-day lives that state officials – or anybody else – discriminate in their favour. This only underlines the complexity of the situation. However, this contemporary class structure, which still awaits proper analysis, is surely now dominated by a *political* class, drawing power from its operation of state services and mobilised around the ideology of cultural tolerance and social and economic inclusiveness, and with a mission to integrate subordinate, culturally specific communities into a common national system. The vital challenge is to do this without neglecting the concerns of poor white groups, for there is a risk of failure unless their plight is addressed along with those of marginalised minority ethnic and poor migrant groups.

The events that have taken place in Tower Hamlets over the last few decades suggest that such a balancing act may not be sustainable in the long run, certainly if carried out in the present manner. There is a danger in accusing long-term residents of Britain of racism or xenophobia when they object to newcomers' speedy access to national resources. This strategy seems to us not only to risk deepening existing divisions between cultural communities but to aggravate class antagonism too. The resulting conflicts in Tower Hamlets have been contained only because central government has stepped in with decisive support for the Bangladeshis. If such strife were to occur on a national scale, and to involve many cities containing large minority ethnic and poor white communities, then the centre would not be able to act so unambiguously in providing minorities with support. Civil disturbances in northern cities a few years ago, the growing numbers of candidates from extreme right-wing parties standing in local and general elections, divisions over the Iraq war and Middle Eastern policy, the emergence of some political extremists in Muslim communities, plus growing antagonism nationally to asylum seekers and refugees, all indicate that this point may yet arrive. In order to avert this it is important to appreciate that discontent is not based on irrational sentiments alone – although that is certainly an element in some people's thinking – but also on feelings of grievance which no political system can afford to ignore.

We suggest in our conclusion that the 'culture of entitlement' in contemporary Britain may itself need to be reconsidered if further breakdown of order is to be avoided. Not only does it appear to be eroding the legitimacy of the welfare state, but it may be working against the integrity of society more generally. All societies have to deal with conflict and competition, but some ways of doing this are more constructive, and better at pulling minorities into the system, than others. When competition is channelled into serving national goals, and putting something *into* the community, then its effect is likely to be increased solidarity, as happened during the war. Michael Young himself said in an interview with the historian Peter Hennessy towards the end of his life that, 'There had been an extraordinary object lesson in the power of fraternity in the war, and when the war was over it was as though that experience could be wiped out.'[3] When competition revolves heavily around drawing on welfare support it prompts a contest to take something *out* of the system. This may undermine the sense of shared endeavour which any nation needs, and which a culturally diverse nation needs more than most.

The present Labour government has rightly declared a commitment to promoting social cohesion. But some of this has meant that by – understandably – attacking racism even more vigorously, there is a failure to carry some parts of the white community with them, thus perpetuating the cycle of division and resentment. So, for example, supporting equal-opportunities schemes to address racial discrimination and helping newcomers such as refugees to access their rights more easily, however ungenerous these rights may seem, is not enough. It must go hand-in-hand with addressing the exclusion, poverty, marginalisation and hostility faced by poor white communities.

The lesson we would draw from our study of the roots of conflict in the East End is that in some places an approach concentrating on minorities alone is adding fuel to the fire. People like our white informants have a perception that nothing is being done for them and plenty – too much, even – is being done for others. It would be a misreading of the argument to believe that in giving a voice to the feeling of dissatisfaction and resentment among some white Londoners we are presenting a justification of racist and retrograde ideas, as some might allege. Hostility to people perceived as threatening, whether as sources of competition over scarce goods or simply as incomprehensible strangers, must be better understood before being written off as wicked or stupid. Depending on circumstances it may be either or both, but we should surely try to find out exactly what is going on in people's minds, and why.

Tower Hamlets has its own unique place in the history of immigration. Most British cities with large minority ethnic communities today were not centres for international migration until the 1950s or 1960s. In that sense they are different from the East End of London which, like only a few other places such as Liverpool and Bristol, has been receiving wave after wave of new immigrants for centuries. If the East End does have anything from its own past experience which it can teach the rest of the country, it is surely this: the traditional processes of immigrant settlement which East Enders have developed over the centuries may be a better way in the longer run to produce a strong, secure bonding between communities. A willingness to learn from history – and from people at its sharp end – might help to generate a more stable society now.

One of the last Jewish shops remaining on Brick Lane in the early 1990s

Chapter 1

Old Bethnal Green and New

Our story revolves around two communities in one small part of London, whom Matthew Arnold might prophetically have described a century earlier as

> Wandering between two worlds, one dead,
> The other powerless to be born.
>
> ('Stanzas from the Grande Chartreuse', l. 85)

But not quite: one of these communities lives on, fitfully, in the memories of its older members; the other has already burst into vigorous life, although – rather like the adolescents who comprise so much of its membership – it remains uncertain of its identity, its sense of cultural belonging, its future in a land and a city it sees as half-alien, half its own. The first community is the historic working class of east London, which Michael Young and Peter Willmott memorably described in their 1957 book *Family and Kinship in East London*. The second is the Bangladeshi community that has grown up alongside it during the last thirty years.

The Lost World of the 1950s

Family and Kinship was the first major publication from the Institute of Community Studies (ICS), which Michael Young had founded in Bethnal Green three years earlier. Unusually for a work of sociology, it became an instant bestseller and remains one of the true classics in its field.

But *Family and Kinship* was also criticised at the time of its publication, and more fundamentally later on by sociologists such as Jennifer Platt, for presenting a distorted and sentimentalised view of East End working-class life in the 1950s. Such comments had a powerful influence on subsequent research at ICS, although in retrospect it seems clear that much of this criticism was unjust. In particular it failed to acknowledge that the authors and their subjects took for granted the harshness of life in a way that people from more comfortable backgrounds elsewhere perhaps could not appreciate. Traditional cockney chirpiness, which the study echoed, was no mere facile optimism but an awareness that the power of communal life could overcome adversity. It was surely the portrayal of this collective strength which endeared Bethnal Greeners to Young and Willmott's readers.

Many of the book's detractors were advocates of central state support who felt that family life stood in the way of an efficient welfare system, yet by the beginning of the twenty-first century the heavy hand of the state appeared to have to dismantled much of the old community spirit without replacing it with a viable alternative system of personalised support.

The world described in *Family and Kinship* was one of a richly shared communal life, through families into streets and neighbourhoods. In particular, there were strong bonds between mothers and daughters. Mothers helped to raise grandchildren when their daughters became mothers themselves, and this support underpinned extended three-generation families. The family reciprocity which this entailed was at the heart of local community life.

> And so it goes on – the daughter's labours are in a hundred little ways shared with the older woman whose days of child-bearing (but not of child-rearing) are over. When the time comes for the mother to need assistance, the daughter reciprocates, as reported elsewhere, by returning the care which she has herself received. (Young and Willmott, 1957, p. 39)

Married daughters seldom lived more than a few doors from their mothers, both because they depended on this system of support and because they obtained housing through an informal system of allocation – first through rent collectors for private land-lords, later through the council – which worked on close shared knowledge of families, their social traits and above all their reliability.

Sons left school early and followed their fathers into factory or warehouse jobs, al-located in the same informal way: your father had a word with the governor, and if the governor knew your father to be a good and reliable workman then he could rely on you too. As a result, small neighbourhoods showed a quite extraordinarily close and complex social organisation based on ties of kinship. But as the study stressed – and here was its deeply political conclusion – all this could easily be blown away. It was already beginning to be undermined by ill-judged policies of rehousing and dispersal to distant estates on the edge of London, or to the new towns that were being built beyond the capital's green belt. Better by far, was the message, to appreciate the value of local community life and rehouse Bethnal Greeners where they had always been, even at the expense of higher densities and more crowded conditions.

This message is still valid today. But it had a real freshness in the now-vanished world of the 1950s, within which the research was conducted and the book was written. This was a time of momentous transition – although the processes of change were only just beginning to make themselves felt. The new queen had been crowned four years earlier, amid a huge outpouring of patriotic emotion. The British Empire was still more or less intact, with the conspicuous exception of India, which had achieved independence in 1947. Class divisions were still entrenched, particularly in London: a huge social gap separated the upper-class West End and the working-class East End, which seldom met. This was partly because they did different jobs: east London was still the home of the docks – in the course of being overtaken by Rotterdam as the largest port in the world – and of traditional industries such as clothing and furniture. Employees earned a weekly wage packet; bank accounts were unknown to them, credit cards unimaginable. They could be hired and fired at the whim of the boss; in the docks, they were still employed by the day. The shadow of the workhouse may have been lifted at the end of the 1920s, and the National Health Service was a recent reality (although most local hospitals were still barely converted workhouses), but this remained a deeply hierarchical, conformist society, where people knew their place and where the governing class established what was fit for the lower orders. When the publishers of *Lady Chatterley's Lover* were prosecuted for obscenity in 1960, counsel Mervyn Griffith-Jones famously asked the jury whether they thought it was fit to be read by their wives and servants.

However, that prosecution failed, and indeed for some years previously there had been intimations of change. In May 1956 John Osborne's *Look Back in Anger* had opened at the Royal Court; its central character Jimmy Porter became the first Angry Young Man. During the summer, Rock and Roll riots erupted in British cities. In October of that year, huge demonstrations against government action in Suez blocked Whitehall. Soon, Mods and Rockers would begin to engage in ritual fights on the beaches of seaside resorts popular with East Enders. Both styles were largely creations of the indigenous East End tailoring industry, now for the first time catering for a newly affluent working-class market. At the general election of 1959, Harold Macmillan could be memorably misquoted as telling the country 'you've never had it so good'.

Family and Kinship anticipated some of these changes, and can be interpreted as a kind of paean for a world that was just then beginning to disappear. It revealed the value of what it had found, and made a Canute-like attempt to stop the processes of social and economic transformation. It certainly did not succeed in doing so. In the four decades between the late 1950s and the 1990s, the real income of the average British family quadrupled. Housing conditions were transformed beyond recognition: facilities like bathrooms and central heating and telephones, which would have been regarded as upper-class luxuries by the average Bethnal Green household in 1957, became almost universal. Technological change meant that video recorders and personal computers, unknown in the 1950s, were common articles in working-class homes. Hard-earned weeks in Clacton or Broadstairs, or picking hops in the Kent fields, were replaced by extended holidays in exotic tropical locations. Tens of thousands of East Enders left the terraced ancestral streets and their rich communal life for the isolation of a new home in an Essex cul-de-sac. The local extended family was replaced by the welfare-state-friendly nuclear family – a change recorded by Young and Willmott in their 1973 survey *The Symmetrical Family* – and then by a progressive unravelling of household structures into a complex skein of single-person households, consensual unions, gay partnerships, step-families and a thousand and one other varieties. Lifestyle increasingly became leitmotif. Living patterns, like consumer durables, could be acquired and traded in at will.

By the early 1990s it was time to find out what exactly had happened to East End life in those forty years – and, in particular, to discover how far the generations that followed our 1957 respondents were living in new ways, and even in new places, and how their now-ageing parents had responded to the change. After the 1950s, the interests of ICS had spread out to many other places and issues, and increasingly to strategies of social action rather than to social research. This had been productive, but by the early 1990s it was clear that much of what was new and challenging in Britain was happening right under our own feet. We resolved to embark on a new stage of local enquiry, to renew our understanding of it. We would go back into the east London streets, retracing the footsteps of Young and Willmott, to find out what had happened in the intervening years.

So we started the 'restudy' survey. This took the original questionnaire from *Family and Kinship* and added questions about how respondents felt that Bethnal Green had changed, and about contacts with relatives living outside respondents' own households. This new survey was carried out for us in the autumn of 1992 and analysed in 1993 by BJM Ltd, a social and market research organisation. A random sample of adults living in wards corresponding to the old borough of Bethnal Green, which became part of Tower Hamlets following boundary changes in the early 1960s, was selected from the electoral register. Full interviews were completed for 799 residents, aged 18 up to 94, who gave information not just for individual respondents but for all members of their households as well. This provided data on 2,565 people living in the 799 households, as well as on relatives of respondents living outside their households. Altogether data on 8,370 people, including the 799 respondents, was collected and analysed.

What we found was that Bethnal Green had changed so profoundly that it was hardly any longer the same place. The area had been transformed beyond recognition, and in ways which could not have been predicted from that first study. Its older members had died but, more importantly, others had moved away – to outer east London, to neighbouring Essex, or even farther afield – while some of its children had joined the middle class in other parts of London. Ironically, the process that one of us foretold in a book written just after *Family and Kinship* was published, *The Rise of the Meritocracy*, proved only too prescient for many East Enders. Some had been adopted by the new meritocratic class; most were rejected by it. Either way, as we show later, the old community was no more. Our research problem, we soon saw, would be not to identify the changes that had taken place, but to find any continuity at all.

The East End as Port of Entry: Jews and Bangladeshis

Simultaneously, we found that entirely different processes had generated a new community in the area, the existence of which Young and Willmott did not recognise because in 1957 it hardly existed. This was the Bangladeshi community. From the late 1950s and early 1960s it began to occupy the dense streets of Spitalfields on the extreme western borders of Bethnal Green. By 1991 it constituted almost a quarter of the population of Tower Hamlets, and its children made up nearly half of school enrolments; by 2001 these figures had risen to a third and three-fifths respectively. This settlement naturally had profound implications for the character of the whole locality.

It also reflected an aspect of East End life which – although not covered in the ICS work of the 1950s – was thoroughly traditional to the area: that is its role as a point of entry for minority groups into British society. Over the centuries east London has contained some of the highest proportions of immigrants in Britain. The cycles of conflict, competition and eventual accommodation between such groups and local residents, who include, of course, many descendants of previous waves of immigrants, have been a recurring feature of local history. This is commonly portrayed as a pageant of incorporation of exotic newcomers into British national life, as was vigorously and colourfully marked in the millennium celebration by an exhibition of tapestries, produced in local schools and community groups and representing the different groups which have lived in the area.*

Spitalfields had been London's main Huguenot district and later a Jewish neighbourhood. Close to the port, it and neighbouring Whitechapel were first stops for many aspiring immigrants. In the sixteenth and seventeenth centuries Bethnal Green was a haven and staging-post for Huguenot refugees escaping from persecution in France, who made an enormous contribution to the architectural, economic and demographic history of east London, and continued to bring in newcomers until comparatively recently.† During the nineteenth century, large numbers of families found the East End sweatshops – in spite of popular anti-Catholicism – preferable to poverty and famine in Ireland. To this day a large proportion of the white people in Bethnal Green have Irish surnames.

Then, in the last quarter of the nineteenth century, Jewish refugees from the pogroms and expulsions in eastern Europe flooded in. Following the smaller wave of Sephardic

---

*'*Stitches in Time*' – *A Tapestry for the Millennium* was shown at a number of locations during the year 2000. Longer-term marking of the role of migration in the history of the area is found at the Museum of Immigration in Princelet St in Spitalfields, in a building which formerly housed a historic synagogue.

†One of the authors, Geoff Dench, whose natural grandmothers were both Huguenots born in Victorian Bethnal Green (and whose Huguenot *step*-grandmother was born in France), can remember as a child in the 1940s having numbers of elderly French-speaking relations living in London.

Jews who had arrived at the end of the previous century, they stamped their own culture and identity firmly on the area. A large percentage of the refugees arrived in the Jewish quarter of the East End, which steadily expanded through Stepney, Spitalfields and parts of Bethnal Green. William Fishman, the great historian of the Jewish East End, considers that '1888 was the year that the "problem" of foreign immigration finally broke surface ... with high local unemployment and housing shortage constituting a major pressure gauge'.[1] The MP for Stepney, Major Evans Gordon, wrote in 1903, as others do today, that 'east of Aldgate one walks into a foreign town'. By 1912 there were an estimated 142,000 Jews in Whitechapel, Poplar, Mile End and Stepney (all part of the present-day Tower Hamlets) out of a total population of around half a million.

Like the Bangladeshis who followed them into these streets, many of the Jewish immigrants of the 1860s and 70s went into clothing sweatshops or set up as tailors. Others, as described in a portrait by Alan Palmer,[2] were cigar and pipe makers, furriers, jewellers, furniture manufacturers, boot and shoe makers and street traders. The street traders (costermongers) in particular found themselves in competition with the Irish, who became anxious about being upstaged by hard-working new arrivals. Widespread hostility to the large Jewish community in the East End contributed to the introduction of the Aliens Act in 1905 and costermongers (street-traders) spoke up against aliens in campaigns for the 1906 general election 'from their own carts or barrows. Their particular grievance is the competition they are meeting with from a host of alien costermongers'[3].

Similarly, Huguenots had complained of the Irish themselves a century earlier, when the competition from incoming workers had, in Walter Thornbury's expressive phrase, 'set these turbulent workmen in a state of violent effervescence'.[4] East London was widely recognised as having a uniquely impoverished and competitive working environment at this time, and the casual and disorganised nature of employment served to keep the area poor at the same time as labour in other European industrial centres was becoming organised.

It was in a part of Bethnal Green known as Jew's Island that verbal harassment turned in 1903 into physical violence, as Jews were beaten and their properties looted. An elderly Jewish woman, born in 1900, told us that she remembered the decade before the 1914–18 war as being marked by violence. Though she surely overstates it, it was clearly a searing memory:

> Bethnal Green was the worst. It was the thugs that lived in the borough. If a Jew had a beard, he soon didn't have it. It was pulled off; he was murdered. Yes, it was very bad. I'm talking about when I was a child.

The rapid arrival of Jews led to an escalation in overt working-class anti-semitism, manifesting itself in conflict over housing, a conflict later only too familiar to Bangladeshis. There is a large estate in the north-west of the borough built in 1901 to replace a notorious slum area, the Nichol, depicted in Arthur Morrison's 1896 novel *The Child of the Jago*. It still stands: large brick tenement blocks, now occupied largely by Bangladeshi families. When it was built, half of the housing was allocated to Jewish families, which gave rise to the now common complaints of favouritism and preferential treatment for the immigrants. It may be, as Raphael Samuel has suggested,[5] that the reaction against the new Jewish tenants was made more violent because the slum housing which had been replaced had been occupied not by Jewish immigrants but by the poorest elements of the indigenous working class, who no doubt felt they should have had priority in the new tenements. In fact, apart from the new immigrants Bethnal Green had the highest proportion of locally born residents in London. It was an inward-looking community, and Jews were blamed for the decaying squalor of the older housing, much as the Bangladeshis are today. Overcrowding was seen both as voluntary and as leading to conditions of extreme poverty rather than vice versa.

By the final years of the nineteenth century, Beatrice Potter (later Webb) was claiming that the strengths of the Jewish community in the East End were developed at the cost of poor relationships with other residents, evocative in several respects of criticism levelled at the Bangladeshi community today:

> The inner life of the small Hebrew communities bound together by common suffering and mutual helpfulness has developed other qualities, but has also tended in its own way to destroy all friendly and honourable intercourse with surrounding peoples. Social isolation has perfected home life; persecution has intensified religious fervour, an existence of unremitting toil, and a rigid observance of the moral precepts and sanitary and dietary regulations of the Jewish religion have favoured the growth of sobriety, personal purity, and a consequent power of physical endurance.[6]

Communal conflict, perhaps inevitably, continued. The Jewish community of east London was associated with Bolshevism, communism and anarchism, all threatening new political ideologies from the East. In a telling parallel, just as the whole Muslim population of Britain has been erroneously regarded by some in the last few years as a monolithic group bent on terror, so were Jews seen by some as a community of political extremists aiming to destabilise the country.

The local economy stagnated after the collapse of the late 1920s and early 1930s, and after the tenement-building decades of the 1890s and 1900s the infrastructure of the East End was neglected until the post-war redevelopment of the 1950s. Oswald Mosley found the East End a fertile recruiting ground in the 1930s. By 1936 there were regular attacks on Jews and their property in Shoreditch, Stepney and Bethnal Green. Actual physical violence against Jews was always a minority action and, as has been shown by Christopher Husbands, tended to occur most often in areas such as Hoxton and Bethnal Green – lying *between* zones of immigrant settlement and more stable localities – in which there had been an established 'tradition' of xenophobia since at least the nineteenth century.[7] However, it is important to note that even in the late 1930s, the heyday of the British Union of Fascists (BUF), their candidate for the LCC elections in

Bethnal Green polled just 23 per cent of the votes – higher than anywhere else in Britain, but not enough (ever) to win them a council seat.

At the time of *Family and Kinship* the Jews represented the main surviving local minority group, although they comprised only 8 per cent of the interviewees in the original survey.[8] But, percolating by then into mainstream national life, and spreading out into the wider population, they were not felt by Young and Willmott to require specific or special attention. Although Michael Young wrote in a letter in August 1953, 'in Bethnal Green we are now interviewing a lot of Jews who fled from Russia at the beginning of the century',[9] there was no specific discussion in *Family and Kinship* of the Jewish community as a whole. Even before that period, the children and then grand-children of many successful Jewish immigrants had migrated out of the area, north to Stoke Newington and Stamford Hill, north-west to Golders Green and Finchley, east to Gants Hill and Chingford; and the traditional clothing trades, which so many of the original immigrants had made their own, were being deserted: *schmutter* business had no appeal for new generations of doctors and lawyers.

So immigration was not a significant dimension of East End life in the 1950s. It no longer seemed an issue, in retrospect mainly because of the Jewish dispersal to subur-ban London, and because others had assimilated into what was an unusually stable local community. John Gross has written a fascinating account of growing up in the East End in the war years and after. As well as mentioning the 'unmistakable low-key pride' in Britain's role in the war, he also contrasts the rigidities of London's social and occupational classes with the greater flexibility and mobility seen after the 1960s.

> Nowhere were the appointed roles and rituals more strongly marked than in London. Stockjobbers, market porters, rag-and-bone men all dressed for the part. Institutions and traditions were firmly in place, sustained by a degree of confidence which has long since been lost. The rules were there to be kept.[10]

Then, as the Bangladeshis came to live in the streets that had once been Jewish, the names above the store windows too began to change: eventually, the Brick Lane syna-gogue – which had started life in the 1740s as a Huguenot church – became a mosque. By the early 1990s it had long been impossible to deny the significance of the new local im-migration. Our initial survey strongly confirmed this, and the subject of this book is the nature and impact of this rapid and substantial Bangladeshi immigration to the area.

Beyond the Golden Age

The arrival of Bangladeshis represents the most visible transformation of Bethnal Green since the 1950s. However, it has not been the only major change in the area, nor perhaps even the most significant. At one level it does not mark a real change at all, for in the longer rhythms of East End life the periodic absorption of immigrant groups has been a regular feature. The appearance of a new minority community may be less novel than some other recent processes. Locally, this would certainly include the closure of the London docks and their replacement by Docklands – which constitutes a unique expansion of the City of London into east London territory. Nationally, too, there has been an unprecedented decline of local community life and democracy in the face of growing centralisation, bureaucratisation and individualisation of British society around the evolving welfare state. Another change – one which may be related to this – has been the inexorable extension of the middle class. This has led to the gentrification of huge swathes of old working-class London, finally extending in the 1980s and 1990s to the former hearts of working-class community and culture. These changes have all influenced the context in which Bangladeshi settlement has been played out. Indeed, it is arguable that the development of that community might not have taken place without them. Equally, it may well be that because of these changes the Bangladeshis will be the last minority to have their original heartland in this particular location.

By the time of our restudy the combined effect of all these factors had taken the shine off post-war optimism. The much-vaunted opening up of society had not turned out as expected. Although some respondents were impressed by a sense of new worlds unfolding, many who had been in the area for most of their lives felt that their general place in British society had stayed pretty much the same. There seems to be a long-term continuity in Bethnal Greeners' (and indeed East Enders') experience of class position – as a community largely excluded from mainstream opportunities. After half a century of social revolution, during which there have been constant public messages about the openness of society and importance of opportunity, those now left in the East End feel as undervalued and excluded as they have ever been, and probably much more so than in the 1950s. This has led to a sense of local loss which for many people is both bitter and hard to ignore:

> After speaking to the [East Enders] who contributed their stories to this book, I would argue that they do not believe that they threw away their old world but that it was snatched from them – by bombs and housing policies, other people's notions of progress and the pressures of consumerism. It is these which have destroyed their communities and left them stranded. (O'Neill, 1999, p. 297)

With the benefit of half a century of hindsight, it is now evident to us that the early 1950s were indeed part of a golden age in the East End: a time of brilliant new promise and an amazing widening of horizons. The authors of *Family and Kinship* did not quite see this for what it was at the time, perhaps because it was too close. But much of the confidence and enthusiasm which was picked up in that study was tied to specific historical circumstances in the aftermath of the Second World War. Throughout Britain social relations were changing radically between state and citizens, governing and governed, rich and poor. And as we detail later on, these changes were felt with particular relish in the East End. For most of the preceding millennium it had been a poor and heavily subordinated part of the nation, remaining despised and inward-looking. But in the middle of the twentieth century, because of the war, the chains of this long captivity were loosening dramatically. *Family and Kinship* was written when this liberating experience was in full flood, unleashing local aspirations and expectations, and this exerted a tremendous influence on our findings.

We can also now see that this will have affected the reactions of local people to events in the decades that followed. Periods of high social anticipation, or 'revolutions of expectation' as they are sometimes known, are often followed by serious disappointments, proportional to the hopes aroused. The year 1957, when *Family and Kinship* was published, probably marked the high tide of that brief golden age: a kind of sunlit upland plateau on which the working class basked in their newfound enfranchisement and prosperity. They faced all too soon a precipitous decline in which – both as they perceived it, and partly at least in reality – their hard-won gains melted away. Not surprisingly, in consequence many East Enders developed a sense of grievance at promises broken.

All this raises questions about the balance-sheet of post-war social development. Most social historians emphasise the material improvements which have taken place as a result of the war. But the more that we have delved into the detail of change in the East End, the more we have been tempted to feel that in some ways the golden age of post-war anticipation may have been just a temporary blip in a more enduring story of inequality and exclusion.

The blip was exciting while it lasted. When the golden age dawned it was the young East Enders who led the way most enthusiastically into the mainstream, helped by the unifying effect of national television. This was most obvious in the form of the new youth culture which was epitomising the growth of personal freedom and the sense it gave of universal membership of society. Young East Enders suddenly started making the short journey to the 'other end', the West End. A disproportionate number of them, such as David Bailey, Arnold Wesker, Steven Berkoff and Barbara Windsor, became prominent figures in the counter-cultural scene and/or joined the glittering firmament of cultural/pop/showbiz celebrity whose natural talent was the basis for their subsequent emergence as the popular elite. The extraordinary success of such people was due partly to their inner sense of escaping from exclusion, and consequent eager response to new opportunities. But that was only one aspect. It also came from outside, and reflected a national rejection of tradition which gave former outcasts a head start. Cockneys already had their own anti-establishment counter-culture and style before the sixties erupted. This pulled them centre-stage, and made them fashionable when the cultural and lifestyle revolution stormed the drawing rooms of middle-class taste and morality.

So it came to be that the end of London which for centuries had manifested the outcast nature of the lowest social orders turned around to symbolise the overthrow of class distinction and the new extension to everyone of personal respect. Furthermore,

the traffic went in both directions: the East End of London became an evening destina-
tion of choice for the movers and shakers of the West End as they discovered the thrill of
slumming it with the fashionable gangsters of the day. Joan Littlewood's Theatre Royal
at Stratford, while not exactly set in a den of thieves, may in its early days have been
helped by this fashion. After its launch in 1985 *EastEnders* quickly became television's
most popular soap series and is still periodically the most-watched programme nationwide. The outsiders captured the heart of the modern nation.

But while the sixties rocked and grooved into the seventies, style images were recast
and young East Enders were making it and moving west, the East End as a *community* was sinking imperceptibly into crisis. More businesses were relocating to satellite
towns like Harold Hill, to new towns like Basildon and Harlow, or to expanded towns
like Haverhill or Thetford. Academics began to note the first evidence of precipitous
decline in manufacturing employment, not any longer because of out-movement, but
due to closure: the firms, many of them housed in small workshops, simply could not
compete in an environment that was beginning to globalise. Then, to top it all, the root
source of much work in the area withered as the Port of London transferred its dockside
operations to larger and more mechanised locations further downriver – to be followed
by many residents of working age and their families. A vacuum was created which government policy arguably made worse. In the post-war period of optimism the need to
rebuild the area had been welcomed as an opportunity to devise bold and futuristic
solutions, but the planning process did not fit well into the British political and legal
system and progress was slow. So the whole area stagnated during the 1970s as plans
to rebuild the docks became disputed and deadlocked. By the 1980s the local rates of
unemployment, poverty and welfare dependence were the highest in the country.

This local economic decline was eventually and dramatically reversed under the
Conservative government of Margaret Thatcher. Deregulation of markets produced a
massive expansion in the financial services sector and relaxation of planning controls
allowed the City to break out from the straitjacket of its ancient walls. Against ferocious opposition from local authorities, the government set up the London Docklands
Development Corporation, with sweeping powers and plentiful funds, to regenerate
the old port; the idea, borrowed from America, was that state money would 'leverage'
much larger sums from private developers. And leverage they did. The builders poured
in, to develop riverside apartment blocks and then – through the arrival of a Canadian
company in 1986 – to build a huge commercial development designed to rival the old
City of London itself, at Canary Wharf on the Isle of Dogs. The character of this rebuilt
east London is not at all like the people's Jerusalem-which graced post-war Labour
drawing-boards, and which was partially realised in the rebuild from 1952 to 1980. The
new economy is now in place, bringing in affluent workers, new-age labourers at the
cutting edge of the finance and communications industries, to live alongside old East
Enders and Bangladeshis in the new East End.

The New World of the 1990s

The diversification of east London's population has from the outset had a class as well as ethnic dimension. The old East End was almost wholly a working-class domain: the 'largest working-class city in the world', according to Engels. This remained true for a couple of decades after the war. The continuing shortage of housing meant that there simply was no space for newcomers to move into, and certainly not newcomers who were other than poor. The first signs of a changing population were perhaps given by the re-emergence of squatting in the late 1960s. Squatting was not itself a new phenomenon. The post-war period saw a series of politically motivated squats, organised by communists and other radicals to draw attention to delays in the promised programme of rebuilding. These protests do not seem have been popular with ordinary, that is politically inactive, residents, who regarded them as a way of jumping the queue. None of them lasted for long.

The movement in the late sixties was rather different. Firstly, it did not involve local families but mainly single middle-class students from other parts of the country. Most of them were not homeless but simply wanted to live in or near central London and could not or would not pay high rents. The planning blight in parts of Inner London, and in the East End pre-eminently, meant that there was a large stock of empty and neglected properties awaiting redevelopment. As Steve Platt has reminded us,[11] squatting these was readily portrayed by educated, articulate, high status young people as a principled statement against government incompetence, municipal parochialism, corporate greed and a general failure of the system to come up with adequate resources to meet people's needs. The squatting movement proved adept at making deals with local government officials and influencing local policies and plans, and was influential in pioneering new lifestyles in city centres. In the East End in particular we shall see that it had tremendous impact on the political priorities of the Labour Party at the expense of traditional working-class interests, and affected the whole ethos of the area.

So by the end of the twentieth century the East End had been transformed. Inward movement of middle-class residents, rapid settlement of ethnic minorities and the departure of many younger white families had together severely undermined traditional local identity and solidarities. Having declined more rapidly than other parts of London through the twentieth century, the population of Tower Hamlets was the first to start growing again as these newcomers arrived. In 1991 the borough was the only one in Inner London to show an increase on 1981: in fact the only one in the twentieth century as a whole not to register continuing depopulation. In 2001 many other boroughs registered intercensal growth too, but Tower Hamlets was second only to the tiny City of London in its rate of increase. From the exalted pyramids of Canada Square and sleek urban marina of Limehouse to tinted glass palaces in Aldgate, the overflowing City had converted much of the East End in just fifteen years from a crumbling relic of Victorian squalor into London's most dynamic and forward-looking district.

But the other side of this coin is the dislocation of the old community, and loss of local activity. In the fifties the bulk of Bethnal Greeners had been born locally, with 53 per cent born in Bethnal Green itself and 83 per cent within London's boundaries. Many of the rest had locally born spouses. By the end of the century these territorial ties had weakened drastically: the ICS survey carried out in the early 1990s, which provides fuller data than censuses, shows that even then only a minority of people resident in the area had long-term connections with it. By 2001, census data revealed that 35 per cent of the population of the entire borough of Tower Hamlets had been born outside the UK, including 31 per cent born outside the EU.

The changing nature of the borough's population is also reflected in the census ethnic data, which shows that only just over half (51.4 per cent) of its residents were white. The largest other groups were, by percentage, Bangladeshi (33.4), Black African (3.4) and Black Caribbean (2.7). Similarly, much greater religious diversity was recorded, with very nearly as many Muslims (36.4 per cent) enumerated as Christians (38.6). The only other group in double figures were the 14.2 per cent who described themselves as having 'no religion'.

Doing a 'Restudy'

When we began our fieldwork we did not know exactly what we would find, although we were aware from the outset that the changes since the 1950s meant that our study could not expect to follow the style of the original work as closely as we would have liked. *Family and Kinship* was concerned analytically, as this present book has turned out to be, with the effects on local community life of a centralising, even revolutionary govern-ment more fascinated by its own great plan than by the lives and ideas of people subject to it. But unlike the present report it was dealing with a local group which was not only extraordinarily homogeneous and stable but also remarkably self-contained, and as such was highly accessible to traditional face-to-face ethnographic methods of study. Much of the informality and intimacy of that book flowed from that accessibility.

The new Bethnal Green is not like that. Although we carried out our initial inter-viewing in 1992 within the same geographical boundaries as were used in 1953, the old borough of Bethnal Green had long since been merged with Stepney and Poplar into a larger Tower Hamlets. Most of our subsequent enquiries were carried out on this larger stage. Moreover, social life is now stretched over considerable distances, and family ties now compete with rather than reinforce local neighbourliness.

Equally, the opening up of educational opportunities has meant that successful local children acquired qualifications enabling them to become less dependent on their fami-lies and to live how, and where, they chose. With social mobility comes geographical mobility. Many of these young meritocrats have moved some distance away, and have been replaced by incoming middle-class yuppies (or 'young professionals') who live in the East End but are not of it. They belong to a new cosmopolitan urban elite, import national class differences into what was formerly a working-class district and increase local diversity and social division. This class gap may be even more significant than the cultural divide between the Bangladeshi newcomers and the old white working-class residents in the area, most of whom are the offspring of previous immigrants.

This all adds up to a far more complex and fragmented East End population than the community explored in *Family and Kinship*, and makes it harder to capture the nature of the place. Our new survey showed the current population to have three main sectors – the remnants of the old white working class, new (and transient) yuppies and Bangladeshis – plus a number of smaller elements. All of these had family and social networks cutting across the geographical boundaries of the area, and often national boundaries too. So the territory no longer contained the lives of its residents. Neighbourhood had become the interface for a collection of overlapping universes.

In spite of all these differences and difficulties we have tried to retain some of what we feel to be the most important features of the original study. We have kept statistics to a minimum and tried to draw mainly on our informants' own accounts of their lives and problems, using where possible their own words. The Commission for Racial Equality generously gave us a grant to employ two bilingual Bangladeshi researchers, who interviewed in Sylheti/Bengali and then translated their recordings. This meant that we were able to access the sentiments of migrants even where they spoke little English. Language, however, was not the only barrier. In such a fragmented situation it is not easy to present personal testimonies, but this very complexity itself makes it all the more essential to do so. Where people are the same as each other, and express themselves in the same way, their common humanity is self-evident. Where they are different, and are guided by contrasting conventions, it is both harder and more important to see and to demonstrate that humanity.

For that reason we have selected a few characters at the outset to help exemplify our subjects. In the original study a number of informants stood out as particularly colourful, without having attention directed to them. But this was within a context of considerable homogeneity, where the prominent individuals and the general collectivity could represent and reinforce each other in a natural and easy manner. The diversity of our new cast makes this impossible. So we have picked out a handful of key respondents who appear in more than one part of the study and have created for them a set of short profiles, to illustrate here the variety of people involved. All names have been changed. These informants should not be seen as fully representative: they are just some of our new Bethnal Greeners.

Some of Our Characters

The oldest of this core group of informants, who has lived in Bethnal Green for longest, is **Joyce Darty**. She remembers the war and post-war periods, and her experiences illustrate the sort of life that many elderly white Bethnal Greeners have had. Significantly, while she expressed hostility to Bangladeshi newcomers as a group, she personally knew and was very friendly with several individuals. Although in her late sixties when first interviewed, she was still working part-time as a cleaner in the same Globe Town school that she had attended as a pupil before the Second World War. In 1997 she celebrated fifty years of marriage to Harry, whom she had married a little while after he came out of the wartime army.

Joyce was born in 1927 off the Old Bethnal Green Road, which was then the centre of a flourishing local furniture industry. It was made up of specialist craftsmen working in collaboration, for instance one making seats, another legs, another doing upholstery. A typical street sight then was a barrow loaded with legs or tabletops or chair frames being pushed from one workshop to another. She had many memories of her childhood. In her family she had five sisters – she was the youngest. They were poor, like all the people around them. 'The lady opposite where we used to live, she used to shout out "Florrie" (my mum was called Florrie), and she used to say, "Yes," and she said, "Is Ted in?" "No, why?" "Lend us his suit will you, so I can take it up to the pawn shop?" And my mum used to say, "Let us have it back by Friday will you?" ' Times were hard but it was a wonderful time to be a child. The street was a playground. 'Children don't play like they used to. We used to put a rope up and swing on it and all the mothers would stand outside their doors to watch. I mean we did have a fantastic time. Kids of today don't know what it's like.'

Joyce feels that life generally has changed since the war. 'People now are more greedy. If they know so-and-so has got something then they've got to have it too.' Then there are changes in family behaviour, especially sexual. She and her husband have known each other since they were eleven. 'Me and him have never had anyone else: never had anyone else.' But that was then. 'The world has just changed so much it's not a nice place any more. Nowadays people just live together. Years ago you wouldn't dream of going in a fella's house. Girls are sleeping with anyone.'

Not many Bangladeshi respondents had reached retirement age. One who had, **Faruk Miah**, was only in his early sixties when we first saw him, but was already in much less robust health than Joyce Darty – possibly as a result of long years spent in demanding factory labour. He had first come to the UK in 1962 from Sylhet, in the north-east of what is now Bangladesh, and spent the next quarter of a century working as machinist in the same Brick Lane sweatshop. In 1982 he had been able to bring in his wife too, and two years after that his children, who had been born in Sylhet. A few years later while in Bangladesh he had suffered a mild heart attack. Since then he had been partially paralysed and unable to work.

Like many of his generation, he had originally not intended to settle in Britain, but just earn some money to improve his family's position in Bangladesh. The money he sent back from his wages had not only helped to support his mother (his father had died young) but was also used to buy land. It was a family investment. But he had assumed that one of his sons would go back to Bangladesh to farm it, and this had not happened. 'I worked hard and bought twenty-three acres of land. Now nobody is there to look after my property. I had high hopes of my son. I paid for him to become a graduate, and at the end of it he is not good for anything. So now I have rented out my land, and the house is locked. I have three big houses in the village, and I wanted my children to go back and take charge of all I have.'

Shortly before bringing his wife over from Bangladesh, Faruk married a second wife there. She then came over herself a few years later, and since then they have all lived together under the same roof. At our first interview, Faruk's household consisted of himself, his two wives, a grown-up son from his first marriage (plus his wife and children) and an adolescent son from the second. He said that his wives got on reasonably well. 'She knew I was going to marry again. When two [wives] live under the same roof there are bound to be some differences. But my first wife is a quiet type of person ... She has got older now, and spends most of her time praying.' He recognised, though, that his situation is unusual and that polygamy is not something that people can practise these days. 'It was right in our time. Nowadays women would leave a husband if they did that. Especially girls born in this country. One of my nephews got married to a girl who refused to cook for him. She just wanted money and her husband to take her to the cinema in a car. That marriage has not lasted. Would you accept a wife like that?'

When we contacted Faruk three years later his grown-up son and his family had moved out following an argument over the son's continuing reluctance to work the family farm. Faruk is now left with a household comprising himself, his two wives and the son by the second. He misses his grandchildren. 'I don't know how my grandchildren are at the moment. When they were here it was good, and the house was full. Now it feels empty. My youngest son is big now, and the grandchildren are gone and I feel empty. A house feels good when there are children in it.' Faruk's life exemplifies that of many men in his generation, whose attention and concerns are divided between alternative homes and lives. Now that he has been in Britain for so long, there is much to leave if he goes back. But his life here is not giving him the rewards he expected, and so he finds himself in a sort of limbo.

Someone who was born into the same world as Joyce Darty, but a generation later, and who is now finding it all changing around her, is **Kristin O'Keefe**. She is a local girl, married to fellow Bethnal Greener Patrick and living with him and their six children in a small flat off Roman Road. Their lives could almost come out of *Family and Kinship*. Patrick has a small business which binds him into the local community. Kristin is in and out of neighbours' houses all of the time (and they hers) and goes out every day, shopping and visiting, and talking to people all the time. 'I'm out every day, and everybody comes and talks to the kids.'

Family relationships are central to this social network. Kristin's most valued ties are with family, and (also traditional) her husband's relations figure prominently in this. Her best friend is her husband's brother's wife, and Kristin rarely goes on holiday without one or both grandmothers to help look after all the children. This close family group is essentially a female club. Although she traces key relationships through her husband, he is only marginal to its activities. 'Women make families stronger. Men can take it or leave it.' She often goes out without him. 'If we've eaten and the kids are in bed, I might say to Pat, "I'm just popping down your mum's for half an hour." ' Her mother-in-law's house is the hub of the family.

There is a clear difference from Bethnal Green in the 1950s: none of Kristin's side of the family lives any longer in Bethnal Green. Over the years they have all moved out to Essex, in the search for better housing. Contacts with them are still close and frequent, but these no longer coincide with local neighbourliness. Given her own large family, Kristin is obviously drawn herself towards moving. They need more space, were on the council waiting list for ages and cannot afford to buy anything locally. At the time of the interviews they were wondering what to do as in desperation they had finally bought their flat from the council under the right-to-buy scheme, but could not sell it on. They had even asked if they could sell it back to the council and go back on the waiting list, but had been told this would not be possible as they would have made themselves 'intentionally homeless'. She and Patrick would talk about this often, and significantly (and, again, as in the fifties) it is Patrick who, even though (or perhaps because?) he is the one with all of the nearby kin, is in principle the one more amenable to moving out.

Although not themselves migrants when seen, Kristin and Patrick's lives had already been heavily influenced by migration – both by that of kin moving out and of strangers moving in. Their own position had become fairly tenuous, and they almost certainly give us an example of what would be characterised as a 'white flight' family shortly before it actually takes flight.

None of the Bangladeshi families surveyed have been around for so long as these native Bethnal Greeners. However, **Shohel Uddin** comes from a Bangladeshi family which has been linked with the UK for several generations. His grandfather was a seaman who settled in Stepney between the wars and married a second wife here who was a white girl. She eventually left him and he returned to Bengal, at that time part of India, feeling very critical of white women. Shohel's father then came to Britain as a young man in the 1950s. Shohel himself was born in Sylhet just before the 1971 war of independence from Pakistan. He was brought to east London when he was three. Thirty years later he speaks perfect English and works as an accountant in the City. People who have spoken to him only on the telephone are surprised when they see him and realise that he isn't a white Englishman. He is amused by their discomfiture. There is much in Western lifestyles that he finds appealing. He regularly gets up early to have a workout in a gym before he goes to his office.

Since coming to London, Shohel has been back to his birthplace several times. On his first visit he was 12. 'I hated it. I wanted to be back in London with my creature comforts. The sanitation, or lack of it, disgusted me and so did the rubbish. Five years later, in 1984, I made my second visit and fell in love with the place and felt that was where my roots are. My village is thirty miles away from Sylhet town – the biggest town in the agricultural district in the north-east of Bangladesh. The village is where my heart is – the greenery, the wildlife, the open expanses, the clear, quiet mornings. The greenery is so vivid. It's quite vibrant. It plays on your heart.'

Family life is central to Shohel. He is the fourth oldest child in the family, with two older brothers in their forties who are machinists in the rag trade. Most of the English branch of the family live in two quite large adjoining houses just off Bethnal Green Road, including his parents and his four brothers who are living at home and their children. 'All the cooking is done in one home, by daughters-in-law under the supervision of my mother. I live a hundred yards or so away in a house I have bought.'

Shohel is close enough to be able to take a reasonably full part in the life of his extended family. But he is also a little bit removed from them. The others are living together almost under one roof. Shohel is at the edge of the compound, half in, half out. This is largely because he recently broke with Bangladeshi custom (but less so his family's) by marrying a white girl, from Liverpool. He says it would have in some ways been easier for him, and much easier for her, if he had moved right away, and this is what usually happens in the rare cases such as theirs. But he had no wish to desert his traditional family, his religion of Islam or Islam's political stance – which crucially for him does not approve of the secular welfare state – or his culture generally. 'I want to retain my characteristics and not become a complete Westerner. I don't want to lose touch with my own people, and I don't want my son to either.'

Because of his work and his marriage to an Englishwoman, Shohel is more integrated in British society than most of his compatriots. He has, however, maintained strong ties within the community, and this may well give some indication of likely trends among Bangladeshis as more move into white-collar and professional occupations – with or without marriage to non-Bangladeshis.

Our next character, **Mandy Charlton**, is one whose own life embodies graphically the transformations that have occurred in the neighbourhood. Born in Bethnal Green, around the time that *Family and Kinship* was published, she married a lad from Poplar, David, and spent the years when her children were young leading a fairly traditional East End life in Bow. As time passed she found David increasingly tiresome, especially his hostility towards Bangladeshis. When we first interviewed her this dissatisfaction was being fed by the moral support that she was getting from colleagues in a municipal women's project where she had taken on some part-time work.

Four years later when we saw her again she had split up with her husband, who was now living with his parents. She was now working full-time for the council on a multi-cultural community project, and moving confidently into a new and wider world opened up by this position in the public realm. She was buying her council house under the right-to-buy scheme, active in many community activities – including as her street's representative on local residents committees – and sending her children to school in central London to give them a better start.

Mandy consciously relates this flowering of her identity to the split from her husband and his racist family. As a single mother she feels freer to form her own opinions, and to be an autonomous, responsible citizen. She can follow her own conscience, not someone else's. Much of her earlier life she now repudiates. Her daughters stay one night a week at their father's house, and she worries about the influence that he could be having on them. However, she remains close to her own parents, who live just round the corner and help out a lot with the children.

In many ways she helps to show how the welfare state has enabled people, and especially women, to develop themselves in ways that would have been impossible in the 1950s when family ties were stronger. It is important to note – given debates on the collapse of families – that while she uses her independence to distance herself from her former husband, she is still close (though perhaps not so close as she would have been) to her husband's kin.

Unlike our other key white informants, **Tony Hicks** is not a native Bethnal Greener. But he has been living here now for half of his life, and he illustrates the sort of influence that post-war *white* migration has had on the area. He grew up in suburban Surrey, and came here as a student in the late 1970s to live with friends in a collective squat near Brick Lane. After a few years of threats and confrontation, the council allowed the squatters to form a housing association and take over some run-down houses. When he first saw us he was still living in an association flat, along with his partner and two children, and was working as a teacher in a nearby school.

Some years later when we interviewed him again he had moved into a nearby studio flat – again through the housing association – and was living by himself, in rather a chaotic state. His son and daughter, now teenagers, usually came to stay from Friday night until Sunday morning. Apart from that he saw little of any family members, though he does have a new (Asian) girlfriend and has some contact with her local family.

Tony does not regard himself as a sociable person. He says that he has difficulty with permanent relationships, and prefers to spend his spare time painting and sculpting. But he is active politically in tenants' organisations, on anti-racist issues and as a teacher. Through all of this he knows quite a few local people. In the time that he has been living in the area he feels that there have been considerable changes. He had a lot to complain about regarding government neglect of education, and the general consequences of that, but he said that many things locally had got better. When he moved in there had been much more hostility towards immigrants, the area was dilapidated and the council was not as forward-looking as it is now. On all counts the area was looking up, but he still considers that one day, when his children are grown, he would like to leave and live somewhere completely different. 'Somewhere quite wild, like Wales.' He feels no real roots here.

Although clearly not a member of a new ruling elite, Tony does embody a number of characteristics distinctive of the meritocracy. He values education greatly, and uses much of his energy promoting it in one way or another or generally standing for an open society. He does not feel that he belongs to the local community and is more comfortable serving impersonal causes such as teaching than personal ones involving his own family.

Our youngest character, **Naveen Mannan**, was a bright and lively sixth-former when first interviewed, just about to sit her A-level examinations, and hoping for good enough grades to be able to go on to read for a degree in law. She lived about twenty minutes' walk from her school, in a flat off Columbia Road with her parents, two brothers and two sisters. A half-brother, the son of her father's first wife, who worked in a nearby restaurant, had also lived with them until recently, but had moved out to a new flat on getting married.

Naveen's father is unemployed. He worked for over twenty years in a mill near Sheffield before eventually coming to London around the time that Naveen was born. The factory in Poplar where he took work as a machinist closed down in the early 1980s and he had not been able to find anything since. Naveen had not seen her father much when a young child, as she had grown up in Bangladesh in the maternal grandparental home while her mother waited for a UK visa. From the age of three she went to school in Bangladesh, and her mother also arranged private tuition for her in English and Bengali when she was four. So when she came to London aged seven she had already made a start in English, and was able to progress rapidly in primary school. By the time she moved to secondary school she could speak English well.

We saw her at an age when questions of identity are becoming important. This was influenced by her relationship with her parents. They wanted her to retain her Bangladeshi culture, but also to adapt to life in the UK. 'They don't want us to speak English at home, they tell us off. They say to keep Bengali at home, and English at school ... They want you to be a Bengali, but a British Bengali.' This is because her parents also relied on their children to help them cope in Britain. 'I know more about what's going on compared to them in terms of language and things ... They often come to me for advice when they don't know what to do.' But she also feels for her own sake that she wants to stay Bangladeshi and keep her culture and religion. 'I think at the moment I'm going through the process of thinking out what to believe. It's important to me in the sense that I don't want to, you know, when I have children I don't want them to lose it, and I don't want to lose it myself. I don't want to completely lose my religion and become westernised, because it has things to give to me.'

At the same time there are aspects of English culture that she prefers. She loved growing up in Bangladesh in her grandmother's house, and enjoys her occasional visits back very much. But now she is no longer a child it is not so straightforward. 'I would like to go there, but I think you get a lot of marriage pressure at my age. My parents are good and will not pressure me. But you'd still get pressure from relatives. You'd get hundreds of wedding proposals even if you say, "No, I'm not getting married!"'

What Naveen perhaps illustrates is that it is far too simple to assume that young Bangladeshis will adopt English ways if they do well here. Though she may change after university, when interviewed she showed no intention of losing her Bangladeshi identity. Any blend of British Bangladeshi that she creates seems likely to contain a generous helping of the latter.

Loss of Localism

These brief sketches reflect much of what has changed in Bethnal Green since the 1950s, and a little of what has remained the same. If we are correct in guessing that Kristin O'Keefe will have moved away by now, this would underline the processes described later.

Among our survey respondents barely a sixth had been born in Bethnal Green, and less than a third in the much larger area of Tower Hamlets. This is in spite of the fact that the 1992 sample included 18–21-year-olds. These were not sampled in the fifties, and were the group of adults in our new survey most likely to be locally born. Less than half of the sample had been born in London at all, and nearly a third were members of minority ethnic groups – virtually all of whose adult members were immigrants themselves. Even if we focus on the white respondents in the survey, including teenagers living with their parents, only 27 per cent had been born in Bethnal Green (compared with 53 per cent in the 1953 survey), 46 per cent in Tower Hamlets generally and nearly a third had come from outside the London area.

Many of the old Bethnal Greeners who do still live locally now feel abandoned by the flow of history, dispossessed of the comforts of family-based community life and betrayed by their former patrons. Labour is still the dominant political force in the borough council, but listens to different voices, such as that for example of Tony Hicks, who moved in during the late 1970s when, in his own words, it was still populated by 'petty criminals and barrow boys'. Tony felt that the borough had improved considerably during the time he had been there. It was not so solidly working class, 'Not so rough as it used to be', was less squalid visually, and the growth of home ownership meant that people looked after their houses. But in spite of some new art galleries there was not much to do in the evenings apart from go to the pub, and he had to go to the West End for most of his entertainment. So he was still reluctant to say that he lived in Bethnal Green. 'Living in London, I prefer to call it.'

Fournier Street, off Brick Lane. On the right is the London Jamme Masjid, originally a Huguenot church and built in 1743.

Chapter 2

Settlement of the Bangladeshis

Few Londoners, let alone those from beyond the M25, have ever heard the name Sylhet, or could begin to find it on a map. They would have a reasonable excuse, because it is 5,000 miles and over ten flying hours away. But in the corner of Bethnal Green towards Whitechapel, and increasingly in its heart, almost everyone knows Sylhet, because they were born there or because their parents were born there.

True, everyone has heard of Indian restaurants, and most have visited one more than once. And some might be aware that virtually every so-called Indian restaurant in Britain is in fact Bangladeshi owned and operated. But almost no one realises that these Bangladeshi cooks and waiters come – as does almost the entire Bangladeshi community of east London – from one district in the north-east of the country, roughly 100 miles from the national capital Dhaka.

Apart from Sylhet town, which has many businesses and some hotels, an airport from which regular twenty-minute flights leave for Dhaka and a large district of comfortable 'Londoni' (the expression used to describe Bangladeshis living in Britain) houses set in gardens, most of Sylhet district consists of small villages set in trees among paddy fields. Rice is by far the major crop, using over 90 per cent of all cultivable land, with other vegetables and fruit grown seasonally around villages for local consumption. Tea, from the plantations in the small hills near Sylhet town, is still an export crop, despite using only 3.6 per cent of the cultivable land in the 1990s.

Sylhet is also famous as the land of the Muslim saint Hazrat Shah Jalal, who brought the Islamic religion here in 1303. Legend has it that the saint, who came from Delhi with his band of 360 disciples to preach Islam and defeated the Hindu Raja (king) Gour Gobinda, transformed the followers of the Raja into the catfish which are still to be seen in the pond adjacent to his shrine. Seven hundred years later, the shrine is still an object of pilgrimage.

The population of Sylhet is predominantly Muslim; in the 1981 census the proportions were 81.3 per cent Muslim and 18 per cent Hindu.[1] This was a significant change since the beginning of the century: the breakdown of population by religion in Sylhet in 1905 was 53 per cent 'Muhammadans', 37 per cent Hindu, 1 per cent 'animistic tribes' and 9 per cent 'other persons'.[2] The greater number of Muslims today is partly the result of continuing conversion to Islam, and also the consequence of the large in- and out-migrations following the partition of India in 1947. Nowadays, in some areas from which Londonis come the proportion of Muslims is even greater; for example in Biswanath *thana* (a collection of villages which make up an administrative district),* to the west of Sylhet town, there were 94.6 per cent Muslims and only 5.3 per cent Hindus in 1981.

Bangladesh is one of the poorest countries in the world but it is developing fast in some respects. For example, literacy rates have been rising: in 1981 rural literacy rates were 20.3 per cent for men and only 9.6 for women, and in Sylhet they were only slightly higher, at 22.1 per cent for men and 10.9 for women. By 1991 literacy rates in Sylhet were 40 per cent for men and 27.5 for women, and for 2003, in Bangladesh as a whole, they were estimated to be 54 per cent for men and 32 for women. Similarly, other amenities are spreading in rural Bangladesh, albeit from a very low base: 8.6 per cent of rural households had an electricity supply in 1991 compared with only 1.6 per cent in 1981. Roads are still mainly unsurfaced: indeed, as another writer has pointed out, movement is easier for many in the flood season when people can travel by boat.[3]

Despite this development Sylhet district is still poor in absolute terms, even taking into account the relative prosperity of many families with migrant workers who are sending money from overseas. Of the 918,000 households measured in the 1981 census, 68 per cent lived in houses constructed of bamboo, straw and mud walls.[4] Only some of these houses are roofed with corrugated iron, the others have straw roof coverings. More recent figures on Sylhet district, taken from the 1991 census, show that by that date only 19 per cent of households had radios, 1.03 per cent had telephones and 2.23 per cent had refrigerators, indicating the poor distribution of electricity.

The villages from which migrants departed, whether permanently settled overseas (as they are in Britain) or working temporarily (as they might be in, for example, Kuwait or Saudi Arabia), typically number around 2,000 people. From the tarmac roads leading from Sylhet town, the villages are hard to see. The houses are surrounded by thickets of tall trees and bamboo. As one approaches on foot, houses emerge beneath the trees. Most housing is arranged as a series of households in separate or linked buildings around a courtyard in which women hang washing to dry, chickens pick at grain, children play, fresh produce dries in the sun on grass mats and older men sit and pass the time of day. This household compound is known as a *bari* and the members of a *bari* are almost always related as part of the same patrilineal kin group. In some respects it resembles the 'turnings' of old Bethnal Green, where many related people lived in the same street or block of flats. One difference is that the *bari* is exclusively for the same kin group, with the exception of agricultural workers or other servants who are not related by blood, and yet are defined as being part of the kinship system. Another difference is that *Family and Kinship* showed that kin living together in one turning or block of

---

*This is not the only *thana* with such a high percentage of Muslims; it is given as an example of a typical Londoni *thana* which has been visited by one of the authors.

flats tended to be related matrilineally, with Mum, the eldest matriarch of the family, responsible for arranging the housing of her daughters and their families.

A *bari* visited in 1994 by one of the authors was one of the largest in the village, and included some of the very few houses made of plastered brick rather than *kutcha* housing, with bamboo and mud walls, which was a good illustration of the relative wealth of 'Londoni' families. One son and a married daughter of the elderly household head and his wife were living in London, two other absent sons were working in Saudi Arabia and another one in Cyprus, making 'Londoni' something of a misnomer for the family as a whole, although they described themselves as such. With four sons away working and one daughter living permanently in London, the principal household consisted of the elderly couple, their eldest son's wife and her three children, their second son's wife and their youngest (unmarried) son, who helped his father manage their land.

As well as the family members there was a woman servant who slept in the house and two young men who helped with agricultural work and slept in a shed across the *bari* yard. These last three were unrelated to the family and the woman was a widow with two small children living elsewhere. It was clear that to maximise the income for the family as a whole it was preferable for sons of the household to work overseas and for the extra labour on the family land to come from paid labourers. The paid workers were not related, as we have said, yet lived in the *bari*. They were partly assimilated into the kinship network by using terms of kinship to talk to other household members, but they fitted in to the household at a lower generational level because of their inferior situation as servants and non-kin. So, for example, they called the two daughters-in-law of the household head 'aunt' despite being older than both of them. In other words, they were incorporated into the group at the lowest level, that of the generation of the youngest children in the *bari*.

Other households in the same *bari* were positioned around the same central open area and shared the same hand-pumped borehole water supply. One consisted of the two widows of the brother of the first household head. At the time of the visit they were living with the son of one, whose own wife and children were living, estranged from him, in London. Another was a poorer household, in a building built of bamboo and mud walls rather than plastered brick, in which lived another more distant male relative and his wife and seven children. He did not seem to have any direct links with anybody in London and the relative poverty of his household, despite being in a prosperous *bari*, showed the limits to which kin will share resources. This family was looked after, to the extent that they were helped with rice and other foodstuffs, but they enjoyed nothing like the same standards of food or clothing as members of the other households. So in this *bari* migrant workers had increased the prosperity of the households considerably, to the benefit of all members but to varying degrees depending on the closeness of the relationships.

Other *baris* visited at the same time followed the same pattern: several households, of varying degrees of comfort and prosperity, positioned around one common open area and usually sharing a pump for fresh water and a pond for washing and other purposes. The sight of a spacious, plastered-brick house in a walled compound in this part of Bangladesh invariably indicated a Londoni family, and many such houses were uninhabited or were being looked after by caretaker relations of the owners living elsewhere. The caretakers sometimes lived in extremely modest mud homes built within the same compound or near the main house. Again, these kin were trusted but not equal. It may not often be admitted, but there can be an uneasy relationship between property owners living in Britain and their kin in Sylhet. A rhetoric of mutual support and reliance may be belied by distrust, treachery and dishonesty. Faruk told us about the difficulties his friend was having in establishing his personal rights over land in Sylhet:

> We had a serious discussion to make. That was about my friend Abdul's brother; they are from my village [in] Sylhet. Let me go back. Abdul's brother is selling a plot of land which he inherited from his father. Abdul thinks he has to buy that land since it is his family's land and his prestige would go down if someone else buy his family property. Abdul has already asked his two sons, who are working in restaurants, to raise 200,000 Taka [approximately £3,200 at mid-1990s rates]. Money is not a problem; he can borrow from other relatives who are in this country. The problem is, since it is his brother's land it will be difficult to get possession. There is a chance of quarrel between brothers. I advised him, since his family sentiment is involved with that piece of land he should buy that land. But before the payment he should go to Bangladesh and call village elders and make the payments in front of them, so that Mohammad, Abdul's brother, does not do any procrastination in handing over the land.

Abdul's problem seemed to be that he could not trust his brother: whereas he was confident that he could raise money in England, and substantial sums by the sound of it, he clearly thought it was possible that his brother might cheat him out of ownership unless the sale was acknowledged publicly. This is not to say that similar conflicts of interest and inter-family disputes would not happen if all the protagonists were in Sylhet; they likely would. Katy Gardner reported in the mid-1990s that, as migrant *gushtis* (patrilineal kinship groups) have prospered, land values have risen and the number of disputes over land has increased, whether the warring *gushti* members are living in Sylhet or overseas.[5]

The First Bangladeshis in Britain

The migration of Bangladeshis into Tower Hamlets began well before the period covered by our present study. It goes back to the end of the eighteenth century, when lodging houses were set up in east London for Indian seamen from the ships owned by the East India Company. Administration of the Sylhet district had been assumed by

'John Company' in 1765, more than a hundred years before it became part of Assam and almost two centuries before it became part of East Pakistan at the partition of India. From then on a special relationship was created between Sylhet and the British merchant navy. The first export from the district was lime from Chattok, used for building and other purposes. But in the nineteenth century this was quickly overtaken by tea, which was the crop that ultimately brought prosperity to the plantation owners of Sylhet. Tea was already growing in Assam and was introduced to the few but fertile hills around Sylhet town in the 1850s. By the 1890s the tea industry was well established, the plantations usually owned by British, often Scottish, landlords. The tea gardens were largely worked by migrant labour imported from other, even poorer, parts of India.[6] Although a significant industry, tea was never as important in Sylhet as in the rest of Assam. It did, however, provide employment for Sylhetis in providing river transport to ports, and this in turn nurtured the earliest migration.

The growing trade contacts between Sylhet and Calcutta (and thus the rest of the world) and the easy river access to Calcutta provided an environment where young men were well positioned to become entrepreneurial migrants. No doubt there are several factors which stimulate this kind of highly risky enterprise. Whatever the other reasons, the report of the 1921 Assam census remarked that large joint family households were at that time more prevalent among Muslims than Hindus, and this may help to explain migration from the predominantly Muslim Sylhet district. Large joint families could more easily afford to lose the labour of a member on a risky enterprise, and to invest collectively in any costs of migration, with the migrant's own earnings forming part of the joint income.

With the traffic of goods moving from Assam and Sylhet to Calcutta by inland waterways for onward shipment to Europe, Sylheti men were able to travel to Calcutta and look for work on British merchant navy ships. Once an extensive trade became established, which continued until the Second World War, men would find work on ships through the middlemen known as *serangs* – in effect 'jobbers' or agents responsible for appointing crews for the shipowners. *Serangs* would act as magnets for the young men from their own village or kin group; indeed, they were the pivotal figures who could help or hinder aspiring Lascars.* *Serangs* acted as employment agents for the Calcutta Shipping Office, which would appoint them to engage the crew for each voyage, but they also acted as agents representing the interests of the seamen themselves by negotiating the employment terms with the Office.

These Lascars, working in tough conditions on uncomfortable ships, were usually employed for one voyage at a time and returned to their home villages with their pay

---

*Lascar is defined in the 11th edition of the *Encyclopaedia Britannica* (1911) as follows: 'The name in common use for all oriental, and especially Indian, sailors, which has been adopted in England into the Merchant Shipping Acts, though without any definition ... [The word has] referred to sailors as early as the seventeenth century.' For a story illustrating the importance of *serangs* see Kipling, 1998.

at the end of the trip. Once steamships were being used by the merchant fleet, Sylheti Lascars were used as stokers; they were believed to be able to cope more easily than Europeans with the extreme temperatures of the ship's engine rooms. They were also employed as cooks and to do any of the other jobs that required them to be closeted in the airless bowels of a ship. As early as the late eighteenth century there were destitute Lascars in east London applying for relief to the offices of the East India Company. These were men who had not found places on ships leaving London, or who had lost the money earned on their outward journey. By 1795 there was a lodging house for such men, and there continued to be so, based in various sites but always in east London, always near the docks, establishing the link between the East End and Sylhet.

Some of the Lascars jumped ship in the east London docks and joined those who could not get jobs on voyages back to their homes. Along with ships' cooks from galleys almost as hot as the engine rooms familiar to the stokers, a number opened cafés in Britain to serve the seamen staying between voyages in the seamen's hostels. Some men we talked to in the 1990s told us about their family link with the merchant navy right up to and including the war, like the grandfather of one of our informants. Although travelling in a convoy with naval escort vessels to protect them, his ship was torpedoed by a U-boat. Only eleven crew members survived: three white officers and eight Lascars hung on to a plank for seven days until they were picked up by a British submarine and taken back to England, in his case to Whitechapel.

The small number of men who stayed in the UK for longer periods, choosing to work in Britain rather than remain in the merchant navy, were also temporary residents, planning to work for a few years to build up a sum of capital for investment back in Sylhet. The newcomers expected to work and return to their own country to buy land and live off the fat of it, in this like the nabobs of the East India Company in reverse. Robert Lindsay, the first Company Governor of Sylhet, and others in the eighteenth century, returned from having made their piles of money to set up affluent establishments in the hunting and shooting areas of England and Scotland. The returns of the small restaurant owners of Brick Lane would be far more modest.

As the sociologist Muhammad Anwar has well described,[7] the long-term aspirations of the early migrants from the Indian subcontinent were bound up with improving their lot in their place of origin rather than settling permanently in their place of work. In the case of the Pakistanis of whom he was writing, and equally of the Bangladeshis described here, this was the main reason for the delay in bringing other family members to the UK. Migrant workers were only that: workers settling for long enough to make money to invest at home. As we shall see, this prevailing idea led to the Bangladeshi migrants of the mid-twentieth century being isolated from the rest of the British population both at work and at home.

The main factor encouraging migration from Sylhet was the pull of economic opportunity, rather than the push of oppression as experienced, for example, by the Jewish communities of eastern Europe and Russia. But one push factor which did promote migration from Sylhet was the partition of India in 1947. The division of East and West Bengal meant that the seamen of Sylhet, now in East Pakistan, were cut off from Calcutta, their main port of employment and embarkation, and seamen already on ships were stranded. As well as destroying the *serang* system, partition meant that more seamen took up residence in the East End. Uncertain of being able to get another voyage if they went back home, they stayed in London instead. Indeed, it has been claimed that Aftab Ali, a prominent Indian trade unionist, issued advice that, with Calcutta lost, East Pakistani seamen should leave their ships at British ports.[8] For one thing they would not then be caught up in the Hindu–Muslim riots in Calcutta.

By the 1950s several hundred East Pakistani men – there were no women stokers – had settled in east London and into rather more secure jobs, in restaurants catering for their own people and for whites who were developing a taste for curry. If not in restaurants or hotel kitchens, their jobs were usually in clothing or leather manufacturing. The Jewish-owned clothing businesses of east London employed a number of the new arrivals to work in their small factories in Spitalfields, Whitechapel and the other areas on the border of the City.

Apart from the traditional occupations already established for ex-seamen in the UK – the hotel, catering and clothing businesses – the arrival of larger numbers of them after partition coincided with the growing need for labour in the industrial north of England, especially in the textile and steel industries. By the early 1960s, most of the new arrivals did not take jobs in London but went directly north, where the textile factories of Lancashire and Yorkshire were using cheap labour as a way to survive. The Bangladeshis (as they became in 1971) were more willing to work on night shifts than local whites were. The Bangladeshi foreman, with some words of English, did the recruitment and the organising of labour, just as the *serangs* in the Calcutta docks had done. Ignorance of the language was no great handicap for people on exclusively Bengali night shifts, in the lodging houses shared with other of their countrymen, or in the largely Bengali kitchens of Indian restaurants, though a lack of English later made it that much harder for them to break out into other occupations.

This tapping into new sources of work in the north was achieved largely through an extension of existing migration chains based on village and kinship ties. Looking at our own informants in Bethnal Green in the early 1990s, one older man, 78 at the time he was interviewed, told us that he arrived in 1955 on a ship which docked at Liverpool. He travelled with an older relative whom he described as his uncle, and they were met by his uncle's friend, a man from their home village who had already arranged jobs for both men in a north of England steel foundry. Another man we spoke to had arrived alone in 1959, aged 20, and was met by his father and older brother who were already established in the UK. His brother was working as a kitchen porter in the Savoy Hotel and had arranged for him to be employed there also.

Similarly, another informant arrived in 1962 aged 31 to join his younger brother, who had arranged a job for the new arrival with a Jewish-owned tailoring business in Brick Lane. Finally, another man arrived in 1963 aged 30 in company with a large group of men who already knew each other and had employment vouchers. The group was met by friends and relatives and they all went to Blackburn, where our informant worked as a house servant for a Bangladeshi supervisor in a textile factory: 'he was from my village'. After three years as a servant he started working in the factory himself. These examples are typical of the pattern of immigration through the 1960s: single men arrived with contacts, housing and work already established for them. No surprise then that the migrant district in Bangladesh is so concentrated, just as the residential area in Tower Hamlets is too.

Focus in the East End

Through all of this, the centre of gravity for Bangladeshi life in Britain remained in east London. At the beginning of the 1960s this amounted to a few lodging houses at the southern and western edges of Bethnal Green and Stepney, where seamen stopping over briefly between contracts and migrant labourers on their way to or from factory jobs in the north or looking for work in London hotels crammed together to minimise their costs. Although they did not realise it at the time, this residential strategy was crucial in presenting them with a chance to recreate a local Bangladeshi community. For by congregating in the most run-down properties in these boroughs, where post-war redevelopment had yet to take place, they were then well positioned to benefit from it when it did.

One of our non-Bangladeshi informants in the 1990s, Carl Johnson, who is mixed-race and described himself when invited to choose an ethnic category as 'belonging to the neighbourhood', lived as a child in a dilapidated corner of Brick Lane around this time, before being taken into an orphanage. His memories give an idea of what that place was like:

> When I was a lad in Brick Lane it was very cosmopolitan – Greek people, Turkish people, Chinese, Jewish people, Asians, blacks. A lot of us were half-castes, being the fact that when mothers were younger than the fathers they used to stick together. They weren't welcome in a lot of places, the mothers with the half-caste kids. They used to live in hostels that didn't let the men in. They had to be out by a certain time each day, in at a certain time each night. So they found bomb-damaged buildings, they chose the one that was the least knocked about, then they'd clean it up and get together there during the day. As a group of young girls who'd fallen in love with older guys they'd stick together; not bosom pals for the rest of their lives, but they'd go on seeing each other.

During the 1960s the fortunes of the western corner of the new borough of Tower Hamlets remained uncertain. Fired with enthusiasm for change by Harold Wilson's administration, the new borough had decided to develop its western flank into a new business district that the City could spread into. But local opposition to these plans meant that they became bogged down in appeals. So instead of revival there was a period of yet further stagnation. This meant that Bangladeshis, who had been living mainly in privately rented accommodation near the docks, faced little resistance when acquiring property in the Aldgate area. Some local Asian businessmen, including a few Bangladeshis, had profits that they were able to invest in buying run-down properties to rent out to compatriots. The account by Charlie Forman of changes in the Spitalfields area reports that in 1961 only one address in Brick Lane was listed as having residents born in East Pakistan. By 1971 this had risen to more than twenty – with a total of more than 200 residents between them – plus another sixteen addresses in Princelet Street, off Brick Lane, with a similar tally, and more spread around other streets. Each house would contain several households, which at the time would typically consist of between three and eight men sharing a couple of rooms.[9]

But this cramped existence did not matter much to the groups of largely young Bangladeshi men who were living in the district. Life for a single male was casual and chatty, and many of the older men now living in the area look back to that period as their own golden age – of freedom and sociability. Hassan Moin, coming up to retirement age when interviewed but already dependent on a disability allowance after working long hours in a sweatshop, remembers his first ten years here as enjoyable. Since giving up work, he had brought his wife and children over from Bangladesh:

> I arrived in 1963 on a plane from Pakistan which was full of young Bengalis like myself, and came straight to Brick Lane where I had an uncle. He looked after me until I found a job.
>
> My first job was as a kitchen porter in a big hotel in Charing Cross, called Lyons. One of my brother's friends was working there, and he took me along a few weeks after my arrival. Then I took a kitchen job in another hotel – I can't remember the name. I worked there for a couple of years and then I took many jobs and left many. If a chap told me this or that hotel was giving good money, better money, I used to take that job.
>
> It was easy to leave. You just waited for the week's wages and then you do not turn up the next day. You send a message to the chef via a friend. Sometimes money wasn't important. Say I found a group of good friends working together in a hotel, I used to join them for maybe less or equal money. That time I was young, and friendship mattered more than money. There were lots of people my age from Bangladesh at that time. So it was easy to make friends.

Shiraj Mizan remembers that part of the solidarity arose out of being Muslims together, and needing each other's help in order to maintain their way of life and uphold Muslim tradition:

> We all used to share food together. We used to buy chickens and slaughter them secretly in our bathroom so that English people did not know.

Helal Ali too, who arrived around the same time, enjoyed that atmosphere even though, as we shall see later on, he later regretted coming to Britain in the first place.

> It was fun at that time. We were all single people, staying together and cooking together. It was not bad at all. At that time the English people were good to us, too.

Our key informant Faruk (see chapter 1) also remembers it as a good time:

> Our plan then was to earn enough money to be able to go back and buy some land. People did not start to bring their families over until after the [1971] war so we were all single. But we had a good time. I used to go to meet friends, have a gossip and cook a meal, then eat and come back home. Some people used to play cards. I never took part, as I do not know how to play. Also my mother told me, before I came here, not to play cards.

Although not present, families were not forgotten and provided the key motivation to earn and save money, which in those circumstances was not too difficult. Faruk again:

> When I started to earn money in this country I didn't let my mum struggle. I used to send money every month. My governor was a good man, a Jew, and he helped me to learn my work and to make good money. I used to bring work home to earn extra money. When I joined the factory [in 1963] I used to earn £7 a week, and another £25 from overtime – because that was not taxed. That was more than enough for me. Rent was £1 a week and a packet of cigarettes, which I could manage for two days, was less than a pound. So I was able to make property in my country and spend money on my children.

Others, like Shiraj Mizan, were able to 'make property' in London as well. Mr Mizan worked in a number of factories in the Midlands before coming to London in the late sixties and taking a job in the clothing industry around Brick Lane. He did well out of this, becoming a local landlord himself:

> I worked for various tailoring factories, I can't remember all of their names now. I started at £15 per week and later used to get £50 – though prices had gone up by then. In the beginning I lived with a group and we used to share the food costs. Rent was £1 a week and food not more than £2. The rest of the income was saved, then used to buy land in Bangladesh. A third of an acre of land was £50. Then I jointly bought a house off Brick Lane with one of my friends for £1,400. My contribution was £500. I had two rooms and he had three. It was good and close to my work, so I could come home to have lunch.

In addition to the houses owned by Bangladeshi landlords, there were also a number of flats in Victorian tenements in the neighbourhood occupied by Bangladeshi tenants. Often they had to pay inflated deposits, 'key money', in order to secure a tenancy in the first place, so they chose to sub-let intensively to friends and relatives. Tenements became more viable economically when overcrowded. This enabled savings to be made and remittances paid but kept men in a totally Bengali-speaking environment.

This led to a catch-22 situation. Single men without families stood a negligible chance of being allocated council housing. They could manage by themselves in cramped circumstances, but it was hard to break out and to get more space into which they could fit their families. The standard route to collecting enough points was by starting a family in privately rented housing. This was not available to them as there was not enough space in the premises they occupied to accommodate families in the first place. Family men had little better chance. Those who already had wives and children in Bangladesh could not think of bringing them to the UK to live in that sort of housing. So even existing family men could not normally aspire to family housing here, unless they were particularly successful in their business.

However, there were changes taking place in their right to leave and enter the UK which were making migration more difficult, and creating incentives to settle properly. People born in the empire – while it was one – had been regarded as having a right to live in Britain, but the Commonwealth Immigrants Act of 1962 introduced a system of employment vouchers which put restrictions on this right. After the Act it was no longer possible to enter freely from a British colony or former colony. The system was further tightened in 1965 by regulations which limited vouchers to skilled workers and to those applicants who had jobs promised and waiting for them. In practice the latter could only be arranged for men who already had kin living in Britain.

Despite these and other restrictions, it has been estimated that up to 70,000 Bangladeshis were living in Britain by 1971.[10] Two events in the early 1970s changed many men's minds and motivated them to think differently about their long-term plans. Firstly, there was a particularly severe cyclone in November 1970 which caused devastation in Sylhet, as in other parts of Bengal. Secondly, and more serious still, the civil war to gain independence from Pakistan broke out in 1971. It was a ferocious conflict, with great loss of life in Sylhet, and many people were left destitute.

Political instability followed the violence. This war and its aftermath were the shock which persuaded many of the married men already in Britain to try to get their wives and children to England, despite all the hardship they might be forced to bear in an increasingly hostile country and the cramped, poor-quality housing that they would have to endure.

There were other factors pushing Bangladeshis towards the area. One of the rules of the Commonwealth Immigrants Act of 1962 had been that, although wives and children could enter the country, no son or daughter should be allowed into Britain after they had reached the age of 18. Many of the men who had come to Britain in the 1950s or early 1960s and went back to Bangladesh on a visit soon afterwards to marry now had children approaching that critical age. In addition, unaccompanied dependent children could legally be admitted only if it could be proven that the parent already in the UK had sole responsibility for them. So, if parents wanted one son to join his father here, it was usually necessary for the whole family to accompany him.

Concurrently the textile industries in the north of England were going into the most serious decline in their history. In the early 1970s, many mills closed down completely. This led to a further migration, within Britain now, from the north to Tower Hamlets and other parts of London where job prospects at the time were not so grim.

On top of all this there was yet another turn of the legislative screw. The Immigration Act of 1971 would, when it came into operation in 1973, close the door on new work-seekers and restrict future entries to the dependants of those who had got through the gates before they were shut.

Back in Sylhet, remittances from migrants were starting to fuel inflation, especially in land prices, so that fewer workers could anticipate retiring to the homeland in great style. Even though more Bangladeshis in the UK were now unemployed, the benefits provided by the welfare state were taking on a new and added significance. It may not have been an easy life for them in Britain, but there was a free health service (immensely important to a community with much higher than average rates of diabetes, heart disease and TB, the combined result of early poverty and poor working conditions in England), unemployment and disability benefits, political stability and, importantly, schools that were both free and better than those in Sylhet. All of this reinforced the growing conviction among Bangladeshis that the best place to unite or re-unite families was on British soil.

Through the 1970s the queues for visas began to lengthen at the British High Commission in Dhaka. Families were beginning to discover what became even clearer as the years went by: that getting permission was by no means quick or straightforward. Immigration officials regarded applications, especially from large families, with suspicion. One of our informants, Afia, had experienced this within her own family:

> [My sister] came five years later because there was an immigration problem. The people in the immigration office, they thought she wasn't our sister because she had darker skin than us, and none of them would believe that she was our sister. And then all these tests were taken, at the end [paternity] tests were taken. They were taken and then she had to come later. I was thinking, if they are going to let her come, why not let her come in the first place? And they didn't let her come, did they. Five years it was.

The Bangladeshi men, insofar as they were differentiated by their white neighbours from other immigrants, had not been perceived as much of a challenge when they were just men on their own. They were living and working almost invisibly. Living in poor quality privately rented housing and working in Bengali-speaking environments, whether in catering, clothing or light industry, they did not give rise to any complaints about housing or benefits. But when they began to be joined by their families things started to change. Each man became six or seven, eight or ten people. And they were not visitors; they were potential settlers. As the numbers increased so did the shops which served them with the kind of food they had at home; there was talk of mosques – mosques in Tower Hamlets! – and the new people were regarded by some as more and more of a threat to working-class life. The country from which they came was, the locals presumed, teeming with millions of people waiting to come to England. The whites who had 'owned' the place by right of long residence feared that they would soon be overwhelmed by a mass of new and strange people living next door but behind a wall of mutual incomprehension.

From the beginning, the greatest pressure was for housing. A few of the Bangladeshi ex-seamen had gone on to the waiting list. As far as the council's housing department was concerned they were non-persons, and council workers did not go out of their way to tell them what their housing rights were. When the wives and children arrived they too were often non-persons, packed in a limbo-land waiting for a policy. The officials and the Labour councillors were united in wanting the newcomers to go away, back home, to the north of England, anywhere. But as more and more came, and found housing with other Bangladeshis who were already living in conditions of dreadful over-crowding or in semi-derelict buildings which had been condemned, it was clear that they would not go away unless they were forced to, and that was not going to happen. If it had there would have been nowhere better for them to go. They would have been no more welcome in the boroughs where the British political class, which was facilitating their settlement, were living themselves.

The Squatting Initiative

Some of these reunited families, in desperate straits, were prompted to follow the trend of moving into houses that were empty. They saw all around them young English people who were taking the law into their own hands. This was the heyday of the squatters' movement and quite a number of young white squatters, like our Tony Hicks, were being drawn to the Brick Lane area by its central location and the planning blight which, as in other parts of London, was making a growing number of properties vacant. Some Bangladeshi men, seeing that apparently respectable white people were succeeding in this illegal endeavour, put aside some of the humility with which they had borne their lot in a country where they were the strangers, and joined in. They had even more to gain from it than the whites, students mostly, for whom squatting offered accommodation that bore no comparison to what they were used to at home. But for most Bangladeshi families a squat provided more space and facilities which, although usually inferior to those in council housing, were still greatly superior to anything that they had or could afford through private renting. Squatting, although alien to their own concepts of property and propriety, seemed to the Bangladeshis to fit in with local British custom and practice. More specifically it offered the beginning of a political alliance with the new left which was becoming increasingly active and dominant in municipal politics. This emerging alliance, perhaps more than anything, encouraged the community to put down roots in Spitalfields, and to use it as a base for further settlement in the East

End. As a strategy, squatting offered Bangladeshis a chance not only to do something for their families and establish themselves in the area physically but also to become part of the community both ideologically and politically.

Some Bangladeshi men started moving into empty properties in 1973 and 1974 in preparation for the arrival of their families – many of whom were as a result united for the first time. The first mass Bangladeshi squat took place a little later, over the summer of 1975, in some houses along Old Montague Street, off Brick Lane. This was organised by Abbas Uddin who was, significantly, later to become the first Bangladeshi councillor in Tower Hamlets, for the Labour Party. In February of the following year the Bengali Housing Action Group, BHAG, was formed, to unite the various squatting groups which had sprung up. Its title neatly straddles the two cultures: *bhag* in Bengali means 'tiger'.

The formation of this movement symbolised a crucial stage in the development of a Bangladeshi presence which was adapting positively to the conditions of East End life. BHAG brought together several hundred families in a collective bid for somewhere to live: a foothold which could turn into a bridgehead. It set up a waiting list and market for squattable properties, and as the list grew and the occupied properties deteriorated, it put pressure on the Greater London Council, at that time the main supplier of public housing in the Spitalfields end of Tower Hamlets, to rehouse the families in decent flats. Through these campaigns people in the emerging Bangladeshi community were developing an awareness of their rights as British citizens – rights which moreover proved effective in delivering to many if not most of the newcomers, over the next twenty years, the tangible benefit of reasonable housing and material security.

With the benefit of hindsight it is easier to see that this alliance worked for both parties to it. White squatters welcomed squatting by Bangladeshi families as it strengthened their own legitimacy and compromised municipal reaction. Councils were reluctant to send in bailiffs and police to clear a squat if they knew that poor Asian women and children would have to be evicted too, all under the hungry gaze of reporters and TV cameras. So at an ideological level the alliance enabled the white squatters to portray themselves heroically as part of an international working-class movement combating British imperialist oppression. Spitalfields was not alone.

This high-publicity collaboration on the left of the Labour Party during the 1970s proved critical in modernising the local party. It has been a key axis in it ever since, had a tremendous effect in encouraging similar movements in other parts of the UK, and arguably became stronger and more significant as time passed and New Labour evolved. For the Bangladeshis, the early and middle seventies were the period when key attitudes were formed, with defining decisions and struggles taking place around housing. Bold public action, using the force and concentration of the *bhag* to grasp citizenship rights instead of just waiting to be given them, was revealed as the mode of collective behaviour needed to unite and look after their families. The second half of the 1970s then tested the resolve of the community, as the resistance of resident whites to the Bangladeshi exercise of these rights was mobilised.

A Battle of Principles

White resistance was informed ideologically by a concept of tenancy allocation in public housing which revolved around membership of community and contribution to it. Early ICS research shows how the 'sons and daughters' principle followed by private landlords, which allowed established tenants to secure new tenancies for family members (and pass on their own), gave a collective property right to tenants' families. It offered families who behaved well and were good neighbours the means to remain part of that community.[11] Another traditional practice, which was also adopted by municipal housing managers as local government took over from private landlords, was the 'ladder principle', whereby the more desirable housing would be reserved for those tenants who proved themselves most deserving. This principle meant that the best flats were occupied by loyal tenants of long standing, pillars of local society, who had waited patiently for them and thrown themselves into neighbourhood affairs. This administration of housing was closely attuned to local interests and networks. In a situation of scarcity it was commitment to local community – involving concern for the needs of *others* – which served you best in the end.

These practices, which attached a lot of weight to communitarian values, were considered fair in traditional working-class morality. Even if the supply of housing was limited, and waiting periods were long, the eventual allocation reflected and rewarded local participation. It allowed those who wanted to get on to the ladder the chance to do so eventually, and then to inch their way up it. The radical housing commentator Charlie Forman later criticised the system as hopelessly judgmental and old-fashioned. But even he readily acknowledged its legitimacy among ordinary white residents in east London, as shown by a letter in its defence he quotes from the *East London Advertiser*:

> Over the years and with a growing family, we have gone from one estate to another, a little better each time until five years ago when we moved to the Glamis Estate. It took me 27 years to achieve the best but I appreciate it because I've also had the worst ... So fair's fair. Let everyone work their way up the housing ladder and prove they deserve the Glamis and Exmouth estates.[12]

As welfare became more centralised and individualised, this communitarian principle was put under growing pressure. The new principle that housing should be provided according to need created severe problems in public housing, where there are limits to the volume of resources available in any particular locality. So legislation was required to reform the way in which supports were provided to citizens. The level of personal need became identified by Whitehall as the overriding criterion for allocation, at the expense of long residence in an area, length of time on a waiting list or 'good behaviour'.

The comprehensive 1966 Local Government Act included provisions to help local authorities meet the needs of Commonwealth immigrants. But the real turning point for housing came with the 1977 Housing (Homeless Persons) Act, which specified homelessness as the key to public housing entitlement. This well-meant act was later found to have unanticipated consequences. In overcrowded areas it was eventually to push council housing away from the long-term 'respectable' poor and towards those who depended on public support. It helped to revive the only recently defeated notion of welfare as charity and was part of a push in social policy in an Americanised direction, which continued under Thatcher and New Labour.[13]

This modernisation of welfare resulted in a system different in both its ethos and its implications from that operating in the early post-war period. Ideas about welfare as an insurance principle or commonly owned and shared pool which was simply administered by the state started to give way to a view of the state as a powerful and benevolent agent for engineering social change by meeting personal needs in a manner compatible with universal and progressive social justice. It took control of citizenship benefits away from the local community, and underlined the power of state experts and bureaucrats to define acceptable rules and objectives. No longer would it be possible to work your way by patience and good behaviour to the head of the queue: a set of central and invariable rules, dominated by the absolute requirement to house the homeless, would override your claim. The squatting movement rode confidently on this new wave of policymaking, against increasingly bitter local white sentiments.

It was also a shift which boosted the cause of minorities. Immigrant groups had been served badly by traditional community-based welfare, but under the new system they could expect to move to the top of the list if they were able to demonstrate the greatest deprivation and need. The weight given to the homelessness principle quickly opened up the East End to settlement by outsiders and loss of local control.

The Battle for Spitalfields

The squatting initiative was a crucial step for Bangladeshis towards the decisive identification of Spitalfields as the heartland of the new community. BHAG and some other local groups formed the Spitalfields Project to keep up constant pressure on the GLC. They demanded recognition of Bangladeshi needs, reversal of planning priorities which ruled out the construction of new residential properties in the Brick Lane area, and the refurbishment for reletting of those existing empty (and squatted) properties which were not beyond repair. After a period of confrontation, a major breakthrough occurred in 1977 when the Conservatives took control of the GLC and wrongfooted their Labour opponents by offering the squatters an amnesty and the promise of rehousing.

National public opinion had been shifting in relation to the housing needs of immigrants, not least as a result of publicity given to the plight of the Bangladeshis in Spitalfields. The 1977 Homeless Persons Act placed a statutory obligation on local authorities to give priority to the homeless, and this no doubt was a factor behind the

GLC's U-turn. The offer to squatters in return prompted a number of associations of Bangladeshi private tenants to petition the GLC for immediate rehousing. So by the beginning of 1978 the overall demand for council housing in the area was rising significantly. This threatened Tower Hamlets' cherished but dormant plans for office development on the borders of the City.

The rapid build-up of Bangladeshi pressure soon brought to the surface a growing conflict of interest between them and white working-class council tenants. In 1977 there were 15,000 applications to the British authorities in Dhaka from Bangladeshi dependants seeking leave of entry to the UK. Many of those families which had already arrived over the previous few years had shown a strong preference for settlement in the Spitalfields area. This was not just because they felt safer there but also because women coming from Bangladesh understood little English and valued the social contacts and support that proximity to a Bangladeshi community provided.[14] Both GLC and Tower Hamlets housing officers had tried to cope with the demand from families by dispersing them with offers of flats on estates in other parts of the borough. There was little available within Spitalfields itself at that time, but many Bangladeshis felt that they should have been offered flats in estates nearer to it. They suspected that housing officers were excluding them from a planned 'white cordon' of newer and nearer estates.

Many Bangladeshi tenants who had been pushed to the eastern part of Tower Hamlets moved back to Spitalfields as soon as they could, often following harassment by neighbours but sometimes just because of their social isolation. Some of the returners became squatters for a second time. Indeed, a number of the original Bangladeshi squatters in Spitalfields in the first years of the seventies had been early-arriving families who had already been rehoused in the east of the borough following slum clearance of privately rented property, and were desperate to get back to the area of first settlement by any means open to them.[15]

Given this strong attachment of Bangladeshis to the Brick Lane area, the new GLC agreement to rehouse them was perhaps bound to be interpreted by some white residents as a precursor to their own displacement. This fear, duly played on by National Front agitators, was then given an opportunity to explode into panic by the way in which the GLC attempted to reassure BHAG that as many Bangladeshis as possible would be accommodated in the Brick Lane area. Early in 1978 BHAG had drawn up a list of estates within that area where it felt that Bangladeshi families could be housed safely. Soon after this a document was leaked to the *Observer* which referred to plans being drafted by the GLC. This included 'setting aside a few blocks of flats in or near Spitalfields specifically for the occupation of people from Bangladesh, in co-operation with the leaders of the Bangladeshi community'. It also suggested that white tenants were already *choosing* to move out. This document, at once dubbed the Ghetto Plan, was discussed at a crowded and acrimonious public meeting in the middle of June 1978, at which GLC officials declared, amid considerable confusion, that its allocations were in fact to be made solely on the basis of need, to whites and Bangladeshis alike.

Blood on the Streets

It was in January 1978 that Margaret Thatcher had famously spoken on television about the fear of white people that they were being 'swamped by people with a different culture'.[16] White panic had already been triggered and was not allayed. Bangladeshi tenants had been encountering increasing harassment, and violence had already started to boil over on the streets. The National Front had stepped up the provocation by setting up a stall to sell their newspaper on the corner of Brick Lane and Bethnal Green Road, and on 4 May 1978 Altab Ali, a 24-year-old machinist, was fatally stabbed in Whitechapel, just south of Brick Lane. Seven thousand people joined a funeral march to Downing Street and 8,000 police officers were brought into the district for the occasion. Several public demonstrations took place over the summer, culminating in a National Front rally in late August. The whole extended episode in 1978 was a scaled-down but still forbidding version of the Battle of Cable Street of 1936, when the police clashed with anti-fascists and local residents who had built barricades to prevent Oswald Mosley's British Union of Fascists marching through the East End.[17]

This joint defence of Bangladeshi territory by community members alongside representatives of the British state marks the effective baptism of Brick Lane as the centre of the Bangladeshi community, and the point at which it ensured a future for itself in the area. It also coincided with a concentration of power in the hands of the Bangladeshi youth movements and political activists who had overcome white resistance in the secular world, and at the expense of traditional voices urging placation of local white people. Through this episode the values of Islam became (at least temporarily) overshadowed by the standing of the secular tigers. It was they who were showing how to meet the needs of ordinary Bangladeshi families in the real world, and how to lay claim to a new homeland on UK soil.

Over the next few years a great deal happened to housing in Spitalfields. Old properties were renovated and the construction of new housing was accelerated, by both the GLC and Tower Hamlets council, and for the first time a substantial proportion of local offers were made to Bangladeshi applicants. Much of the work for this new planning and provision was carried out by housing associations and co-operatives, in which the local authorities collaborated with central government and groups of local residents. This was especially valuable for the Bangladeshi community as it increased their direct say – and in particular the influence of women – over the character of their housing. It also confirmed the loss of power of the hostile parts of the local white majority.

The wave of building and conversions which got underway at the end of the 1970s gave Bangladeshi settlement a boost by creating a local environment which began to resemble Sylhet town in its retail outlets, amenities and, in small parts of the borough, in its population. This is reflected in the growth of the Bangladeshi community in the three decades since the 1971 census. In that year, the number of people in Tower Hamlets born in Pakistan was some 3,500, of whom fewer than 500 were women. Ten

Figure 2.1 **Known arrival dates in the UK for Bangladeshi subjects and other household members**
(Number of men, women and women with children, by period)

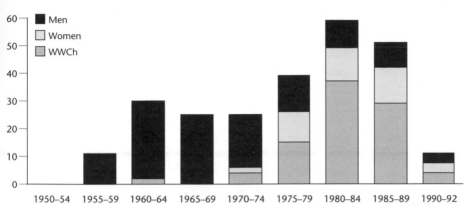

Note: 1990–92 data for three years only.

years later the comparable figures were over 9,800 born in Bangladesh, of whom just under 3,500 were women. By this time too there would have been a number of locally born Bangladeshis. The number grew steadily during the 1980s, as is shown in figure 2.1 which plots the known arrival dates of the men, women and children in the households of 171 Bangladeshi respondents (approximately 250 arrivals in total) in the 1992 survey. The top sections represent the arrivals of men, most of whom came alone in the earlier years, a pattern peaking in the years 1960–64. The men arriving in the 1980s and later are more likely to have been joining their fathers already in Britain, or joining wives who were already British citizens. The middle and lowest sections show the numbers of adult women coming alone and accompanied by their dependent children, respectively. It seems clear that the majority of men were joined by wives who already had dependent children and that the peak years of the unification of these families were 1980–84, or twenty years after the peak arrival dates for men on their own.

Against the trend in the rest of Inner London, the population of Tower Hamlets grew between 1981 and 1991. By 1991 some 37,000, or just under a quarter, were Bangladeshi and by this time too the ratio of men to women was nearer equality. However, the Bangladeshi population was still very much concentrated in the western end of the borough, comprising nearly two-thirds of all residents in the Spitalfields ward itself, in a neighbourhood with a clear majority of council tenants. By the end of the century the number of Bangladeshis had risen to marginally over one third of the borough population, over 65,500 people. It is one of the most rapid settlements ever to have taken place in the East End.

There are few places where children can play in the most crowded parts of the borough.

Chapter 3

Spread and Conflict

The battle of Spitalfields was decisive in enabling the Bangladeshi community to put down roots in east London. It proved, however, to be only the beginning of their struggles. There continued to be sustained opposition from parts of the existing white population – themselves including many descendants of Irish and Jewish immigrants who had faced similar opposition as incomers. Such opposition was present from the outset in the case of Spitalfields itself, and for a while even after the battle of the late 1970s there was pressure to disperse new Bangladeshi tenants to outlying estates in the borough. But it has been equally true of other parts of the borough that Bangladeshis have moved into, in which there has been fierce resistance to their perceived encroachment.

Once it had established a heartland in Spitalfields, the Bangladeshi community grew steadily through further immigration of dependants and a traditionally high birth rate. It needed to look further afield in order to find vacant housing, and the conflict spread as new settlement took place in other parts of the borough and was met by white reaction. To many Bangladeshis this expansion may appear to have been painfully slow, precarious and uncertain, but in terms of historical replacement of population the turnover has been sudden and dramatic.

The Spreading Settlement

We have seen that information on the size of the Bangladeshi community is limited for the early years of settlement. The 1981 census asked about birthplace, but not about the ethnic origin of people born in the UK. This omission mattered less for newly arrived settlers such as Bangladeshis than for longer established groups, but it does nevertheless mean that we do not have a very sharp picture. All that is clear from the 1981 census is that by then most settlement appears to have been in Spitalfields, on the western edge of Tower Hamlets, with some movement into areas to the south such as Whitechapel and Stepney.

The 1991 and 2001 censuses both contain fuller data, allowing us to trace the movement of Bangladeshis as they spread from this western corner into other parts of the borough. When considering the nature of this flow and looking at individual wards, we realised that the borough could be divided into four 'blocs' of adjacent wards with broadly similar Bangladeshi profiles and characteristics. Comparing rates of change in these four areas gives a clearer view of the main pattern of spread of the community. To make things more complicated, between 1991 and 2001 the ward composition changed, with many wards changing name, some disappearing and most modifying their bound-aries. But the same broad blocs could be reconstructed reasonably well from the new units. The first bloc, occupying the south-west corner of the borough, contains the origi-nal core of the Bangladeshi settlement. It comprises the wards of Spitalfields – the com-munal *heartland* and now fittingly renamed Spitalfields and Banglatown – plus, in 1991, St Mary's, St Dunstan's, Shadwell and St Katharine's. These were the first areas settled by Bangladeshis in the decades before families were reunited. Parts of this bloc, as along the Wapping waterfront, are pockets of mainly white (and now middle-class) residence. But every ward in it contained at least 35 per cent Bangladeshis at the time of the 1991 census, in total some 20,000, representing 41 per cent of the total ward populations and 61 per cent in the case of Spitalfields. Of these Bangladeshis, 11,000 were under 18, which was 78 per cent of the population in this age group. For the 2001 census data this area is covered by Spitalfields and Banglatown plus Whitechapel, St Dunstan's and Stepney Green, Shadwell, and St Katharine's and Wapping. In 2001 these wards had increased their Bangladeshi population by a quarter, to 25,000, representing nearly 45 per cent of the bloc population. It is noteworthy that this increase involved a general consolidation through most of the bloc (apart from Wapping) rather than an intensification within Spitalfields, where the statistics show a slight reduction in the proportion of Bangla-deshis, although changes to ward boundaries make exact comparisons difficult.

The second bloc, which we have called the *outer core* of settlement, consisted in 1991 of Weavers, Holy Trinity, Redcoat and St Peter's wards, located on the northern edge of the heartland. For the 2001 census this area was covered by Weavers, Bethnal Green North, Bethnal Green South, and Mile End and Globe Town. This was the first area into which the Bangladeshi community started to expand from the mid-seventies onwards, already making up one quarter of the population in these wards by 1991 and approach-ing 38 per cent by 2001. Together these first two blocs constitute the western half of Tower Hamlets, containing four-fifths of the Bangladeshis in 1991.

The eastern half of the borough does not divide up quite so neatly. Extensions of the Bangladeshi community have moved out from the heartland along the Mile End Road (which becomes Bow Road) into Bromley-by-Bow, and down Commercial Road (becoming the East India Dock Road) to the Limehouse and Poplar area. They have cut into a ring of almost exclusively white territory, dissecting it into a number of white enclaves. Some of the islands created are large enough to have retained a predomi-nantly white character. Others are not, and are the scene of greater competition. This difference forms the basis of our division of eastern Tower Hamlets between a 'zone of conflict' and the 'white corners'.

The most obvious resistance to Bangladeshis for most of the late eighties and during the nineties was located in the east-central area of the borough, lying across these main arterial channels. This delineates the bloc three we have designated as the main *zone of conflict* during the nineties. In 1991 it consisted of Limehouse, Blackwall, Bromley, Lansbury and East India wards. In 2001 the area was covered by Mile End East, Bromley-by-Bow, Limehouse, and East India and Lansbury. At the 1991 census, the wards of Lansbury and East India still contained less than 10 per cent Bangladeshis, and still made up an effectively white enclave. But by 2001 the proportion had risen to 30 per cent – and to nearly a third for this bloc of wards as a whole. This has been the area in which greatest change and conflict has been taking place while our study was being conducted.

The two longest surviving white enclaves in the corners of the borough together make up our fourth bloc of wards. In 2001 the northern part comprised Bow West and Bow East and is the area south of Victoria Park. The southern part, basically the Isle of Dogs, consisted of the large ward of Millwall in 1991, but in the 2001 census the ward structure was contained within a rearranged Millwall plus Blackwall and Cubitt Town. The south-east corner now therefore contains a slice of conflict zone around the East India Dock Road. Apart from this small northern strip of Blackwall the proportion of Bangladeshis in 2001 ranged between 10 and 15 per cent for the wards in this bloc. Including the strip, the overall percentage for the bloc reaches 15 per cent.

The two maps below show the density of the Bangladeshi population in all the borough's wards in 1991 and 2001. In order to show clearly the pattern and direction of the population movement we have not labelled individual wards, but the maps show where, and by roughly how much, the Bangladeshi population grew as a percentage of the whole in the various parts of the borough over the course of the decade.

The accompanying tabulation (table 3.1) presents data showing the profiles of the Bangladeshi populations of these areas in 1991 and 2001. In 1991 Bangladeshis in the 0–17 cohort already formed a large majority in the west of the borough. Even in the eastern half of the borough they constituted a sizeable minority of that age grouping. This is why there was such a strong sense in the borough throughout the decade that the Bangladeshi community was still growing fast.

Table 3.1 shows that the young population in the heartland bloc appears to have peaked and, as we argue generally, it was within the zone of conflict that the young Bangladeshi population grew by the largest percentage during the decade. The fact that the 0–4 population in this bloc was proportionately even higher than the 0–17 age range seems to imply that the rate of growth may well continue in this part of the borough.

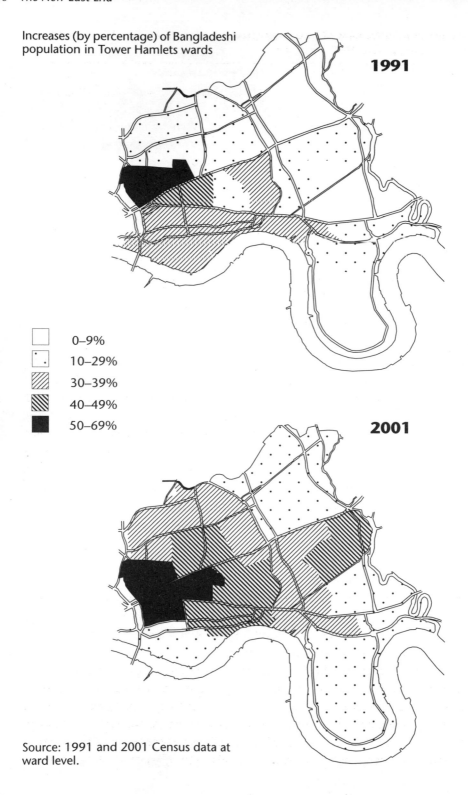

Increases (by percentage) of Bangladeshi
population in Tower Hamlets wards

1991

0–9%
10–29%
30–39%
40–49%
50–69%

2001

Source: 1991 and 2001 Census data at
ward level.

Table 3.1 **Bangladeshi settlement of four Tower Hamlets blocs (Bangladeshi percentages of area population, 1991 and 2001)**

Bloc	All ages:		0–17 years		0–4 years
	1991	*2001*	*1991*	*2001*	*2001*
1. Heartland (SW)	41	45	78	74	69
2. Outer Core (NW)	25	38	58	64	63
West of borough	*34*	*41*	*70*	*69*	*66*
3. Conflict zone (Central E)	14	33	38	52	56
4. White corners (NE & SE)	7	15	20	33	32
East of borough	*11*	*24*	*30*	*45*	*47*
All Tower Hamlets	23	33	54	58	58

Sources: Base figures derived from 1991 census research report, Tower Hamlets Corporate Policy and Equalities Division, April 1997. 2001 figures from 2001 census.

Changing Population Structures

We can also learn something about the roots of inter-community relations by looking at differential age structures of the populations of these zones. The first settlement of Bangladeshi families took place in run-down parts of the borough, alongside young white childless newcomers. These two groups shared from the outset an interest in opening up the area. They then also discovered considerable complementarity of needs and lifestyles. For their part Bangladeshi families, often arriving with large numbers of children, needed school places and access to local social services. There was far less competition for these from the incoming whites than from existing working-class families. At the same time, the presence of Bangladeshi families gave many yuppies a lot of satisfaction. Sharing public space with families that were quite external to their own lives and needs meant that they could enjoy the sense of belonging to a cosmopolitan community without having any demands made on them.

The result of this affinity between the two incoming groups has been that the age composition of areas with high-density Bangladeshi settlement has remained distinctive. In spite of some attempts by housing officers to promote a more mixed community by placing white families on estates in the west of the borough, the population still shows a noticeable deficit of white family households.

To explore and illustrate this we sorted the 1991 census data into four age groupings.[1] Those aged 0–17 we counted as family dependants, those 18–34 as young adults – who among middle-class newcomers at any rate are unlikely to be parents, the 35–54 age group we assumed to be mostly parents and the over-55s we treated as (family) elders unlikely to have direct responsibility for children. These four groups were then pooled into two major population sectors. Dependants (0–17) and parents (35–54) were brought together as a 'family class' whose lives revolve significantly around the bringing up of children. The young adults (18–34) and elders (55+) are by contrast those most free of day-to-day family responsibilities, and in domestic terms can be seen as together constituting something of a leisured class.

The family class as defined here has of course been in decline nationally over the last twenty to thirty years, as families have become smaller and more people have postponed or decided against having children at all. The decline in Tower Hamlets since 1971 has been noticeably steeper than elsewhere in the country, including the rest of Inner London, certainly when we look specifically at the white population (which we can separate out in 1991). The rate for this sector has fallen by a quarter between 1971 and 1991, compared with a sixth for Inner London as a whole, and with just one thirteenth for England and Wales. The percentage of children in the white community in Tower Hamlets fell by more than a third. White families as defined here have disappeared much faster in Tower Hamlets than in any area of comparable size in the UK that we could find.

This direction and speed of change for Tower Hamlets reflects the rapid gentrification taking place in the borough as young childless professionals replace the traditional population. But it is also bound up with Bangladeshi immigration, and there is a positive association between the deficit in the family class among the white population and the density of Bangladeshi settlement. This is, of course, the sector of the white population that we would expect to be in most direct competition with immigrant families for scarce local facilities and services – especially in housing and education. On that basis they would be the most liable to feel squeezed out, and to decide that life would be better elsewhere.

Sure enough, our data show that in the western wards where Bangladeshi settlement is high the proportion of white residents in the family class is extremely low. In the areas of low Bangladeshi settlement in the east of the borough, which do include several districts of gentrification, the levels of white family-class occupation were higher, indeed rather more so than the rate for Inner London as a whole. So at the beginning of the 1990s the eastern part of the borough seemed to have retained some white families 'holding out' against Bangladeshi settlement.

Evidence from School Rolls

School rolls are a further source of data which helps to map the spread of Bangladeshis through the borough from the mid-1980s to the end of the century. Under the Inner London Education Authority schools monitored both their ethnic composition and the mother-tongue usage of their pupils, at regular intervals from the early eighties onwards. Their recording system was taken over and improved after 1986 when the

GLC was disbanded and responsibility for local education was devolved to Tower Hamlets, although figures for the early years of this monitoring are not wholly reliable. Numbers of Bangladeshis were small, only a sample of school registrations was dealt with, and the main purpose of the exercise, which was to apportion Section 11 funding,* may have influenced its conduct. But the data still offer useful measures, because they deal with different sets of behaviour. Given this, the parallel between these findings and data from other sources is telling.

What we find is that primary schools within the Bangladeshi core areas already had a clear majority of Bangladeshi children by the mid-1980s. If anything, the outer core appears to have had a higher proportion of Bangladeshi school-age children in relation to its overall Bangladeshi population than the inner. This presumably reflects the pressure on school places inside the core, where there were at the time relatively few schools. Many Bangladeshi children therefore needed to go further from their homes to find places. The schools in the outer core may not have been much further, but what it does mean is that there will have been a daily pull in the same (northward and eastward) direction for many families, which could have helped to speed their residential shift in those directions too. This regular spilling over of educational demand will have helped to familiarise them with other parts of the borough into which they might then move. To the south of the inner core is the river, and to the west is the City – with virtually no residents and negligible social facilities. Settlers requiring services not available within the core would have needed to move north and east, and education is likely to have been a key determinant of such expansion.

The movement of children to schools east of where they were living confirms that during the early 1990s competition for social resources was building up between white and Bangladeshi families in the east of the borough. This is supported by the fact that there was a higher rate of family-class residence in the east of the borough among Bangladeshis themselves than in the west – though not so much higher as that among whites. This could in part be a consequence of housing market factors during the 1980s, with an increase of supply drawing more families to the area, but even without this we would perhaps expect higher proportions of Bangladeshi children in the east. The longer established Bangladeshi migrants, with older or adult offspring, have always been concentrated in the western heartland. When those offspring marry and have children of their own, they are likely to move away from the overcrowded conditions of the heartland to the margins of the community in order to find new accommodation. It is therefore not unexpected that the east has a more youthful Bangladeshi profile.

---

*A special provision for language teaching to non-English speaking children later changed to the EMAG grant – see details in chapter 7.

White Resistance

In 1991, less than a generation after the battle for Spitalfields, Bangladeshis constituted nearly a quarter of the overall Tower Hamlets population, and a decade later had become marginally more than a third. Behind these figures, however, lies a great deal of conflict. The state authorities had accepted the right of immigrant families to be here, and did their best to protect them as citizens, but many old East Enders resented their presence.

In the early years the migrating children found themselves heavily outnumbered at school. Their relative isolation left them open to bullying, often brutal. This was not necessarily from other pupils. Shohel Uddin estimated that one in twenty of the children at his school were from Bangladesh. He himself never had any problems, and in fact had lots of white friends, many of whom called him the 'Perfect Paki' – in part because his spoken English was so good. But others were not so fortunate, and he remembers an attack during the first week at his secondary school in Spitalfields in 1980 when he was 11:

> There was a lot of racial tension at the time, a lot of tension, and various attacks, and I was at school one day when some older boys came into the playground at break-time and pulled one of the eleven-year-olds into a lavatory on the side of the playground. He had attended junior school with me. They took him into the toilets, shoved his head down the bowl, flushed it several times, broke three of his ribs and smashed his face onto the sink. That resulted in him losing three or four teeth and a broken nose. They were older boys with bovver boots and shaved heads. They left him with his head poked down the lavatory. They were not part of the school themselves, but they had friends in the school. I'm sorry to say he never returned to the school again. He didn't attend school for a good few years, and had special tuition.

Few attacks like this have taken place inside school premises. More common are scuffles in the street between groups of teenagers and, particularly disturbing for families, the harassment of people inside their flats. As we arrived to interview our informant Arshod Alom two policemen were leaving his flat following an incident. Earlier that afternoon some white children from flats across the road had been throwing stones at their windows, and some glass had been broken. Mr Alom and his wife were frightened as their baby son had been in the room near the window. They had rung the police three times before the officers eventually attended. The police had visited the culprits, given a caution and advised Mr Alom to contact them immediately if the problem recurred.

Another respondent, Maryum Dutta, living at the other end of Bethnal Green, has experienced hostility quite often, although she seemed surprisingly philosophical about it. 'A few days ago some kids threw stones at us in the street when I was picking up my children from school. But they were only kids, and we are foreigners. Even if they are racist we have to bear it. You have to get on with people of other races.' However, her family had fallen out with a white neighbour, and her husband had given up work as he is now afraid to leave the family alone. When they moved into their current flat, the neighbour had started to complain that they made too much noise: 'He started to bang on the ceiling if he heard any noise. Then it got worse. He came round and kept kicking our front door. So we reported it to the police and complained to the council. The council warned them not to do this again, otherwise they would be evicted.' At her request, the council has now put them on the transfer list.

This sort of experience is common. Many families have found it necessary to move, and often to refuse an offer of housing, because of their likely reception. Naveen Mannan's cousin Ruksana went with some of her family to look at a flat they had been offered on the ninth floor of a tower block. They had hostile racist remarks made to them by the white neighbours and an elderly woman was heard to say to a white boy of 11 or 12, 'Go on, go and hit them, go on.' The council worker advised them to accept the flat because under the regulations currently in force the council was obliged to make only one offer of housing. However, Naveen's family helped the couple to insist on being made another offer because of the racial harassment they were obviously likely to encounter. A few weeks later they were offered their present maisonette and accepted it. Despite the fact that there are only four Bangladeshi families in the block, everybody is friendly.

As the numbers of Bangladeshis have grown, so has their ability and inclination to fight back.[2] Young people increasingly form defensive gangs. Shohel saw this happening over time:

> As the Bengali population grew things gradually got better. I can remember my form teacher one year saying – this was when I was getting older, when I was in the fifth year – that she had always seen the Bengalis as a very passive race. Very loving and affectionate. But they've become more aggressive, more willing to defend themselves. She said she didn't know if it was a good thing or a bad thing. But certainly when the Bengalis started to stand up for themselves and were more willing to fight back things did quieten down. So in a sad way it took violence to quieten violence. And by the time I was finishing in the sixth form things were vastly improved. The population grew to a size where they could defend themselves. Those little boys who were beaten in the playground as first years and second years were no longer willing to turn the other cheek when they had reached the fourth and fifth years.

The fact that forming gangs clearly had a part to play in protecting the wider Bangladeshi community gave them a legitimacy which they might not have had in different circumstances. One incomer from Manchester, Kalpana Sattar, explained that compared with the school she had been to there she felt safe in Stepney:

> I had racial problems from the first day of school in Manchester. Someone harasses you all the time, you know. 'What is your colour, black? Who are you? Why are you? Why you got such long hair?' Just walking in front of us, 'You stink.' All that stuff, nasty ... But this place is better, it is all good. These days the gangsters; you know the Asian boys, the gangsters. They do try to face all the racism. They try and do something because of our colour. They'll stand up and fight against it.

Comfort in Numbers

The most reliable way of finding safety in numbers lies in staying within or moving back into the Brick Lane heartland. During the seventies most white liberals felt unhappy about the prospect of a Bangladeshi ghetto forming around Spitalfields. But over the next decade, as the community achieved majority status there, and the area became visibly more peaceful, white attitudes changed. The development of 'Banglatown' was increasingly regarded as a desirable objective. It was assisted by the setting up of a police station in Brick Lane in 1978 when rioting was at a peak. This had prevented the situation getting out of hand and restored order. The police presence gave increased protection in Spitalfields, but the first defensive action was usually taken by Bangladeshis themselves. The method used was often a 'telephone tree': someone being victimised would ring a friend nearby who would then alert other friends and so on. A crowd could be on the spot in a short time, often before the police. Even those without a telephone could usually rely on help from countrymen living nearby.[3]

By the time of our own survey most of the informants living in the heartland felt safe there. Mobushir Zaman, for example, had first come to Spitalfields in 1965, and had moved to the north of the borough to get a larger flat after his family arrived. He found a lot of racial tension there. 'There were a lot of racial attacks, and I had to do work [for the mosque] on a lot of the cases myself.' Shortly before our second interview with him in 1996 he had moved back into the Brick Lane heartland. He felt much safer there, and had an active social life in the Islamic cultural centre at the mosque. Perhaps significantly, he seemed relatively more attached to friends and less tied to family socialising than most of our Bangladeshi respondents. He remained fearful of other parts of the borough, and said that he would avoid areas such as Victoria Park and Bow Common Lane, especially after dark.

Another respondent, Mitu Das, had lived near Brick Lane since he arrived as a child in the early 1970s. He too felt safe there, in spite of the violence in the past. He said he would avoid groups of young black youths, but that 'With white people there are no problems generally.' As far as he knew none of his children had been involved in fights. However, his experience of being confined within Banglatown may have left him overconfident. At our second interview he announced that the family had been offered a larger flat, in Poplar, and would soon be moving. He was not anxious about this, and felt that if they were nice to their neighbours they would be treated well in return. 'Bangladeshis are very friendly people if there are nice people around.'

This is unusual. Most recognised that the Spitalfields community was important in giving real protection. Even Nizam Jabbar, who had, unusually, come to the UK as a political refugee (a communist) and was quite hostile to religion, still felt most secure in the west of the borough. 'White people may seem friendly but they don't all show their real attitudes.' He would avoid 'Globe Road and east of that, by Victoria Park'.

Because of the safety factor, many families who had gained even a crowded perch in

Spitalfields living with relatives refused more ample accommodation elsewhere. After the Greater London Council (while it was still one of the housing authorities for the borough) changed its allocation rules in 1984, we were told that 90 per cent of the offers to Asians of council housing on 'white' estates were refused. Whether or not this figure is correct, we know that many took the view that poor quality housing, even very poor quality housing, in a safe and known neighbourhood was better than a relatively good house surrounded by hostile people. Most Bangladeshis had heard only how bitter the white opposition would be once you got beyond the safe zone of Spitalfields. But it was not always possible to stay where it was safe; relatives housing a new family might be unwilling to go on doing so for long. Some people did go, not too unwillingly, south to nearby Wapping if they could get there, or north to Columbia Road or other places which were gradually incorporated into the heartland and had easy access to the great mosque on Whitechapel Road. But the more distant estates in Poplar, towards the east of the borough, were another matter altogether. They seemed much further away than the two or three miles they actually were. Only if there were no other choice would they go, sometimes in fear. But many incoming families indeed had no other choice, hence the gradual movement of Bangladeshis from west to east.

In the Conflict Zone

To confirm our opinion that Spitalfields was in no way typical of Tower Hamlets we decided to look at one of the estates of east Poplar in 1995. We chose the Teviot Estate.

The Teviot Estate is like an island, with 1,041 homes on it at the time we visited, 800 of which were council owned. Only 4 per cent of the households were Bangladeshi in 1995. The only ways out of the island on three sides were through tunnels or over bridges, for it had the misfortune of being cut off on one side by the Limehouse Cut, a section of the Grand Union Canal, on another by the Docklands Light Railway, and on another by the dual carriageway leading to the Blackwall Tunnel. The road could be crossed only via a subway and pedestrians were afraid to go through it to reach the supermarket that lay beyond. The unfortunate people in Tweed House, a block built in 1961 and already ripe for demolition, were only ten metres away from the A12 with its noise and pollution.

The flats facing the canal get the full force of the north wind and this resulted in a great deal of condensation on the inside walls; they were wet through for most of every winter. The estate at night had the air of a deserted town gradually falling down, which it was. Few people ventured out after dark. Most of the flats had been built, badly, in the 1950s. One of the worst was Hillary House, opened by the conqueror of Everest and named after him. Adjoining slab blocks were called Irvine and Mallory after other famous white mountaineers. What a tribute! They were the ugliest blocks in a borough famous for awful tower blocks. Hillary House was literally falling down. Slabs of concrete, like a Himalayan landslip, were liable to descend unexpectedly; at the time we were there a walkway had been closed off to avoid a fatality. (Happily, these blocks were demolished in 2004.)

Many of the flats had steel windows rusted and broken away from the walls, leaving daylight all around them. People disliked the central heating because it was so much more expensive than the coal fires they used to have. The draughty windows did constant battle with the central heating, and cold air funnelled up from below into the pantries built into each kitchen before fridges were commonplace. In some maisonettes the water pressure was too low to send the output from the kitchen water heater to the second-floor bathroom. A 'really mad thing' (to quote one of our informants) that the architects did was to put the central heating thermostat in the coldest part of the flat. The draught from a nearby window made the central heating, and the heating bills, soar. At the time we were told that the 25-year-old German central boiler, which served the whole estate, was defective and broke down regularly every winter. It took weeks for spare parts to arrive from Germany, during which time everyone froze and some old people died. If the boiler failed on a weekday there was immediately a long queue of shivering and despairing people outside the housing office.

The White View

In the local shopping parade there was one small general shop, an off-licence, a Chinese take-away and a dreary, peeling pub. A proposal for an Indian take-away was at one time considered by the Teviot Tenants' Association. Most people were utterly opposed to it. They said they did not want to lock up their dogs to avoid them being put in a curry. One member of the Tenants' Association who was in favour had dead animals left on his doorstep as a warning, and his car was constantly vandalised.

There were almost no trees on the estate and no flowers whatsoever. In an attempt to show how schools could brighten up the place, one of the authors and his wife brought 2,500 daffodil bulbs and arranged with a primary school that the children would plant them on a sad piece of grassland outside the school. The following spring none of them bloomed. The bulbs had been dug up by the children and thrown about in their games.

Before any Bangladeshis arrived on the estate it was already a scene of violence on a large scale, with gangs of local white boys at war with gangs from the Isle of Dogs. Since Bangladeshis came to Teviot, that old warfare had been superseded by fighting between white and Bangladeshi gangs, although the intensity of the conflict, though fierce, was possibly rather less vicious than the all-white battles it replaced.

'It's OK for Bengalis in a place like this,' said long-term resident Phillip Sugden, 'because the flats are so wretched we are all together in our wretchedness.' But he had resented them when they first arrived:

> There is a real problem, because when new homes and flats are built the Bengalis are most likely to get them. Me and other white people may have been waiting ten or twenty years for a new place to move into. It can't be just that they've got so many more children than we have although I know they have. I had six children myself – four daughters and two sons – but we could not get a larger flat. They said if they put me in a flat they'd be making me overcrowded from the beginning and they couldn't do that. But if that were the case for me, why isn't it for the Bengalis?

Into this place came newcomers who were quite often unprepared for what they found. Since there were few shops they had to go elsewhere to buy food, and that entailed a long and sometimes dangerous walk to a local market. There were no Bangladeshi shops on the estate and no buses. Bangladeshi newcomers felt they had to go all the way back to Brick Lane for much of their shopping and they realised each time how good a place that was compared to their windswept wasteland. And always there was the fear of being attacked.

Four years earlier Mr Sugden had acquired two Bangladeshi families as neighbours. There was no street demonstration against them as there sometimes had been. They were allowed, without being harassed, to bring in their beds and their few chairs and a sofa. His new neighbours were easy to get on with, partly because a couple of youngsters in the family spoke English. If they didn't, white children would make fun of them in the universal language of gestures and laughter. He was generally pleased with his new neighbours, although even for him there were aspects of their behaviour which made him feel uncomfortable and more sympathetic to his white neighbours on the estate:

> You've got some bigots, obviously, but there are real points to be made. When Asians are talking their own language and you hear them when you go down the stairs or in the streets, it's like whispering behind your back because you can't understand anything.

However, he thought it was ridiculous to suggest there should be a Bangladeshi-only post office just for them, as some whites had apparently proposed, no doubt fuelling rumours about the extent of Bangladeshi dependence on state benefits.

The Bangladeshi View

Rubel Azad had moved to the Teviot Estate along with his wife and five children. His wife looked at least thirty years younger than him and appeared content. She spent the time of his interview in the kitchen getting an evening meal ready, which included preparing a very large fish imported from Bangladesh, so large it flopped over the edges of the sink. Listening to our conversation next door she would look around the door every now and again and join in. There was no other Bangladeshi family in that block. Mr Azad's health was not good, so they had been given a ground-floor flat, which had lots of disadvantages in other ways.

Mr Azad, with a lined face and a beard beginning to fleck with grey, sat straight-backed in a white tunic in the principal chair, outlined against a large picture of Mecca on the wall behind him. The interviewer sat on the sofa; two of the younger children sat on the floor looking up at the interviewer.

He talked mainly about how fraught times had been since his young wife and children joined him from Bangladesh. They had squashed in with a brother until the one-year qualifying period was over and they could apply for housing as a homeless family. After that it was not long before he was offered this flat. It had been bad since their arrival on the estate. Their children of school age went to the local primary school, and he had no complaint about that, but he worried if they were more than a minute or two late back from school, fearing that they might have been attacked. The children were under strict instructions to stay together, to come as far as possible with some older Bangladeshi boys, and to come straight home. Every afternoon he would keep an eye on his clock around school closing time.

That was not the worst of it. White boys were liable to circle outside their flat and jeer and throw stones at the windows. He had complained frequently to the Bangladeshi welfare officer at the local housing office. As a result a high wire fence had been erected by the council, enclosing his flat. He was hoping that, because of the harassment and his anxiety for his children, he would be able to get a transfer to somewhere safer. He was not one of the Bangladeshis who felt they should stay away from the heartland for the sake of their children, thinking they would have a better chance of learning English quickly than in the Brick Lane area, where many school populations are almost entirely Bangladeshi and so many children start school with little or no English.

One of our young male Bangladeshi interviewees told us in 1995 about a failed anti-racism experiment he had been involved with:

> [Earlier] this year, I did a course on 'tolerance and diversity' at the Youth Club. It was designed to counteract racism by working closely with other [sic] white racist youths. The white boys lived at Teviot Estate in Poplar. It has the worst reputation of being the most racist area, where white boys will hunt down Asians. The course did not last long, because we got into more fights with these white boys. The white boys could not be civil to us and kept called us Pakis instead of our names. One of the local Bengali boys lost his temper and hit back. The course won't continue any more and we are not likely to get any more funding for future joint courses.

One of the local secondary schools was caught up in a disturbance while the interviewing was going on. About 25 per cent of the pupils were Bangladeshi and another 25 per cent from ten or so other visible minority ethnic groups including Black Caribbeans, Somalis, Chinese and Vietnamese. The remaining 50 per cent were white. Six or seven years before it had been entirely white. The practice of forming Bangladeshi gangs had spread from Brick Lane and they had become a real problem to the head teacher and the school. Some time before, a white gang had stabbed a Bangladeshi youth and, although the police apprehended the culprits, when the case came to court it fell apart when, as often happens, nobody was prepared to stand up and testify. Passions had been aroused by the BNP by-election victory in the Isle of Dogs in 1993. On the day after the election a white boy came into a classroom, raised his arm in the Nazi salute and shouted 'Sieg heil'. A gangfight quickly followed.

It was not difficult to see why people in Spitalfields did not want to move here.

A Changing Balance of Power

The shape of this confrontation has changed as the size of the Bangladeshi community has increased, reflecting perhaps the confidence in collective identity that can build up almost imperceptibly with growth of numbers. Ruksana felt this effect even in relation to dress, after moving into a flat where there were some Bangladeshi neighbours. Since her marriage, Ruksana has always worn a sari in public and whenever anyone visits. When she first arrived in the flats she noticed that the other Bangladeshi women were often in Western dress. Now, however, they too nearly always wore saris. She attributed this to her own unintentional influence. The others noticed that Ruksana wears saris and thought that they therefore should. Their conformity to Bengali dress code had increased as a result of her arrival. Perhaps two effects were at work here: the growth in their numbers not only gave women the confidence to express their Bengali identity sartorially but at the same time pressured them to conform to tradition.

In the community heartland of Banglatown, the rapid concentration of population produced a sense of solidarity and well-being early on. Our informant Tony Hicks commented that this in turn may have encouraged the white people most hostile to Bangladeshis to leave. This effect was also suggested by Guy Portman, another local white teacher, speaking in 1995:

> I don't think there are that many racist incidents around here now, and I would imagine that things have got better over the last ten years. Over that period more of the people who would have racist attitudes have actually moved away – as an expression of their racism, if you like. They have been replaced by more Bangladeshis, and that leads to a very nice atmosphere in the area.

The combination of white flight and Bangladeshi mutual protection meant that, in spite of the unwelcome significance to hostile whites of the growing number of Bangladeshis in Brick Lane, it soon became relatively peaceful.[4] At the end of the 1990s Shohel Uddin was able to joke about it – drawing on white-insider 'class' references:

The area around Brick Lane, and Brick Lane itself, had quite a large white community in the 1970s. In fact there were more whites than Bengalis in the area than I can recall as a youngster living in the area. However, as more Bengalis came in the whites at the same time moved out. So with a Bengali influx you saw an amount of emigration of the local white population, most of whom moved out further into Essex – or the few I knew did, so I am making the assumption they moved further east, you can jokingly argue to the homeland of Essex Man. They too went back home again. By the mid-1990s they had virtually all moved out.

As already mentioned, the police had opened up a new station in Brick Lane after rival shows of strength there by the National Front and Anti-Nazi League. Reports for some of the violent incidents they dealt with made it clear that racial motives were involved. In 1982, following the further impetus of the Brixton riots and the recommendations of the subsequent Scarman Report, police began to collect figures for all racial incidents. The statistics compiled since then enable us to trace the subsequent spread of racial incidents throughout Tower Hamlets.

Table 3.2 collects together Metropolitan Police figures corresponding with our four blocs of residence for a ten-year period.

Table 3.2 **Rates of reported racial incidents in Tower Hamlets by settlement bloc (incidents reported per 10,000 population)**

Bloc	1985	1991	1995
Heartland	16	12	16
Outer core	23	16	18
Conflict zone	19	69	66
White corners	10	20	32

Note: The 1991 ward census population has been used as a base figure for all years and numbers rounded to the nearest integer.
Source: Metropolitan Police, Tower Hamlets community liaison officer.

The figures reflect the way in which the area of major confrontation between whites and Bangladeshis moved eastwards across the borough. Confirming what we were told by our Bangladeshi informants, the heartland itself has become more peaceful, certainly in terms of the number of cases and probably in terms of their seriousness too. In the late seventies and early eighties the main conflicts were taking place in the Brick Lane area. However, by 1985 the rate of incidents in this inner core was already lower than in the outer core to the north, and indeed than in the emerging new 'conflict zone' in the east. The table shows that by 1991 the rate in the western half of the borough had fallen further, while that in the east as a whole was up, and had rocketed in the conflict zone. During the nineties the rate in the white margins of the borough climbed above that of the western part.

From 1995 to 1998 there was a steady fall in the number of racially motivated incidents for the borough as a whole, but after 1999 a surge occurred following the murder of a black teenager, Stephen Lawrence, by young white men in Eltham, an enquiry into the police investigation, the subsequent Macpherson Report and related changes in police practice and recording. What, however, is particularly striking about the revival of confrontation is that the direction of aggression, and the power relationships expressed by it, appear to have altered. Until recently the main victims of racial incidents had been Asian and the main perpetrators white or black. In the early years most Bangladeshi violence was manifestly defensive or, as when a National Front office was fire-bombed, carried out alongside left-wing white allies. But as Shohel Uddin explained to us, over time it had become more aggressive:[5]

> I am not one to condone violence. But eye for an eye did really calm things. When we were attacked we used to retreat back home. That time is over. In more recent years when a Bengali is stabbed a white boy would be attacked in retaliation. Defending oneself did work in a curious way. Bengali boys had been those who were picked on. The whites had been physically stronger, but that changed. Bengali boys realised that Bengalis would be picked on unless they stood up for themselves. 'We can give as good as we get', became the attitude. It did bring violence to an end. This applied to Bethnal Green Road and Roman Road as well as Brick Lane.
>
> At first the borough did not have active groups [of Bangladeshis] who went out looking for victims. Now it's the same with Bangladeshi gangs as well as the whites. It has spiralled out of parental control. Stephen Lawrence at King's Cross was knifed to death by Bengalis. Some of them were arrested, and sent down.* Bengali parents used to have control. Now boys at any rate no longer adhere to what their parents say. I used to be home about a minute after three in the afternoon. My father, mother and oldest brother criticised me if I was any later. We always listened to our elders. That's changed. I don't see much respect for elders any more. Of today's [Bangladeshi] teenagers we are looking at 50 per cent who are ready to defend themselves. The skills useful in street-fighting have become popular. Kick-boxing and Thai boxing are both designed for street-fighting. You can learn them from videos as you can martial arts. You can learn kick-boxing at various places in East Ham and at Stratford, and you can learn martial arts at the Brady Centre near Brick Lane and at Oxford House.

This transformation in Bangladeshi consciousness culminated by the end of the decade in a shift of direction of reported racial incidents. In 1998, for the first time, more whites in Tower Hamlets reported themselves as victims of racial incidents than were reported as perpetrators.[6] However, it is difficult to unscramble exactly what is going on here. Police procedures have been put out of gear (and police confidence knocked, it is claimed[7]) by the fall-out from the Macpherson Report. It may be that Bangladeshis are asserting themselves more vigorously. Or it may be that white people

---

*Note that Shohel is muddled here. The (white) boy killed by Bangladeshis near King's Cross was Richard Everitt. See Harris and Robins, 1997.

(perhaps now believing that the police are not on their side) are seeing themselves as victims more – either with justification or as a tactic.[8] Either way, inter-communal power relations in the borough are now in flux. An additional twist has been given to all of this in the last few years by the politicisation of Islam and growing international tensions between Muslim and Judaeo-Christian traditions. As chapter 5 will show, this is now giving increasing relevance to questions of identity which could be avoided when the Bangladeshi community was still in the process of establishing a footing for itself in the country, but which it must now confront.

In Tower Hamlets, spring 2003.

Chapter 4

Bangladeshi Life in London

We have seen something of the life of the people in the villages of Sylhet, and their intro-duction – often difficult, even brutal – to life in east London. Now we will look at how far Bangladeshis settled here are able to reproduce their traditional household structures and family life if they want to. Clearly, the pre-war walk-up apartments and post-war tower blocks of Tower Hamlets, one of the most crowded of London's boroughs, offer no way to replicate life in the spacious and tree-shaded *baris* of the village. Yet many British Bangladeshis continue to live in their traditional extended family households, despite the evident overcrowding this brings. The borough contains thousands of such families, and we were struck by the similarities of these to the white families of the 1950s, in the degree of mutual aid, intensity of contact and extent of local networks.

This way of life is based on deeply felt and deeply shared values. For older Bangla-deshis, the home – whether it is *bari* or house – ideally consists of a couple, married sons and their families, and any unmarried children. They lament the restricted size of most British housing stock – especially the traditional British public housing they find in Tower Hamlets – and the fact that their families are forced to divide by the circum-stances in which they live. A small number of large houses were built in the borough during the 1980s and 1990s, but these have usually been allocated to couples with a large number of children rather than to overcrowded extended family households. Sim-ilarly, in some of the older local authority blocks of flats, two flats have been combined into one by knocking through in order to accommodate large families. The economic situation of most Bangladeshis, and their low level of access to private housing, either rented or owned, means that they are restricted to occupying the housing provided by the state, and they are realistic about what this means. One mother, Mina Basit, explained what they would *like* to have:

> If they gave a big house, I want to live together with all my children ... We want to live with our children, hoping that when I get a daughter-in-law we will all live together, the daughter-in-law will look after us, this is what we want ... Yes, it's good to all live together, isn't it? It's better that way, it's a good way to do things, helping each other, looking after older people.
>
> If only they would understand us, why we need big house, then we wouldn't have this problem. But they don't understand, they don't see our need, you see, otherwise

they would give us Bengalis, any of us Bengalis, four bedrooms at least. Then we could have managed all right. OK, maybe not like the houses in Bangladesh, nice and wide and big ...

You know, you get your son married happily, then there is no privacy for the mother-in-law or the daughter-in-law [in these small flats]. If they have to live away from the parents, what will happen to the mother-in-law? If her daughter-in-law was home at least she could cook her some rice when she is ill, isn't it? ... If I get my son married, shouldn't I live with my daughter-in-law, isn't it her duty to look after me, take care of me and cook for me? Now if there isn't space in the house we go to the council, they will say, 'We will give your son and his wife another house'. So they've taken our son away from us ...

If they gave us a four-bedroomed house, at least I could live with my children and grandchildren happily. We won't ask for six [bed]rooms, will we? I know I could never have one room per person. We would like to live together with our sons. OK, not our daughter, we will get her married, she will be with her husband. So if they give us four rooms we will be OK; I can get three sons married, they live in a room each and us in one room. It's different with the girls because I'll get them married.

Asma Bibi indicated that it would be a matter of shame if her children did not *want* to live in a family household:

I don't know what English children do. And we can't follow their system. We are Muslims and we have to fear God. If our children spread one in one direction and the others in other directions like chicks then it will be a matter of shame. Isn't it so? I don't think my children will do that.

There are several assumptions that emerge in the above excerpts. Firstly, there is the desirability of household co-operation and mutual support among household members. Secondly, Mrs Basit shows her awareness of the limits to what is possible in the different circumstances of life in Britain: there will never be the space that there is in village housing and she acknowledges the reality of what she might expect to get from local authority housing. Thirdly, it is the duty of the daughter-in-law to look after her husband's parents. Finally, in the first extract given above, there is the assumption that daughters get married and leave home, while sons will live with their parents after marriage. Of course there are several factors which affect this ideal picture in practice.

For example, daughters may indeed marry men from Sylhet and have to be accommodated for a while by their own parents or by other kin. For the younger women there are advantages in such a situation: they are relieved of the domestic responsibility for looking after their husband's family and their decisions about working or studying are less likely to be contested by their husband or his family.

Bangladeshi Families in Bethnal Green

In our survey of 799 residents (from all ethnic groups) carried out in Bethnal Green and Globe Town there were 170 (21 per cent) single-person households. The residents of these 170 single-person households described themselves as 'single' (52 per cent), 'widowed' (30 per cent), 'divorced or separated' (14 per cent) and 'married' (4 per cent). It would be most unusual for Bangladeshis in any of these four family-status categories to live alone, and indeed only four of these 170 individuals *were* Bangladeshi. Expressed as a percentage of all the Bangladeshi household members in the survey, a total of 1,021 individuals, only 0.4 per cent therefore, were living alone – a striking contrast to the British population as a whole. The four in question were a 20-year-old single woman, a 41-year-old man with a wife in Bangladesh but no children, a 35-year-old divorced man with an ex-wife and children living in the north of England, and a 27-year-old single man.

Single Bangladeshis tend to live with their parents at least until they marry, and often until they have several children or until a younger sibling (usually a brother) has married. The incidence of divorce and separation is much lower among Bangladeshis than among the white population; indeed, in the 1991 census, taken at roughly the same time as our survey, adult Bangladeshis were less likely to be single, divorced or cohabiting than any other ethnic group in Britain,[1] and the 2001 census found the same.[2] Widows would almost invariably live with one of their children. The care of elderly parents is considered an imperative; it would be most unusual for widows to live alone, unlike their white counterparts. A number of households containing widows were found in the survey: there were three households headed by young widows living with their children; two of these widows were in their early twenties, the other in her thirties. In all three cases their husbands had died in Bangladesh. Since the survey was carried out, one of the widows in her twenties has remarried and is hoping that her second husband will get permission to join her from Bangladesh. There were two widowers living with their children; one was aged 43 and had six children, the other was aged 63 and lived with his son, his son's wife and their daughter. Apart from these three households there were another six widows living with their children, in one case with grandchildren as well and in another case with her three children, her mother and her husband's sister.

Bangladeshi women in the UK who are living alone with their children are more likely to be widowed than divorced; relatively more Bangladeshi women and fewer Bangladeshi men aged 60–64 were widowed than in any other ethnic group in 1991 and 2001.[3] This is partly caused by the large age differences between husbands and wives; the average age difference between married Bangladeshis is greater than for any other ethnic group in Britain.[4] Some early migrants spent many years working in the UK before accumulating sufficient resources to repay obligations to kin and enable them to marry. Other factors also contribute, for example if first wives died in Bangladesh second wives would have been married when in their late teens or very early twenties, the usual marriage age for women, whatever the age of their husbands. Many Bangladeshi men also suffer from poor health and have high levels of long-term illness, especially diabetes and heart disease. These factors together make for a large number of widows, including many with dependent children.

Of the other households identified as Bangladeshi in the survey, only two consisted of married couples living alone with no children. These were not, as might be expected, young and recently married; instead one couple was aged 70 and 60 at the time of the survey, the other 59 and 44. The older couple had two sons in Bangladesh, the younger couple had no children. Although divorce or marital separation is rare it does happen, and the sample also included four women who were divorced or separated but living with their children.

Of the remaining Bangladeshi households, the majority of the sample, 104 (61 per cent) consisted of a married couple and their children, 44 (25.7 per cent) were extended family households (details are given below) and the remaining five came into neither of these categories, yet all but one of which consisted of parts of families.[5] Although our sample is statistically small we suggest that, in this respect, Bethnal Green may be untypical of Britain as a whole; one analysis of 1991 census data found that 83 per cent of British Bangladeshi households consisted of a couple and their children compared with 52 per cent for white families.[6] There are several possible explanations for this, one of which is the absence through non-recording of non-nuclear family members in census responses, another of which is the severe overcrowding in Tower Hamlets, which means that family members have to wait longer after applying for re-housing, or that in order to get housing of their own young couples are having to move out of the borough.

Extended Family Households

What is most unusual compared with the white population is the large number of extended family households, in other words households of related people containing more than two generations and/or more than one nuclear family. As already noted, these comprised more than a quarter of Bangladeshi households in our survey and, as might be expected, some of the extended family households were very large, as figure 4.1 shows.

Among these families, the most frequent household structures were those which reflected the preference for young couples to reside with the husband's parents. Only three households consisted of a couple living with a daughter and her husband; in all three cases the husband had arrived recently from Bangladesh. Another six couples had their daughter and daughter's children living with them; two of the daughters were separated from their husbands and the other four were waiting for permission to bring their husbands to Britain. In every case the (grand)children were very young.

Figure 4.1   **Size of households containing Bangladeshi extended families: proportions of 44 extended family households containing given numbers of residents**

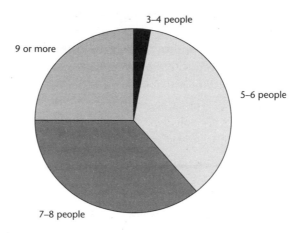

There were also households consisting of married siblings and their children; in each case these were married brothers and in each case they were living in the homes where their parents had previously lived. A few households had more distant kin living with them; one household contained a 'cousin', another the husband's uncle. Finally, one household contained a man, his two wives, a son by each wife and one son's own wife, son and daughter.

What we see in the above, in marked contrast to white households, is the almost complete absence of *unrelated* people living together. Of our white subjects, 9 per cent (including unmarried couples) lived with non-relatives. Only one Bangladeshi subject (one of the five anomalies) did so. The few Bangladeshi households consisting of siblings, married or unmarried, were almost invariably those from which the parents, if still alive, had retired to Bangladesh to live in a house or on land they had bought while living in Britain.

The data from the survey show the large size of many of the Bangladeshi households: just under six people, on average. This is not, however, limited to the extended family households; one small survey we conducted in a class of 9- and 10-year-olds at a Bethnal Green primary school found an average of 6.5 children in the families of the twenty-two Bangladeshi children in the class. As the children in the class were still young, some of these families may have grown since the survey was taken.

The 1991 census found an average household size for all Bangladeshis in Britain of 5.3 persons, with more than 60 per cent of households containing five or more people, against an average household size of 2.5 persons for the country as a whole. Again, in Tower Hamlets the figures demonstrate the overcrowded nature of housing; the average household size among all Bangladeshi families found in a more recent study is 6.6.[7]

This, combined with the limited number of large dwellings in the borough, resulted in there being more overcrowded households in Tower Hamlets in 1991 than in any other local authority. In 2001 the overcrowding indicators placed Tower Hamlets in fifth position in the country, partly a result of members of Bangladeshi extended families being rehoused during the decade.

Values in the Bangladeshi Community

By comparison with earlier waves of migrants to the East End, the Bangladeshi community has achieved a large volume of settlement, with a high level of material security, in a remarkably short time. Part of this point is bound to be disputed. On many formal indicators of social well-being, the Bangladeshis compare unfavourably both with the general British population and also with some other minorities in Britain. They suffer high rates of unemployment, and exceptionally low per capita incomes.[8] They are concentrated overwhelmingly in social housing, with limited facilities, in poor areas. Their health profile is not good. Nor have they shown great success in penetrating elite activities at national level. On all of these counts they are liable to be portrayed as still excluded and in poverty.

But we do have to be careful about such arguments. To begin with, we must remember that poverty is a relative concept – especially in the modern West – so that it is important to compare appropriate groups. There is no real hunger in Britain these days, nor abject poverty of the sort that was widespread here even less than a century ago. Both can still be found in Bangladesh itself, however, and most Bangladeshis born in the UK are shocked when they first visit – though as part of a Londoni family you are likely to find yourself comparatively well off. Jamila noted:

> We've been back, six years ago. I enjoyed it; I feel like going back there again. It's like [our family there] are leading a wonderful life of leisure, that's how it is in Bangladesh, because it's so cheap to do things over there. It doesn't cost much, you can even have a servant for virtually nothing, you know, you don't hardly do anything.

Farzana and Naseema told it together:

> F. Here you don't have anyone starving, do you? Whereas in Bangladesh it's ...
> N. One part is starving and another part is having a feast.
> F. It's like we're probably having a feast here and outside our door people are starving.
> N. If you want to be rich [there] then you have to be cruel to the poor; don't give them any money, don't give them anything, just have everything yourself.

For the poor in Bangladesh life is desperate. Shohel explained with awe:

> Most of the poorer people rent their huts, sometimes squatting in them. The landowners and house owners are either in the few local compounds or from elsewhere. The rents

are collected by members of the owning families, not yet by formal agents. Those who want to settle pay rent, and do not become nomads. The landlords pull the houses down if the rents are not paid. It is quite brutal ... All young people have an aspiration to come to Britain. Would you sponsor me, they say. Get me a work permit, they say ... In London we don't have to worry where the next meal is coming from.

Another way of looking at this is to say, as many respondents did, that the material conditions in Britain, and not least the support provided by the welfare state, made it a much better place than Bangladesh for raising families. This is not understood by many village Bangladeshis arriving here – as reflected in Monica Ali's novel *Brick Lane*, where the heroine Nazneen has to have it explained to her by her new friend Razia.

'Something else: if you don't have a job here, they give you money. Did you know that? You can have somewhere to live, without any rent. Your children can go to school. And on top of that, they give you money. What would happen at home? Can you eat without working? Can you have a roof over your head?' (Ali, 2003, p. 58)

All this is galling to men here who have not yet been able to bring over their families, and are having to support them *in* Bangladesh. Moin Abbas arrived in Britain at the age of 13, and had a marriage arranged for him five years later back in Bangladesh – where he now has several children. Because he has not learnt much English he cannot find well-paid work. And because he cannot afford to bring over his wife and children he has to send most of what he does earn back to support them, while his mother (here) looks after him:

I want to bring my family over but I do not have that much money at the moment. The children are growing up, and going to school. In our country it costs money to send them to school and take them to doctors. In Bangladesh you need money the moment you step out of home. If they come here I will get some help from the government, so I am seriously thinking about ways to bring them here.

Because they have not arrived yet, Mr Abbas has not yet confronted the dilemmas that immigrant parents experience over westernisation. His lack of English limits his social contacts, and he stays at home most of the time. He is aware of cultural differences through nephews and nieces, but regards them only as matters of curiosity:

Our youngsters are becoming English. They go to school and pick up things from other kids. They like chips and fish fingers and are doing things which a Muslim should not do and eating foods which a Muslim should not eat. They are learning Christian things from schools. You can't keep them home, can you? I have nephews and nieces and I find the way they behave and act strange. We have been tied up in this country. They talk to each other in English, and watch TV all the time. They can't speak our language well, and somebody told me that girls who have grown up in this country don't like the arranged marriage system. They want to choose their husband themselves. It is strange, isn't it?

The bottom line here, though, is that most Bangladeshis feel themselves to be much better off materially than their parents and grandparents. And given their different backgrounds and expectations, particular levels of income do not necessarily translate into the same lifestyles as found among their native British neighbours (and other immigrants). Being 'poor' in British terms still allows Bangladeshis to live in considerable relative comfort here. We have to remember too that low incomes trigger state benefits, and once Bangladeshis are on benefits then if they follow a modest lifestyle they can live reasonably well. Apart from a few youngsters who have adopted British habits of spending much of their money on leisure activities, all members of the community can afford to eat well and healthily at home, and most still find enough money left to send some to families back in Bangladesh, where it buys a lot more. In basic terms their settlement has obviously been successful. To suggest it has already failed is to over-estimate greatly the speed of the British state in transforming people's lives, and to ignore the level of poverty and lack of capital of migrants on arrival.

The Balance Sheet of Migration

This is not to deny that some migrants regret their decision to come here. Helal Ali fits that category well, having left Bangladesh without due prior consideration, changed plans many times and then found himself unable to choose whether to settle in Britain or return home. His misfortunes include the incorrect completion of his early paperwork so that he will not be able to claim a state pension until he is well beyond usual pensionable age. It is perhaps in the nature of migration that there will be some cases like this, and we should point out that Mr Ali was interviewed by a male Bangladeshi researcher in Bengali, which probably influenced the degree of his candour. This is the essence of his story:

> I was born in the year 1336 [AH; 1918 by Christian calendar], the year when there was a great flood in Bengal. My age is well over 60 now, but when I came to this country people at the recruitment office put my age down wrongly, so I may never see my pension.
>
> I didn't want to come to this country, as all of my family members are in Bangladesh. But I was a school teacher, and someone told me that 'They are distributing forms to go to London at the District Office.' These were the work voucher forms. I filled in the form and I was in England within a few months. That was a mistake.
>
> When I first came here they handed me a work permit and I got stuck in a factory job in Yorkshire. There was a lady at the Indo-Pakistan Society called Mrs Haque. She insisted that I should not work in the factory, but take a part-time job and study for a teaching degree. If I had followed her advice I would have been in a far better position today. But I was young, and my idea was to work for a while and then go back. I regret that now. There were not many educated people here at that time. The people who had come before me were all *allua-jallua* [lit. fisherman-farmer, i.e. peasant class], and on

Saturdays and Sundays there used to be a big queue of them in front of my place to read their letters. Also I had to write for them.

I did not want to stay here, and so I spent long holidays in Bangladesh. None of my family members was keen to come here. In 1983 I went back intending to live permanently in Bangladesh, and took up a job as a primary teacher in my village school. But I got fed up after some time and applied for my family to come over here. Since they came in 1986 I have not been back. The situation is bad in Bangladesh. Things are scarce in the market now, and the parties are fighting again. Ever since 1947 it has been in decline, and after 1971 I was in real confusion about whether to keep a Pakistani passport or go for a Bangladeshi one. In the end I chose British.

But now I think we made a mistake bringing our children here. Since 1986 I have not been working. I am weak. I get chest pains, and leg pains. I would like to go to see my mother. She is over 100 and might not survive long. But my eldest son has gone for me. My other son can't find a job here, and it is hard finding suitable husbands for my daughters. One lives with her husband in Poplar. I didn't want to give her in marriage in this country, but we had no other way. I wanted someone more educated for her, but we couldn't find an educated man here.

My wife too is unwell now. She has to take lots of tablets for cancer in her throat. She has been given radiation several times, and as a result her teeth have fallen out. We wanted to get a place near her hospital in Westminster. The people there agreed to give us a flat, but they can't do it unless Tower Hamlets release us. They are refusing to do that. It is a fight between the hospital and council. This place is no good; there are too many fights around.

This is a sad account of one family's history in Britain. For the most part, though, our Bangladeshi respondents felt that they had done well by coming here. Taking account of the relative improvement in lifestyle that even being poor in Britain represents, it may even be that it is the *speed* of their accommodation, rather than obstacles to the achievement of parity, which in reality contains greater potential dangers for them. The risk perhaps is that smoothness of settlement encourages migrants to feel that it is safe to dispense (too) rapidly with their own community support structure. For what has enabled such rapid build-up of the settlement to take place has been the commitment of state agencies to immigrants' welfare, and willingness to support Bangladeshis in ways that suited their needs. The argument here revolves around the effect of settlement on the community as a group rather than on individuals.

Culture and Commitment

There is a paradox running through white attitudes towards Bangladeshis in Tower Hamlets, and probably in most other parts of the UK: it is that many of the people who are most supportive of their settlement, and condemning of attacks on them, are at the same time highly disposed to be critical of some aspects of the culture they have brought with them. Typically these attacks focus around ideas about Bangladeshi patriarchal family culture. Daisy Tremain, a trainee nurse from Devon, said that on the one hand she felt that the Bangladeshis had been treated badly and deserved more support, but then added that she felt hostile to the in-home violence she believed was prevalent among them. Similarly, Mandy Charlton commented, 'It's a funny sort of family they have. Females are only allowed to do what they're told.' Then there are fixed ideas about arranged marriages. Shohel found himself constantly having to counter public attitudes on this:

> I've often argued at work about Islam. People don't know what Islam has to say about women. Men and women are equal in their choices. Women can refuse a marriage. Religion teaches that women should be on a pedestal. But maybe it is wrong there; women should be in the same position as men.

Equally, though, as we have seen with Joyce Darty, it was quite often those ordinary Bethnal Greeners more openly opposed to Bangladeshi settlement who tended to feel sympathetic towards Bangladeshi family-centric values, and who often got on well with Bangladeshis at a personal level. Kristin O'Keefe, hostile towards some aspects of Bangladeshi culture, liked many Bangladeshis and thought highly of their general attitudes towards family.[9] Observing her Bangladeshi neighbours from the perspective of her own expressly female-centred (even if bilineal) family network, she saw the women as elbowed out of things – certainly in this country: 'The mums don't speak any English, and the men take over the running of houses. Women don't get no say. When they go out, she's always walking three paces behind him.' But at the same time she complimented their commitment to family: 'Some white people don't see their family hardly at all. But my Bangladeshi neighbours have always got other members of the family there visiting them and playing with the children.' And she felt positive towards them: 'They've always got a smile on their faces. You couldn't get nicer people.'

The implication of this ambivalence, even paradox, is that much of the general support for Bangladeshi settlement may be associated with the idea that it is the *people* who are being admitted to Britain, not their way of life. It is based in a high valuation of individual freedom and opportunity.[10] And this in turn poses a latent dilemma for Bangladeshis, which has emerged more explicitly since our fieldwork was completed and indeed has become quite overwhelming since 11 September 2001. This is that much of the tolerance shown by British liberals towards minorities is based on the assumption that members of these groups who settle or grow up in Britain will quickly seize the opportunity this gives them to abandon any aspects of their original cultures which are seen here as regressive, and then adapt themselves to British values.[11] Many liberals are now reconsidering their tolerance, in the light of national security issues. But the tolerance of some of them has always been strategic. It is not really endorsing pluralism as such, but tends to operate on the idea that the best way of encouraging immigrants to adopt a new (that is, liberal) value-system lies in not pushing them too hard to do so.

In a way therefore the level of acceptance which has been achieved by Bangladeshis so far is provisional. It could be withdrawn if they fail to adopt key aspects of British life quickly enough. Support for migrants from the governing class in Britain has been on the basis of individualised human rights. Those people ostensibly most positive towards them are the last people one would expect to stand up in the longer run for a community's right to maintain imported traditions, and certainly not to organise members' lives around a religious culture that played down individual rights and saw little merit in other cultures.

In short, much of the political support for Bangladeshis has been for them not as an (inward-looking) group, but as an easily identifiable category of the population containing disadvantaged, needy individuals. And this is contingent. For as some of these individuals overcome their background to emerge as successful members of wider society, as more of them become local British-born citizens with an understanding of how to operate the system for themselves, as new and more-needy minorities arrive, perhaps above all if the Bangladeshi community is seen to stand for anti-individualist values, then the support of British liberals (and the state) towards the group will turn out to be ambivalent.

Even before the stimulus of September 11 and subsequent international tensions, members of the community felt themselves slipping down from the privileged position of materially deprived newcomers, deserving of special solicitude, towards the role of obstructive and possibly dangerous fifth-columnists serving culturally regressive interests. At the time of writing (summer 2005) public opinion is re-assessing the values of tolerance and human rights following recent suicide bombings in London. Muslims had already been finding themselves subjected to tests of group loyalty and integration which they had rarely experienced in the past, for example through attacks on arranged marriages.[12] This was particularly disturbing for those members of the group who assumed that they had been accepted.

Sexual Difference and Family Life

One of the few sentiments which unites all generations of the Bangladeshi community is the feeling that white families fail to protect the interests of needy members. White children are seen as left exposed by marital breakdown. Old people suffer because of their children's neglect. Wives are abandoned by uncaring husbands. Such events are rare among Bangladeshis. Even though their successful children may now want to live separately from their parents when they marry, and even leave home when single in a few cases, most still believe in the moral solidarity of the family and the importance of putting family interests before those of the individual. Indeed, in most situations individual interests are seen as best served *by* the family.

However, the priority of the family operates in slightly different ways for men than for women, who therefore do not experience the pressures of white British values in quite the same ways. In Bangladeshi culture, women are regarded as needing family support at all stages in life – as dependent children, as wives and mothers requiring help and protection, and as elders receiving care. As conscientious Muslims, however, men have a religious obligation to marry and be involved in a family life, and are therefore building up *spiritual* capital by performing their family obligations. These obligations are structured in ways which effectively make them dependent on others – and thus to *need* family themselves – in order to be able to fulfil them.

The primary family obligation of a man is to his parents, in particular his mother, to whom he owes his existence. But in order to discharge this obligation properly he needs to marry. His mother needs domestic help such as cooking and cleaning which in traditional households would be provided only by another woman. Also, the best way to repay parents is to have children yourself and carry on the line. So there are moral and social considerations which make men need families and which become impressed on them from an early age. Several young Bangladeshi men reported to us that they were under intense pressure from their mothers to be good sons by getting married.

On the other hand it is assumed that women will want to have children, and will understand the importance of family support in enabling them to do so. They will therefore accept more readily than men the logic of reciprocity within the family, and be willing to take on obligations towards others in return for the help they receive. Potential drawbacks are, firstly, the lack of freedom in the choice of a husband and when to marry – though this depends a lot on individuals' relations with their parents – and, perhaps above all, the requirement to submit to the authority of a mother-in-law. So marriage can be a problem. But whereas white women would have objected in the past to only obtaining a public identity as a result of marriage to a man, Bangladeshi women would be more likely to complain about the way that marriage places them for a while under the private thumb of another woman.

The mother-in-law problem is not something that figures greatly in contemporary British culture. This itself is an indication of the reduced importance of family life. But during the 1950s it was a powerful theme, and the subject of many jokes recorded in *Family and Kinship*. The mother-in-law in question in those days was almost invariably the wife's mother, and the jokes (and related avoidance behaviour) turned on the discrepancy between the formal prominence in British culture of the male line of descent and authority of the husband on one hand, and the reality of dominant matrilineal relationships on the other. Subsequent weakening of marriage ties has eliminated this discrepancy by affirming the priority of maternal links.

This points again to an aspect of white family life that young Bangladeshi women do find appealing. In Bangladesh brides resign themselves to the necessity of serving their husband's mother, and pray that she will not be too harsh or unpleasant. Among Bangladeshi girls in London the mood is more defiant. Schoolgirls we interviewed spent nearly as much time discussing (and said they spent more time worrying about) mothers-in-law as they did future husbands. Naveen Mannan told us what happened to her sister:

> Trying to live with parents-in-law when you haven't known them all your life is a hell of a problem. My sister has had problems with hers, and found it difficult to adjust to it ... They were completely different from my parents, and her expectations did not fit. She was so used to being brought up in our family and when you go to another one you automatically think, 'Well, this is how things should be, so why isn't it?' ... My sister had problems with her mother-in-law because she had very old-fashioned views and she expected my sister to follow them ... My sister hated her at first; but now she has learned to stand up for herself, and can cope with it. It takes a while to get to know everybody and find your own position in the family.

Najma made similar comments in relation to her family, and pointed out that this could be a significant factor in the selection of a bride. Parents often think that it is important for a daughter-in-law to come from the right district, and even the right *gushti* (kin-group), because otherwise they may not do things in the same sort of way. Not that this saves them from criticism:

> The way they cook their meals would be different: the way they cut their fish, these things would be criticised. 'How do you cut a fish; you're supposed to do it that way.' Or, 'Why do you put your onions in first when you are supposed to put them in afterwards?' These are things that a mother-in-law would criticise highly about her daughter-in-law, and say, 'Hasn't your *zat* [caste] ever cooked any meals?' If she put in the coriander a bit late, or if she put dal in too much water, she gets told off. Daughters-in-law face this criticising of every little action all the time. 'Why are you sitting like that? Why didn't you put your headscarf on when this person walked in?' All the time ... Even if they do know how to cook, they don't according to the mother-in-law. That's her way of showing her authority, because that's her area, the kitchen. It's a family tradition that the mother-in-law teaches everybody and the family has a certain way of cooking.

So one of the reasons why some Bangladeshi girls in London are happy to marry someone from Bangladesh itself is that they can then hope to get a husband without acquiring a co-resident mother-in-law too. There is already some shift towards stronger maternal-line ties in Britain – with mothers retaining closer involvement with adult daughters. So far, though, this does not seem to have affected formal emphasis on patriarchal ties, which are, of course, maintained through the converse expedient of local boys marrying girls from Bangladesh who might be more amenable to accepting a mother-in-law's authority.

Women's Domain

To many white Britons Islam is synonymous with the oppression of women. As shown earlier, many of our white respondents, both those hostile to Bangladeshis and those more positive, referred to Bangladeshi women as being confined to the home and not allowed to take jobs or mix with people outside the family. Such ideas do correspond to much visible behaviour within the East End Bangladeshi community. They are nevertheless highly misleading, as they fail to capture the full meaning of the behaviour. So stereotypes of Asians go unchallenged, and fanciful scenarios of social change – revolving heroically around the liberation of women from sexual domination – continue to inform British attitudes and social policy.[13]

For what rarely seems to be addressed in contemporary liberal commentaries is that although many Muslim women do spend most of their lives in domestic contexts, this may not constitute confinement. We should say at the outset that there are indeed cases of domestic violence, mental illness and depression, which cause great unhappiness to women and members of their families. But for most of our women informants, these do not typify Bangladeshi family life. Within Islam the family is considered to be the real and powerful centre of life. So when men are out at work, or doing other errands in the public realm which would be done by women in the white community such as shopping, they see themselves as serving the family, not controlling it. Young Bangladeshi women *can* feel oppressed within families, but this is more likely to be at the hands of mothers-in-law, the effective heads of households, rather than of men. The family power issue is a generational or life-stage matter rather than one of sexual inequality.

The image that white respondents had of Bangladeshi families was largely a reflection of their own values and anxieties. While white liberals were informing us that Bangladeshi men ordered their wives and daughters around, young Bangladeshi women themselves – when talking about their own future lives in Britain – told us instead about the central importance to them of maintaining Muslim family life.

Far from conforming to the notion of compliant 'little women', in our study Bangladeshi mothers – certainly those in the senior generation – emerge in the domestic context as decidedly matriarchal, in firm control of their families. Shohel explained at length how his mother is the organising force at the hub of his extended family. Crucially, she holds the family purse, and all those in the joint household who are working (the men) pool their wages in it. The men are given pocket money, for cigarettes and suchlike and the rest is used for rent, travel and food, or saved for larger purchases such as a car or a family trip back to Bangladesh. The men's wives are allowed to keep their child benefit and to spend it on their own children, but this is the only source of income not controlled by Shohel's mother.

When Shohel's father goes out shopping, for fish and vegetables for example, he asks his wife for some money, and then gives her the change when he gets back. He is involved in decisions about money, but generally leaves them to his wife and regards her as the boss. Not that any family members resent her, or see her as controlling. It is more a matter of trusting her planning and judgment:

> We all hold my mother very dearly. We never criticise her, and even if we do I suppose it's constructive criticism. But we hold her very dearly, and it's just our showing her respect in many ways. We say, there you go, Mother, there's the pay packet.

Because Shohel's family has had long contact with Britain, this behaviour might be taken as a sign of assimilation to Western ways. But we found that almost precisely the same pattern operated in Naveen's family – including on both parents' side in Bangladesh itself. Naveen herself seems to have picked up the idea from white teachers at school in London that Muslim women were downtrodden, and to have been quite surprised and impressed, when she went to Bangladesh, to find out just how powerful women were in daily life:

> Women are very, very strong in Bangladesh ... It is to do with economic power, with money and with providing for your family and things ... Men are lumbered down with one thing, their business or their land. Women are involved with anything, virtually everything. They don't go out; when I went there I did not see women go off and help their husbands in the fieldwork. But I saw that women are very strong in the household and with managing money within the household.

She remembers being surprised to see her father submitting to his mother:

> In my family my grandmother, my father's mother, was the head and all the money had to go to her. She's pretty old; she was about 85, but she was still in control of what was happening with the money. So the money that my father had sent in, or the earnings that they had there, had to go straight to my grandmother. When he needed it, he'd come and ask for it.

Much the same applied to her mother's parents:

> Again, my grandmother is very much in control with finances within the household, and my grandfather is less involved. He's more concerned with managing the land. His great interest is in that. But she's involved in everything – getting all the rice and keeping the workers, housemaids, employing them, she's in control of all that. Then giving money to her children, my mum, or bringing her over.

Not surprisingly, the generation now living in London manages things in the same way:

> With my parents, my father has to bring his money and give it to my mother. It's the same with my aunt. My uncle at the end of the week will give his money to her ... In my family it is not just with my mother and father, but it's my brother-in-law and sister too. When his parents were in Bangladesh, he'd bring his money to my sister for her to keep.

What is important to notice here is that when the mother is absent it is a (senior) daughter-in-law who takes the role over, not a son, as she is the emerging family manager. So it seems that leaving financial management to the woman of the house is a traditional pattern within the community, and something strongly rooted in life in Bangladesh rather than a recent practice adopted following immigration.

Family and religion

Our respondents' views on family life, not least those of younger members of the Bangladeshi community who have grown up in London, suggest that it is a mistake to equate patriarchal culture with male domination. Because of the high valuation of family life, and of women's central place in it as family managers, their effective status is much higher than formal indicators suggest, and probably not very different from 'Mum' in old Bethnal Green.[14] The actual role of women is moreover closely bound up with the operation of Islamic religion – itself clearly patriarchal in form. Westerners tend to regard Muslim men as epitomising a male urge to control women. What comes out strongly in our own interviews with Bangladeshi women, again including those who have gone through schooling in Britain, is just how many of them saw men who were actively religious as being more caring, more respectful of women and generally as more committed to upholding the family values which they as women themselves believed in. Being religious made men better people, in the particular areas that mattered most to women.

In recent years there have been political reasons for religion to be significant for men, in particular young men. But the main underlying reason is surely its role in confirming their place in traditional family life, which can otherwise easily be lost in the UK. Habiba Rahman offers a pertinent illustration of this. She was born in Bethnal Green and went through school here, and had taken a YTS training course shortly before being interviewed. When asked to compare men who had grown up in London with those who came from Bangladesh, she found it hard to be positive:

> Some of them you can trust but some you just can't ... [Boys raised here] are totally different actually, in so many ways. Before, you didn't used to get cheeky boys or rude boys. But nowadays they're cheeky to any girl, any girl – it just doesn't matter [to them]. Just walk down Brick Lane. If they see a girl, or woman, it doesn't matter how old or young the woman or girl is, they just start, you know ... it's like that. We didn't have that before. They used to respect us when we used to go down the streets.

The crucial point about Habiba here is that she could in no way be regarded as wedded to traditional values. She does not find people from Bangladesh easy to get on with:

If I had some kind of personal problem ... I would probably go to one of my friends, to try to explain to her, hoping she'd understand more than my own family would ... To tell you the truth, my mother is a different generation to what I am, and I've like got one foot in the Western society and another foot in another society ... I find it more comfortable to talk to friends of my own age, who have been here all their lives, than I would to my parents ... They are actually very different.

She certainly does not see women as dependent on men:

I don't need any support from a man. Not unless it is love and affection. I don't think anything else. I can find a job myself, things like that ... Nowadays, I mean. Before you had to depend on a man to get the money, go to work, do this, do that, but nowadays you can do without a man.

And yet in spite of all these modern sentiments, Habiba still felt strongly that men had an important part to play in bringing up children:

I think that if somebody has a child I think it is best to have two parents rather than just one. You can cope better than you can as a single parent.

And this comes back to the key role of men in helping women to bring up children, and the continuing importance of religion to that role. Habiba's brother is religious, and to her this, more than anything, is what makes him a valuable member of the family:

My brother is religious. (He's upstairs asleep now, by the way. I should have said how lazy he is!) My brother is very religious and because he is religious he's so calm, he's calm about everything. Most people, like my friends' parents, if you do something wrong they'll, you know, grab your throat, they're jumping at you, thumping your throat. But my brother, he sits me down, and he explains things, and then says, 'Don't do that again,' and I say, 'I won't do it again.'

Her father died shortly after she was born, and her brother has in some ways taken his place in the family:

To tell you the truth, I've always thought of him as my father figure. I've never actually seen my father, he's never been there. And my brother's always been there when I've needed anything, any help, anything, he's always been there. In my mind I do think of him as my own father, to tell you the truth.

Although her mother is the head of the family for practical purposes, especially financial matters, it is her brother to whom family members will turn when they want advice on how to deal with difficult personal questions, or help with defending family interests in the outside world. He understands and can explain religious teachings about family life, and has often helped Habiba's friends negotiate problems with their parents, or mediated between their families and public bodies such as schools. And it is his religious orientation, and related belief in the centrality of family relations, which enables him to do this, and inspires confidence in his character and judgment.

This example helps to show why some young Bangladeshi girls who would be expected by white liberals to run a mile at the sight of a mullah do seem to feel safer with men who are religious. Several mentioned how calm religious boys were, and Habiba explained with evident pride how her brother was hoping to become an imam. Men appear to get approval, and authority, by virtue of standing up for the rules and values and behaviour that women themselves strongly believe in.

Boys and Religion

From the point of view of boys, this appeal to girls obviously means that there are reasons far closer to home than fighting holy wars against infidels which make a religious way of life attractive to them. The fundamentalist trend can be seen at least partly as a response to anxieties about the impact of Western values on their families, and about the community's ability to maintain coherent family life while they are living within a dominant culture which seems to value such things so lightly.

This is already an important issue for girls still at school, and Farzana, a bubbly teenager born in London, emphasised that for her the value of living within a large Bangladeshi community was that it made the maintenance of their religious practice so much easier:

> The advantages of a big community are that we can still live like in Bangladesh; it's like we don't lose anything, our cultural background, because here we keep to our culture, plus our religion. That's the most important thing, that we stick to it, because around us we see everyone Muslim, everyone like us, and it's easier to be like ourselves ... At school, here we can talk about our home and everything to our friends and they understand the importance of what we are going through.

So if boys within the community want to impress girls with their suitability as partners, an interest in religion may be just the ticket. But by the same token it restricts relationships with potential white partners. Quite a large number of the early male settlers found English wives or temporary girlfriends, but as the community has grown and come to contain more women, and mosques have been opened, the incidence of intercultural relationships has declined, and also changed in nature. Bangladeshi boys who want to have sex without marriage still tend to go outside of the community to do so, and this is regarded as a particularly harmful white influence. Kobir Ahmed told us:

> What the Asian community are doing, obviously the temptation's in the West, you go to school and they say, 'Oh, what's up with you, I see you have no girlfriend and why is it? Are Asian people not allowed to have girlfriends or what?' So it's like the bullying, you

have to get a girlfriend, you know, so the pressure piles up, so what's happening is kids are in a dilemma and it's your choice, so what you do is they have kind of girlfriends but they see them in a secret place, they talk to them, they send them a letter through some people, and all that stuff, so they can explore the other life, but there is a great fear that if their parents do find out or even if somebody threatens them or blackmails them they will totally fall in pieces. You know, so that is what's happening at the moment. The thing that hasn't happened yet is they are not yet willing to walk in the street hand by hand with [a] white girl.

As Kobir suggests in this passage, almost all then marry within their community of origin. Bangladeshi girls do seem to have strong feelings that marriage should be within the Muslim community. White people can join, and do in very small numbers, through conversion. Farzana explained that this often worked well:

The thing is, in a lot of cases where a white person married into Bengali families, and take on the religion, they are more religious than the Bengali people themselves. They take it very seriously and they are very, more religious. Because they come in and they truly believe that they want to convert or whatever, or take on this culture, they do it more seriously.

She offered a concrete example of this from her own family:

I had a cousin, a girl, who was a law student. At first she was a rebel, she didn't listen to her parents or anything. And then she fell in love with this white guy and she married him against her parents' will and now she's a really good Muslim, it's like she's more strict than her parents. Her parents like them now. They're real Muslims. Her husband, he's really nice, he went to Bangladesh and lived there for a year. So in that way the parents are OK because he can speak Bengali with them.

We also heard another, rather more robust explanation for the very low incidence of partnership or marriage between Bangladeshi women and white men from one of our young male informants who had been asked about the preferred husband for his sister:

Firstly, I don't have a sister and, secondly, if one of my cousin-sisters went out with a white boy I would encourage it as long as he was a converted Muslim. That is unlikely to happen in our family because my cousin-sisters' parents are strict Muslims and will marry them off to husbands in Bangladesh as soon as they are 18 years old. Wearing *burkhas* plays a part in discouraging anyone, whether a Bengali or white person, to actually mingle and getting to know my cousin-sisters. Basically, you don't get to see their faces and therefore no sexual attraction. That's what I call a Muslim girl.

The Importance of Religion and Age for Men

We need to distinguish this view of Islam from that taken by older men in the community. Although there are many shared perspectives, there are also additional considerations for these men which complicate the overall picture, and which have to be unpicked. It is older men who form the visible core of mosque culture in Brick Lane and Whitechapel Road. So it is their values and practices which tend to give people outside the community their sense of the part played by religion in its life.

The first and in some ways most paradoxical point that has to be emphasized here is that until the arrival of wives and children in the 1970s, and above all in the 1980s, there was not a great deal of religious activity among Bangladeshi men living in Britain. We have seen that they spent most of their time with compatriots, both at work and in the little leisure time that they did enjoy, and on the whole they complied with Islamic prescriptions. Some drank and gambled a bit. A few pursued relationships with white women and, perhaps even more frequently than in later decades, married them. But basically their lives were oriented to families and values in what is now Bangladesh. They sent money home, took long breaks there, married there and observed customs that were grounded there. Their lives in Britain, although strongly influenced by traditional values, were largely external to the main Bangladeshi traditions, and in some measure were free from its constraints.

The arrival of Bangladeshi women in Britain has changed that. On the one hand, the need to manage family life here, and to raise children, has forced more explicit recognition of Muslim values and prompted a dramatic revival of traditional religious ideas and practices. On the other, it has multiplied the occasions for contact with British institutions and culture – manifestly in hospitals, schools and social services, as well as among neighbours – in ways that have required ongoing compromise and adjustment to Western influences. For many men this has, moreover, coincided with unemployment, and in some cases may have contributed to it. Shiraj Mizan had a succession of well-paid jobs, and as we saw earlier was able to invest in a house near Brick Lane. But since bringing over his family he has not been able to work:

> What can I say? My bad luck started when I brought my family to this country. I have had to spend most of the time shopping and cooking for them. My wife fell ill soon after she came here, and I had to look after the little ones. I took them to school, fed them, dressed them, and that was all hard work. That caused me this disaster [of partial paralysis].

All this means that the opportunity to play a traditional patriarchal role as a head of family has arrived at a moment when many no longer occupy the position of economic provider that it should be based on. It is a stressful combination of circumstances for them, and this may well have contributed to the high rates of ill health found among older Bangladeshi men.

One of the manifestations of such stress appears to be hostility towards women, or at any rate towards the presence of Bangladeshi women in Britain. Ruhel Mukim, one of our older informants, drew attention like many of his peers to how good life was in the 1960s compared to the present, and then blamed women for the deterioration:

> There were not many Bangladeshis in this country when I arrived (in 1962). In 1963 to 1964 our people came in large numbers, but we hardly saw any Bangladeshi women at that time. They came in later, and our luck vanished because of them. Go out and have a look at the streets. They are full of our women, swarming like maggots. They have taken this country's culture. They have no shame, and no respect. They are drifting away from Muslim values – boys and girls are alike in this now.

The views of Mr Mukim show how older Bangladeshi men may be trying to resolve the ambiguities of their position by adopting strong religious roles. One assumption is that once men have reached a point (in their early or mid-twenties) where they are capable of supporting a family, their main obligation is to support a wife (or wives) and children – which is commonly seen as mandatory on them – and to give alms to the poor and disadvantaged, through the mosque.[15] When they are older they take on a role in the community teaching and upholding values that encourage others to honour this family system. Men who are unemployed in Britain, or forced by ill health to give up work, can help to give some meaning to their lives by adopting this spiritual role sooner.

This helps to explain the surge in religious activity that has taken place in the East End since the mid-1980s and it is critical to emphasise that this is separate from the growth in politico/religious extremism among some younger men. Virtually all of our older male informants said that they prayed five times a day, and on most days, above all on Fridays, the two main mosques in Brick Lane and Whitechapel Road are crowded for the midday prayer. Mustaqin Syed, an unemployed informant coming up to retirement age, gave us an outline of his day's activity, which showed that it revolved around religious routines. He was currently living in a council flat with his wife and young son, Jakir. His eldest son had a family of his own and was living separately. His three daughters were living with their husbands in Bangladesh:

> I am an early riser. I got up at six o'clock, and did my morning prayer. Then I had a biscuit and a cup of tea, and recited the Qu'ran for half an hour. I stopped because I can't read for a long time, as my eyes get sore. I went to bed again at about nine thirty and slept for an hour. Then I had my breakfast, with a piece of toast, an egg and a cup of tea. I went out to do some shopping in Brick Lane, and met a few people at the shop who are my old friends. I came back home at about eleven thirty, had my bath and then rushed to the mosque to catch the midday prayer. If the weather is good I prefer to say my midday prayer at the mosque.
>
> Prayer finished at about one o'clock and I stayed in for some time to hear the *waz* [or *Khutbah*, a religious sermon by an imam]. We came out at about two, that is me and two of my friends. We went to the Aladdin restaurant and ordered tea and samosas.
>
> I spent an hour or so at the restaurant, and the time for late afternoon prayer was

nearing. So we left the restaurant and went back to the mosque. At about four thirty I went back home. Jakir's mother* was moaning because I did not turn up for lunch on time. She had to warm everything up. I had fish curry, dal and rice. She is not an educated woman but she is an excellent cook. I had to go out again because I had forgotten to buy *paan* [betel] for her. I wandered around Brick Lane for about half an hour, but could not find any friends. So I came home, just before you got here. I will say my early evening prayer after you have gone, and then stay at home. I do not go out in the evening.

We can see from this account that although the frameworks of such lives are laid down around religious rules, the actual content also consists of far more practical, mundane matters. Much of Mustaqin's day was spent simply chatting with old friends, or looking for old friends to chat to. Most of these friends have known each other since the 1960s, so that even attendance at the mosque serves to reproduce patterns of male socialising that they have been engaged in continuously since they were young.

A lot of the chat is linked with family business. Men of this age in Bangladesh would be sharing economic pursuits with sons, and busily passing on experience and the control of property to them. Not many can do this in London – though a few, as we will see with Faruk, do try, and probably end up more distant from their sons as a result. In the absence of shared business concerns with their families here, they take a close interest in the ownership and acquisition of land in Bangladesh, and in matters such as the state of the harvest – which affects how much financial help relatives will need. Meetings at the mosque create an ideal setting for conversations and deals on such issues; and even if these men have less power than they think over the events they debate it still gives them a stake, and a role, in the community, in spite of their lack of productivity.

The fact that many of them are not in fact active economically does, however, produce some ethical dilemmas for imams across several areas. Men who are earning are required to pay some of their income as *zakat* (charitable alms) to the mosque, for distribution among the needy. But also, as noted later on, benefit income from the welfare state does not count as legitimate income, but as charity from a non-Muslim (and therefore unclean) source. Most Bangladeshis do accept welfare payments on the 'when in Rome' basis. That is, the welfare state is how things are done in Britain, and so it is wise to compromise with the system. However, what about *zakat*? If you receive welfare benefit, should you – or even 'can' you – pay *zakat* out of it? The question turns on how you define eligibility of funds for *zakat*. If all (including benefits) are eligible, then you should pay if you can afford to do so. If only *earned* income is eligible, and you have no earned income, then you need not, and some even believe you should not. There is a similar debate over whether you can take more than one wife while on benefits, or use money from benefits to pay for a trip to Mecca, and achieve *haji* status

---

*Bangladeshis employ teknonymy, a way of describing somebody by their relationship with a child. In this case Mustaqin refers to his wife by her relationship to his son rather than to himself.

– which, like the payment of alms (but more so), eases your passage and that of your family to heaven. These arguments continue.

There is much less room for disagreement over westernisation, which often seems to mean Western attitudes towards sex, with young Bangladeshis coming in for heavy condemnation for relaxation of proper standards. Ruhel took a particularly damning approach to this when talking to our (male Bangladeshi) interviewer:

> Everything is happening according to God's order. God is ubiquitous, he can see everything. He lets us at large on this earth to act sometimes freely and sometimes he is pulling the strings. All the accounts will be reckoned on the final judgment day. You never know who will be rewarded and who will be punished.
>
> When children are young a father should do everything to keep them in comfort. But a father must be careful that whatever he provides must come from *halal* [legitimate] income. There is another important thing to remember. If a husband and wife make love in *haram* [impure] conditions the resulting baby will suffer. He wouldn't be a good person. Everything has a ritual or right way of doing ... Now our kids who have been born in London are not *halal* babies. They are the result of incorrect acts by their parents.
>
> [INTERVIEWER:] That is a serious accusation.
>
> It is. I don't care. I am telling the truth. They are products of their parents' ignorance or carelessness. I am doubtful about their future. They will suffer in some way ... I hold parents responsible for this degeneration of our children. When most parents are godless their children are bound to be spoiled. Our women are learning bad things from this country. This is a Christian country. Most people are at least honest; their final destination only God knows. Our boys and girls only pick their bad things somehow. They are worse than white kids. (Interviewer's translation.)

Interestingly, Mr Mukim did not see the issue of arranged marriages as being a directly religious question:

> In Bangladesh as well as Britain, girls and boys are refusing to allow parents to select their marriage partners. According to our religion this is OK. But it is affecting us as a community, as a society. Traditionally we hold high respect for our elders. And that is one way of showing respect, by trusting their choice. Do you think a father would make a wrong choice for his son? On the other hand, if a young man is given absolute power to decide his future wife he is most likely to make a wrong decision because of his inexperience. He will be moved by glamour rather than the virtue of the girl. It is also a challenge to the integrity of parents and senior family members.
>
> Performing religious duties is the prime duty, for both men and women. For a man religion is the first priority – then helping out his wife in her domestic work and financially. I do help my wife in the house. Some days I ask her to stop the housework, and I do the cooking on those days. Our men quite often spend the day doing dishwashing for white men and then when they come home they become tigers. I don't mind helping my wife: I don't see any shame in helping her.

Such sentiments as these extend outwards among many men into a generalised hostility towards youth. Shiraj Mizan used a tone which combined hostility, mockery and not a little sympathy – a mixture which is more common than the simple denounce-ment by Mr Mukim:

> Some of our young people are becoming mullahs. They are English mullahs. They go a bit to mosque and they go a bit to dance party. They keep a little beard under their chin and wear Teddy dresses.* Look, we older people in this country have released our chil-dren into a jungle, and we cry to God every time we pray to save them and God listens to our cry and grabs them by their collars and puts them into the mosque. This is God's work. God is forcing them to go in the mosque.
>
> To us this country is a jungle, full of bears and tigers. There are so many temptations to swallow you. Women, alcohol, gambling, horse racing. If you put one step wrong you are eaten, snap. [He claps his hands.] Just like that. We older people always beg to the Almighty to look after our children, and he does. If you go to the mosque you will see our people crying all the time for our children.

As Mr Mizan's comments reveal, the distance between older and young people does not, unfortunately, appear to be greatly reduced by the recent revival of religious inter-est among them. There are generation gaps within the mosques themselves, among believers. The Islam practised in Bangladesh, and in Britain among first-generation migrants, bears traces of local Hinduism and leans towards the liberal Sufi tradition. The resurgent religion which is popular among the young is, by contrast, based on Iranian and Arab models of Islam. It is critical of (Hindu) saris – which are regarded as revealing and seductive – and prefers women to wear the modest salwar-kameez. Some young Bangladeshis have adopted Arabic names – and one of our informants was hard to trace for a second interview for precisely this reason.

Moral Economy and Paid Economy

Thus, the realm of religion is more complex than it may at first seem. There are, however, indications within this that Islam is proving useful in helping Bangladeshis to mediate their transition to life in the UK, albeit different sections in different ways. Also, if the resurgence of interest among the young plays a part in prompting a more general revival of religious activity in British Bangladeshi society, as seems possible, then it could itself prove a long-term adaptation. But this does seem to be closely tied up with questions about what are the needs of Bangladeshi families here. If Bangladeshi family life were to change greatly, then religion might lose its central role and rationale. And whether or not this happens is likely to depend mainly on choices made by young Bangladeshi women.

If the assumptions often made about male domination in Bangladeshi families are

---

*Presumably a reference to Teddy boys' clothing recalled from his early days in England.

largely illusory, we are left with patterns of behaviour which are not unlike the white extended families which formed the backbone of Bethnal Green local life in the 1950s. The tendency among Bangladeshis to import more sons-in-law than daughters-in-law may be leading towards matrilocal instead of traditional patrilocal extended households in the UK's Bangladeshi community, and could strengthen this resemblance even further. This similarity with the old white community is remarked on quite favourably by older white residents. Even where they resent what they see as the privileges of newcomers, many welcome the strength of extended family life among them, and take some comfort from it.

As we shall see in the next chapter, the reason they *need* to take comfort is that since the original study, and most of all during the period that Bangladeshis have been settling in the East End, white extended families as the old-timers once knew them have been steadily losing their own vitality. Local redevelopment has seen whole generations of many families leave. Changes in the pattern of housing mean that virtually no three-generational white households remain. White couples have fewer children, so those children have fewer siblings and, later, fewer nephews and nieces. And conjugal partnerships have become ever more fragile, with growing proportions of single parents, short-term relationships, multiplication of step-ties and a general – and for many older people bewildering – advent of flexibility in living arrangements.

But some of the mutual scrutiny between the two largest communities of Bethnal Green may be based on a misunderstanding of the role that families can expect to play in contemporary society. Since the original 1950s study the welfare state has taken on many of the supporting activities which used to be carried out informally within networks of family and friends, and pulled them into the public arena. A number of important implications flow from this. Firstly, and most obviously, kin no longer need to exercise such vigilant mutual care, as so much is now done by the state. Secondly, and less self-evidently, many of the jobs that women (in the main) used to do as members of these networks they and others do as paid workers within the welfare state. Thirdly, and following from the previous two, because much of the valuable activity which previously took place within it now gets done outside, in the public realm, family life has come to be seen as less important. What may appear to Bangladeshi women simply as impending loss of family may not be what is feared, but rather the shift of family activities into new organising frameworks. Thus, as more of them confront the same choices as white women have faced over the last generation or two, there may be a relaxing of attitudes in that community towards family life. While taking value away from the family, the growth of state social services may also increase the attractiveness of work to women, as it creates so much employment in areas of traditional female interest such as childcare and education.

So it might be misleading to imagine that the continuing importance of religion in the lives of Bangladeshis, and the apparent obstacle this forms to intermarriage, means that the community is bound to stay sealed off culturally. Although still more enclosed than some other minorities, the community is by no means cut off, nor moving in that direction. Bangladeshi women *are* finding jobs in the public sector. As they do so we might see a decline in their demand for a religiously grounded family culture within the community, and a steady secularisation of Bangladeshi lifestyles. One of our white informants, Nora Gerrard, pointed out that young Bangladeshi women have already changed the way that things are done quite a bit; so why not a bit more?

> One of the main weaknesses of the Bengalis is that they try and go against their own beliefs – the young ones especially. Lots of them, they don't believe in the way they're brought up and they don't listen to the old ones. Mostly I've heard young girls talking at the school when I've been helping out. They say they want to pick their own partner and not have the partner picked for them. That's going against their own parents. But lots of them now pick their own partners instead of having them picked.

Individualism and Assimilation

Far from being inward-looking, there are indications that the most successful members of the Bangladeshi community, those who have been admitted to the meritocracy, are indeed already distancing themselves from the rest. Shohel Uddin is in an interesting position here, because he could have moved on a long while ago if he had wanted to. Instead he has stayed near the heartland, and watched others leaving. This is partly because he needs to maintain close ties, given that his wife is white, if he is to remain part of the community. Living near to family has always been seen as indicative of solidarity:

> We are already seeing young Bangladeshis, educated Bangladeshis who are now becoming affluent, who are moving out ... They are effectively living in a cleaner street, which is what they all aspire to, having a home of their own, living in an environment where children can play safely, where there's no noise pollution and dirt pollution, where again there aren't too many other Bengalis living in the area ... Most Bengalis themselves want to move to an area – the educated ones I am talking about – where there are less Bengalis ... The whole idea is to get away from a Bengali community and to start mixing with everyone else in the area ... I can use myself as an example. I still refer to most Bangladeshis as being villagers. I use the term in a semi-insulting way because I find them quite dirty, quite rude, and not willing to integrate into the area or with the rest of the local community. What really annoys me is these people aren't in many ways home-proud, they're not really bothered about the conditions they live in.

Inevitably, the community as a whole is weakened by this outward movement. However much emphasis may still be put on retaining close family ties, and continuing to provide support, a symbolic change is occurring which has consequences. It is the individuals who are manifestly successful in Britain who are choosing to move on, and becoming closer to the British mainstream. Hence those who remain – and the residual group they constitute – are bound to bear some of the marks of failure. They are the ones meritocracy has rejected, so their collective behaviour takes on some aspects of a reaction to rejection.* Shohel found it worrying:

> People who have done well at school to a large extent do move out. There's a worrying trend at the moment that the new generation of Bengalis who are now growing up in the primary schools and the secondary schools are in fact falling very far behind. They are way behind the likes of me who are a generation or two older, who tried quite hard to get out of here and educate ourselves. These people in many ways have now become the least educated people, as a group, in the whole country. Of the people from the Indian subcontinent I would say that we are at the bottom of the pile ... I think there's a downward spiral and the children aren't doing very well at all.

Insofar as any such reaction involves holding on to values that the group came here with, then it is likely to have some positive implications. The Islamicist mood which has been in the ascendant since the early 1990s does, for example, surely contain some reaction to social exclusion, and to failure in educational contests and so on. And this perhaps feeds extremist and reactionary elements in it. But overall its correspondence with homeland culture, and with family traditions, means that it is able to provide satisfying, unifying experiences within the community. It informs a favourable identity for its unambitious backbone. In meritocratic terms they may count as failures, but for the most part they are reasonably content to confine their aspirations within their family and community activities, and find rewards in sharing an ongoing way of life with other group members. Not everyone can be a winner. This is just the sort of function that communities should be playing, whether ethnic or otherwise.

What, however, does give cause for concern in the East End is the behaviour of young Bangladeshi men, raised in the UK, who appear to be responding to failure by adopting aspects of British counter-culture that have nothing in common with the lifestyles of their parents. Youth gangs developed in response to white violence, and by the end of the century had largely taken control of Tower Hamlets streets. But alongside the growth of gang culture there has been a surge of drug abuse and in the thefts and robberies needed to sustain the habits. There is a slide by many young Bangladeshis into an alternative value and opportunity structure, which community elders seem unable to stem.

There is a real dilemma here for Bangladeshi parents in that the more traditional are their attitudes and style of discipline, the more alienated their children are liable to feel and the less amenable to their control. This was explained to us by Najma Sharhid, who appeared herself to have coped with her situation successfully. Najma had just finished a degree in psychology and education at London University when we talked

---

*This is reminiscent of the consequences of failure predicted by Michael Young in his 1958 dystopian novel *The Rise of the Meritocracy*.

to her, and was preparing to go into teaching. She said that many of the decisions she had made were in reaction to her traditional and authoritarian father, with whom she was still living, and that her parents' efforts to influence her had simply increased her determination to be as independent as possible.

> When I was younger, I never used to wear a headscarf. To my dad that was very wrong, because he had a certain status in society. Because my dad was sort of prominent in his circle and in Bangladesh, he has always been a very authoritarian person. And he was brought up in a very authoritarian way by his brothers. That's why he behaves like that with us; he's strong on discipline and that's how he thinks children should be brought up.

Najma felt that her father now understood that, in his efforts to control his children, he had in fact lost them.

> He's changing slightly, because with me and my older brother he was very strict and so we don't really have a relationship with him. He really regrets it now. He can see where he went wrong, so now he is behaving not so authoritarian with my sister and my younger brothers. She doesn't wear *hijab* and he doesn't say anything to her. My wearing *hijab* now was my own choice, but I didn't want him to pressurise me into it ... And my older brother doesn't mix much with Bengali people; he doesn't mix with our relatives very much, just ignores them ... The thing is, because my dad wanted us to be quite traditional and everything, it had an opposite effect.

So parenting in London which tries to be too traditional is liable to prove counter-productive. In Najma's case, and in that of almost every Bangladeshi girl we interviewed, this does not seem to produce alienation from Bangladeshi culture, simply a more liberal interpretation of it. But for boys it may well contribute towards the slide into drug-taking and an associated criminal lifestyle. The wider Bangladeshi community has been slow to realise what has been going on. For a long time, many elders either just indulged in blanket condemnation of westernisation or could not even accept that there was a problem. To older Bangladeshis, the dangerous substance to avoid in the UK, and to which some had themselves succumbed when just living with other men in lodging-houses, was alcohol. So long as they could not smell *that* on their children's breath, they did not worry too much. Now that they are finding out that heroin has no odour, it is too late. A lively drugs culture has already established itself among those young Bangladeshis who are failing in the meritocratic race, or don't believe it is worth winning, but who are too integrated into British life, and perhaps too ambitious, to find consolation within a transplanted subcontinental lifestyle. A pattern is being set for fast-track integration into the underclass, alongside some of the 'poor whites' they have already been through school with. Most Bangladeshis, however, do not see this as a white lifestyle choice so much as black. Many have a premonition of their youth following what they see as a Black Caribbean path. As Shohel himself commented:

Bengalis, young working-class Bengalis, are very much like their West Indian counter-parts – only interested in big flash cars, expensive clothes and music ... They are much more interested than other Asians in fashion, cars and drugs ... We used to be frightened of being attacked by packs of West Indian youths. That time has gone. The gang mental-ity that the Bengalis acquired as a way of defending themselves has been transformed into more of a drug mentality.

It is probably seen this way, rather than as simple integration to majority culture, because for many Bangladeshi elders the behaviour of their youth is thought to be related to a weakness of their own community structure, and to be a particular fate of minority groups. There has been much heart-searching in the last few years to find what can be done collectively to avert this fate for more of the community. And again, part of the interest in Islam springs from the desire to create a stronger community which can resist other values, and protect its children from such outside influences.

All of these changes, affecting above all the younger generation, add to the alienation of the first generation of men. Even in the area of spiritual activity, from which they are not excluded by their economic inactivity, such men seem to be denied the full role and respect which they seek. For all their urgent crowding into the busy mosques on a Friday morning, they remain a generation in limbo – suspended between a Western society that is too liberal for them and a rising generation of Muslims that is less Bangladeshi and increasingly part of a politicised and global version of Islam. As one of our field researchers, Shariful Islam, noted:

It is early afternoon. The imam of the Brick Lane mosque is chanting his call to prayer, 'Allah is our creator, Allah is almighty, Allah is kind ...' There they go, wearing the distinc-tive skullcap and with grey beards. Chewing *paan* and holding cigarettes in their hands they drag their bodies, weakened by decades of hard work, towards the mosque. One, ten, hundreds of them. After all, Allah is the creator. Allah is kind. May Allah ensure them a good life in heaven.

Fruit and vegetables are sold from a cart on the main road in Bethnal Green.

Chapter 5

The New Individualism

At the same time as cohesive Bangladeshi families were arriving in Tower Hamlets, the white community was fragmenting under the impact of lifestyle changes, many of which appear to follow post-war developments in the welfare state. Together with demographic and economic changes, these were altering family life and the way that families linked in with local society. This is shaping the context into which new Bangladeshi settlers are moving and affects relations between the two communities.

Families at the Centre

In the old East End, it was families – and especially mothers and motherhood – which constituted the heart of local community life. Family ties gave people the support and security which made life tolerable, and provided a model for organising relationships with close neighbours. Being a member of a family gave you kin and quasi-kin locally, and made the world a safe place. Many older respondents in the 1990s study recalled this fondly. For example Mrs Sandwich, a frail widow in her eighties living halfway up an imposing tower block to the north of Bethnal Green Road, recounted that:

> Years ago there used to be private landlords (to get flats from), and when people got married they would move into a one-bedroom flat. You used to be able to move around the corner from your mother, or just down the road. Forty years ago the mother would talk to the landlord for you ... When we was kids we used to call the woman above Aunt, and her kids called my mum Aunt. We all used to go to the baths together. The mums used to be in the laundry, and you used to talk to one another. Nowadays a woman would be indoors doing her washing, in the washing machine, with the kids in the bath upstairs. So you miss out on all the talk. We used to go to the shop and get the shopping for her. Your mum would pay at the end of the week. Everybody knew who you were.

Formal marriage was of practical importance in this system as it gave people more relatives to interact with, and stronger claims over them. Family status defined suitable expectations and opportunities, and rituals of status change were key markers for progression through the stages of life. Birthing and baptism (plus, for some, confirmation), marriages and funerals – the stock in trade of parish churches – were all observed seriously, even by those with no other interest in religion.[1] The overlapping lines of personal ties which marriages created between local dynasties were the main weft holding together the fabric of communality, and giving local society its structure and texture.

Marriage was also significant in that it bound men into families and gave them a place in the wider community. It committed a man (and his kin) to providing material support for a wife, particularly where there were children. Public support systems, including the early post-war welfare state, operated mainly to reinforce private family support. A single mother, by contrast, not only lacked much kinship support, but also faced difficulty in securing public support. Poor Law provisions, which ended only in 1948, could not be accessed without experiencing some degree of shame – either at family failure or at personal failure to fit into family structures. So overall there was a marked difference in social position between married mothers, who were honoured for their role in the community, and unmarried, who were liable to be seen as dependent on charity, however hard they might work.

Unlike in modern Britain there was therefore little difference between high valuation of motherhood and strong emphasis on the institution of marriage. Celebrating motherhood did not mean discounting fathers. Indeed, the organisation of men through marriage into socially useful lives as husbands and fathers (bringing in a family income) was an important role that mothers played on behalf of the wider community.[2] This mobilisation of men into active provisioners of the family was especially appreciated in the poorest sectors of society such as the East End, which enjoyed only a slender margin of spare resources. Whether or not people in such communities can be said to have valued the conventions of marriage more highly than others did, they certainly *observed* them scrupulously, as can be seen from official figures on rates of illegitimacy in table 5.1. In the years before the new welfare state began to offer viable alternative forms of support, it was in the poorest parts of London that the illegitimacy rate was lowest – even while the overall birth rate was the highest. It was in precisely such areas that the security offered by marriage, whether shotgun or not, was most needed. And this was the case both during the war, when the birth rate and rates of illegitimacy went up everywhere, and in the pre-war years. It is striking that Poplar in 1937–39 had both the highest London birth rate and the lowest illegitimacy rate. We have included Bermondsey in the selection of boroughs to illustrate the finding; it was a feature of working-class life, rather than of Tower Hamlets specifically.

The senior figure in this traditional East End way of life was usually a matriarch, known generally as Mum to her children and as Nan to her grandchildren. Mum was frequently instrumental in arranging nearby housing for her children when they got married, so that she could keep an eye on them and help bring up grandchildren. She often played an informal role too in helping them find local work, and she was a major source of advice on all aspects of life. Her house was where the extended family would congregate.

Table 5.1 **Birth and illegitimacy rates in (selected) rich and poor London boroughs, 1937–39 and 1940–45**

Borough	Illegitimacy per 1,000 births 1937–39	Total annual birth rate per 1,000 population 1937–39	Illegitimacy per 1,000 births 1940–45	Total annual birth rate per 1,000 population 1940–45
Bermondsey	26	14.2	44	18.2
Bethnal Green	33	13.4	46	17.4
Poplar	21	15.4	50	19.6
Stepney	39	13.1	75	17.2
London County average	*60*	*13.3*	*84*	*16.6*
Chelsea	93	10.3	139	13.3
St Marylebone	118	9.2	172	11.5
Westminster	146	8.2	197	11.4

Source: *Statistical Abstract for London*, Vol. XXXI, London, London Council Council, 1945

The mother is the head and centre of the extended family, her home is its meeting place. 'Mum's is the family rendezvous,' as one wife said. Her daughters congregate at the mother's, visiting her more often than she visits any one of them: 68 per cent of married women last saw their mother at her home, and only 27 per cent at their own.[3]

Thus it was Mum's concern for her offspring which helped to keep extended families local, within the neighbourhood. And when she died the family descent group would soon split up and regroup around her successors.

'It all broke up when Mum died,' said one woman. 'There's been no head of the family, no organisation ... We don't see that much of them since Mum died. Mum's used to be the central depot in this family.'[4]

She was also a figure of great moral authority. Not only did she use her local reputation and connections to promote the interests of family members, but she also upheld rules of fairness within the family. To most people, she was the undisputed leader, and belonged on a pedestal.

The very word (Mum), and the warmth with which it is uttered, somehow conveys the respect in which she is upheld. Since her status as 'Mum' is so high, it is derogatory to call her by any other name.[5]

Bureaucratisation of Caring

The early welfare state built on this informal edifice of face-to-face, reciprocal supports. When the Beveridge Report on health and national insurance was published during the

Second World War it was welcomed by many working-class citizens not simply because it offered material security but also because it seemed to reflect or even embody many traditional working-class practices. Working-class local communities prized not only their extended family groups, but also a host of mutual-aid societies, savings clubs and informal networks for providing personal security through reciprocal support. What Beveridge appeared to do was to take these mechanisms of self-help and mutuality and make them more viable by inserting them into state schemes backed by vastly greater material resources. The give and take practised within local communities would inspire new collectivist public institutions. All citizens would support each other when they were able – that is when they were in work and healthy – and be supported when they were not – that is as children, when unemployed, in old age, or when sick. The nation was re-cast as one mutually supportive community, even one great public family. This would make it more united, because state pooling of risks and resources would provide much fairer and more reliable balancing out of support between citizens in different personal circumstances.

This vision of citizenship looked back for inspiration to a face-to-face society in which long-term personal reciprocity and loyalties were highly valued. Enjoyment of rights within it was bound up with membership of the community and contribution to the commonweal. But such moralistic perceptions of citizenship did not survive as the administration of welfare became more centralised. The promotion of social mobility and 'meritocracy' emphasised rules which would encourage personal freedom by providing more individualised security for those who might be left behind. Massive expansion of higher education was being implemented, to lift ambitious working-class children out of local communities which might hamper their advance and to encourage wider identities and loyalties. The security formerly provided by families became increasingly vested in the 'national' family administered by the state. It took the form of welfare benefits that could be enjoyed by individuals in their own right, without reference to family ties or parental or conjugal restraints, and were transportable to any part of the country. For many people, in particular young people, most of all those who have achieved social mobility, this has undoubtedly enhanced their lives, and enabled them to do things that would have been impossible for earlier generations. But there are also losers in this – especially collective losers such as local communities and the people dependent on them – whose interests are not easily protected in the new relationship between citizen and state.

When the negative side of individualism is considered now, it is conventionally seen as a product of the Thatcher years. But much is traceable further back, to the libertarian policies of Roy Jenkins in the 1960s and beyond. For what has enabled individualistic behaviour and attitudes is the individualisation of citizenship and social support systems which started after the war. Tension between state services and the lives of private families was already emerging when *Family and Kinship* was being researched. The use of kinship to elicit support which could alternatively have been provided by the state was criticised as inimical to individual freedom and corrosive of universalistic social justice. When Michael Young met a group of social planners to present some of the early findings, he drew attention to the important role of extended families, and the fact that 'many working-class extended families operate continuously as agencies for mutual aid of all kinds'.[6]

In the ensuing debate Ruth Glass, an influential advocate of public social services, rebuked him by asserting that the mobilisation of extended family support was a clear indication of the failure of social services to provide adequate back-up themselves. 'The virtues of the extended family ... were often no more than the defects of other institutions.'[7]

Much of this animus towards families derived from the idea that they took women's labour for granted, and confined them within duties from which they could not escape. Promotion of the welfare state was linked to a wish to remove the subordination of women to men, to assert the priority of public roles and relations over private, and secure motherhood as a *public* function. Lynn Jamieson has shown how the growing welfare side of states in the West during the latter part of the nineteenth century, and first part of the twentieth, was giving direct prominence to mothers – as managers of family care and consumption on behalf of the state – while sidelining the role of fathers:

> By the late nineteenth century, motherhood had become a matter of public policy and debate in all industrialising nation states. A corollary of the focus on mothers was the marginalisation of fathers. Fathers were implicitly irrelevant to the intensive management of children expected from mothers.[8]

So the extension of state activity and intervention in family life was welcomed by reformers as rebalancing family power in favour of women. They felt that a measure of exemplary competition from the state, as an alternative material provider, might help to make men more, rather than less, responsive to what women actually wanted. However, what started as an endorsement of mothers' rights, vis-à-vis fathers, gradually seems to have developed into a move towards state management of mothers and motherhood too.

One prominent reforming observer of working-class family life in Britain was Eleanor Rathbone, a Liberal crusader whose ideas were to have a profound influence on the shaping of the post-war welfare state by making welfare benefits payable to mothers. She believed that even where men *did* behave as committed fathers and breadwinners this was not rooted in genuinely caring attitudes but arose out of a male instinct of domination, which she dubbed the 'Turk complex'.[9]

Rathbone believed that the welfare state could best liberate women, while supporting them in their domestic labour, by extending to them full citizenship in their own right. In her decisive contribution to the famous 1945 House of Commons second reading of the legislation which made family allowances payable directly to mothers, she made it clear that motherhood was no longer (just) a private status, but a public one (too):

> If the money is given to the mother, and if they know that the law regards it as the child's property, or the mother's property to be spent for the child, that will help them to realise that the State recognises the status of motherhood.[10]

This perspective gives an additional edge to the post-war speeches made by Labour ministers in the East End reported below in chapter 10, and in particular to the ceremonial handing over to a local mother of the first family allowance payment. Eleanor Rathbone was well known as a local campaigner, and cited the lives of East End women when making her case. This connection, and the repeated references to the wartime valour shown by the civilian population in the East End, among them many women, meant that the creation of the new welfare state was seen as not just a general reward for ordinary British people. It also liberated women from conjugal subjugation. Those who needed public support had finally gained access to it, not in a demeaning manner by playing on their dependence, but positively through behaving as heroines, making an honourable and public contribution to the common good.

The findings of *Family and Kinship* endorsed Rathbone's argument that men became more responsive and supporting partners once the welfare state had diluted their authority. The men interviewed during the 1950s, while still committed as providers, were reported as being more caring and involved in family life than their fathers and grandfathers, and discussed family life in terms remarkably similar to those used by women. The elevation of women to a position of equal status in the public realm appeared to improve relations between the sexes. But the other side of the coin was also becoming evident: as family members increased their slate of rights as individual citizens, families as groups were losing influence in the public domain. 'Putting a word in' for relatives, for example, had already become defined as nepotism.

In the years that followed, intellectuals on the left such as Michèle Barrett and Mary McIntosh encouraged young people to break away from parents, by condemning families as anti-social groupings which compromised the personal loyalty of citizens to the state. The welfare state was moving away from rewarding service in the local community, and it was the young meritocrats, eager to escape from cloying family ties, who grasped most enthusiastically the personal freedom offered.

Mothers – or perhaps motherhood – have experienced a more complicated outcome. There are many women who have been able to wield the new freedoms to improve their own lives, and widen their horizons, and those of their children too. But this has been as meritocrats. Eleanor Rathbone's passion was to improve the general status of motherhood and domestic life in British society, by defining it as *public work done for the community*, rather than privately for a husband. But in the East End, it would be hard to say now that the lives of women as mothers have been greatly improved by the changes that have occurred.

Families of Choice

In fact a new type of family life seems to have emerged, which was neither intended nor anticipated by earlier reformers. Marriage is no longer seen as a publicly defined and regulated institution determining public status, where the rules are known and agreed by everyone. Instead, many people emphasise private, customised relationships, governed by personal choice, about which society in general has no right to pass judgment. This follows logically from the general proposition that people should be free to determine for themselves how they live, backed by rules allowing them to claim benefits as independent individuals as easily as (some would argue *more* easily than) if they were living with others.

All this has made research in the field much harder. In the fifties you could knock on a door and ask who lived there and what their relationships to each other were. And the answers would be unambiguous. By the 1990s it was not just difficult to find an agreed terminology to use; you could no longer even assume that your questions would be answered.

Many people now are living in very casual, fluid households, or in more than one place, or in unconventional relationships. On top of this, the rise of strategic single parenthood (see below) means that many are engaged in undisclosed cohabitation which they simply do not discuss – certainly in a short interview – for fear of losing benefits.

Some respondents did trust the interviewers enough to admit this openly. Francesca Dacosta, who called herself Mrs Dacosta even though she had never been married, was a single mother with two young children and claiming all possible benefits. We interviewed her in a converted second-floor flat from which she was hoping shortly to move. There was a man present when she was seen, but she did not want him to be recorded as living there. She insisted that she had boyfriends to stay only occasionally, and lived most of the time just with her children. She had never worked, and said that she could only just make ends meet. So she felt entitled to conceal her friend's existence in order to protect her benefits and her children's well-being.

Melissa Terry dealt with this differently. She did acknowledge the existence of a steady boyfriend who was in her flat, but argued that he did not cohabit with her and was not a member of the family. Melissa lived in a three-generation female household which would have been remarkable in Bethnal Green in the fifties but seems not uncommon now. It consisted of Melissa herself (unmarried), her mother (described as a widow) and Melissa's daughters. The boyfriend was a visiting partner, said to stay occasionally but to be living elsewhere most of the time with friends. No one in Melissa's household was a wage-earner. Nor was the boyfriend. So again the pattern of residence can be seen as tactically linked to safeguarding income from benefits.

Being married is itself no guarantee of conventional behaviour. When talking about the state of modern families, Mrs Woodcraft commented, without any evident display of irony:

The old strength has gone, of close-knit East End families. You don't have several members of the same families in one street very often. Children all move further away these days ... But my family is very close. *I even see my husband regularly, and we are separated.* I also see his family, and have days out with his brothers and sisters still (emphasis added).

In the fifties, when married couples either lived together or were at war, this would have been an unusual set-up. But not any more. Sometimes, though not in Mrs Woodcraft's case, such household arrangements of married couples are, like those of unmarried ones, linked to playing the benefits system by maximising their rights as individuals. Marion Daly's family is an interesting and complex example. As described later in chapter 8, Marion and her two children were living separately from her husband. In spite of this, and also of the fact that her children have lived with her mother for periods, Marion, like Mrs Woodcraft, did not see her family as collapsing. Both she and her husband were dependent on benefits, and living apart ensured that they were treated as separate claimants and so could receive more money, although their costs were presumably also greater. At the same time, and rather bizarrely, we shall see that they were collaborating to sue Tower Hamlets Housing Department jointly for the loss of a flat which they formerly occupied together. When it suited them they could act as a couple. When it didn't they stayed apart.

One rather paradoxical aspect of this is that whereas the original emphasis on personal choice seems to have been intended to benefit women, in a poor area like the East End it may end up allowing the greater freedom to men. For an implication of giving women fuller direct access to citizenship, not mediated by relationships with men, is that men may lose their positions as representatives of family interests in the public realm. They are then the ones liberated. This was anticipated by Conservatives when the post-war welfare state was being designed, but the public mood was so strongly in favour of change that they did not push the objection very hard, even though there was obviously a danger that by discounting traditional family obligations the new legislation could weaken men's commitment to marriage and sense of responsibility for their offspring. Lady Apsley, a Conservative MP, spoke against Eleanor Rathbone's proposals on those grounds during the second reading of the Family Allowances Bill, and criticised what she regarded as Edith Summerskill's romanticisation of mother-centred systems:

[I]t seems to me perfectly easy to retain the typically English tradition based on the Greek concept of the father as head of his family ... but to enable the cash to be drawn by the mother. Some hon. Members have spoken as if it were something new and modern for the mother to be in the head place of the family, but that is not so. The matriarch is a very ancient form of social life. The hon. Member for West Fulham (Dr. Summerskill), who made such an eloquent speech just now, mentioned Australia. I wonder if she saw the ancient Australian aboriginal tribes, living in the state of our forefathers in the Stone Age. If so, she will realise that it was the mothers who did all the supplying and feeding of the family, while the father was merely the warrior ignorant of all other responsibilities for his family. Matriarchy is an extremely primitive type of civilisation alien to the English tradition ... It would be a great mistake if we did anything to undermine the position of the father as legal head of the family.[11]

The point was not taken. But now it is looking as if, by trying to create more symmetrical partnerships between men and women, welfare provisions may in the longer run actually have increased the imbalance. For while women have stepped up their participation in the labour market without losing their domestic responsibilities, men seem to have collectively reduced their productive contribution without picking up additional family work in return. There is still a powerful lobby in Britain urging that if men and women are treated the same, they will behave the same, and that any remaining sexual divisions of labour should and will soon disappear, and are in the process of doing so. We are not so sure.

It rather depends on what you measure. Those studies by analysts such as Jonathan Gershuny which regularly monitor the domestic labour inputs of men show that those living in heterosexual couples now report themselves to be doing (marginally) more housework and caring work than in years gone by. Even if these survey responses are taken at face value, though, it has to be borne in mind that such studies do not consider the way in which many men are avoiding parenting obligations altogether, by not living in couples or families. The life stage which has multiplied most since the fifties is that of the child free, and this category contains many more men than women. There is marked and growing asymmetry here.

Marginal Men and Disappearing Fathers

Those men in our study who were living as parents were still much less restricted by parenthood than women in their interactions with the world outside; even the few lone fathers had a relatively easy ride. Take Doug Carter, for example. Mr Carter had been unemployed, with a full-time working wife, when he was first interviewed in 1992. Two years later we found him divorced, still not working, but with main custody of the children and claiming to be the main child-carer. He justified not looking for work by arguing that he needed to spend his time looking after his children. However, he was not wholly alone. His (ex) mother-in-law lived a few minutes walk away, and his own mother was not much further. So he frequently took his children to spend time with their nans, and normally had several days and nights a week completely child free. He fell well short of the role-reversing house-husband which he liked to regard himself as being.

His lifestyle was shared by Tony Hicks. Tony considered himself to be something of a New Man, on the basis that his teenage children came to stay on a Saturday night. But his use of time did not appear seriously impeded by parenting.

These cases illustrate how older women too may now be picking up extra parenting duties, as grandmothers step into the breach following a conjugal breakdown. Since their separation, Mandy Charlton's ex-husband was looking after their children for two nights a week. But he had moved back to live with his parents, so was able, like many male carers, to share this responsibility with other people – *female* others, moreover – who were probably happy to put themselves to considerable trouble in order to maintain a precarious link with their valued grandchildren.

The outcome of the recent changes in family life may therefore be an intensifying focus of family life around women and female descent lines, with men becoming increasingly individualised and marginalised. This goes beyond merely dropping out from family life, and extends into lesser community participation and a whole range of reduced contributions to social life. The findings of sociologists Katharine Mumford and Anne Power in other parts of east London, where there are more young white men around, indicate that for many families today the presence of males is experienced negatively – in relation to crime, drugs and disorderly behaviour.[12]

Some of our informants considered that the root of these problems lay in male unemployment, which during the early 1990s was over 20 per cent in Tower Hamlets.[13] Caroline Ives was a single mother with one child and a visiting partner when first interviewed, and then cohabiting with a new partner later on, and subsequently alone with two children when seen last. She felt, like many others, that relationships are much more difficult when men had no work to go to, not so much because of the economics but because men get under your feet.

> That's why my husband and I broke up. He was out of work and we were arguing all the time, and him being around the flat all day really got on my nerves. So we were rowing all the time. I think things are getting worse, really, with all the unemployment.

But in the view of others, unemployment is merely a symptom of the redundancy of men in poor households which are bound to be better off on state benefits. Father Reilly pointed out that, because women can expect public support when they become mothers, there is no compelling reason for them to get married, nor for men to become involved. Responsible fatherhood was the main casualty. The contemporary family was much like that of the 1950s, but without a stable male presence.

> It's all mother-centred still – more so because of the break up of old family structures. If there's a crisis, it's a crisis of fatherhood. Women have changed. Young men are afraid of some of the young women. They're afraid of the aggression of some women. They are liberated women. A new feature is male suicides. Women have a different route now, not into marriage. Once they have a child, motherhood gives them a route into housing and benefits. There's a framework for them to survive in. I conducted a funeral last Thursday. A man there was boasting he had eight children from eight different women.

What the changes in family over the last forty years may show is that unless men are given incentives to take a responsible part in family life, they are content to play a marginal role. Sometimes men remain semi-detached simply by keeping a short distance from other family members. Several non-resident fathers of young children in our survey seemed to live near by, without being closely involved in daily care. They were near enough to stay in touch and be available if needed, and perhaps to derive some satisfaction from the relationship. This may also be quite compatible with what some single mothers want in a partner. Dave Mansfield, for example, originally from Nottingham, was living in Bethnal Green in order to be near his three-year-old daughter. He did not have frequent contact with her, and at the time of interview was seeing her only once every few weeks. But even this slender routine seemed to give him enough sense of purpose, and a connection here, to enable him to play a part in local life and hold down a job.

There do seem to be basic sex differences present here, which current family ideologies fail to comprehend. The very first interview carried out in our main survey was with an elderly man living alone who had rather a quiet life, although his responses indicated that he was genuinely satisfied with it. However, our interviewer could not understand this, and peppered her report with comments to be followed up by us in later sessions. Why wasn't he demanding more help from social services with this and with that? Why didn't he ask to be housed on the ground floor where access was easier, and more people could come to visit him? Why didn't he get more involved in community organisations? Shouldn't we be contacting Social Services for him, if he was unable to do so himself?

This contemporary failure to acknowledge male detachment may contribute to the growing sexual polarisation of behaviour. The assumption behind current social policies relating to family, and work, is that men and women have the same disposition to be involved in family and community life, and so if treated in the same way will behave the same. But perhaps their disposition is not the same. It is interesting that when their relative indifference was openly accepted, men often seemed to end up with higher levels of commitment to family life and ability to fit themselves into it. Kristin O'Keefe, for example, who lives a very traditional life, had a clear sense of men being different. 'Family is for women,' she believes. But she was perfectly happy with this, and used her husband as a link to the many women in his family, with whom she passed most of her time, without worrying for a moment that he was not nearly as involved in it all as she was. But because she was willing to do this, he then became drawn in himself – to a level that he felt comfortable with. So in addition to serving as an affinal link he was probably less marginal to family activities than many other men of his generation. By being treated as *different* from women, he was enabled to become more *like* them.

Rediscovering Family and Marriage

Most of the women we discussed these matters with in any detail felt that family life had changed for the worse. More to the point, virtually all mothers did. References to the growth in Britain of a singles culture are a little misleading. It is not marriage, or even having a partner, which makes the real difference. It is children. They create the watershed. Single people with children do not play much part in the so-called singles culture. Young married people without children, on the other hand, do share many life-style characteristics with childless singles. The principal change in domestic life since the fifties may just be that more people are waiting longer before having children, or even avoiding parenthood altogether.

Thus the key area where choice does have pertinence lies around fertility. *Family and Kinship* argued that it was the demands of rearing children which trapped women into domesticity and dependence on men. Mothers were slaves to their children. 'Being a prisoner to child-bearing, the wife could not easily mend her finances for herself by going out to work.'[14] This is still the case; it is between women who are mothers and those who are childless that the greatest differences of lifestyle are now evident.

The first Bethnal Green study also found that having children pulled young women into extended family life, and underlined sexual divisions of labour. Findings in the new survey show that this process is now less formal, and more drawn out. But it is essentially the same. Within our own detailed case studies, we found few mothers who seemed comfortable with the fluid, more casual relationships common among the childless. Some of those young mothers who were not married were refugees from an unsatisfactory relationship, and in the course of re-assessing and re-ordering their lives. Most of the rest were actively discovering that they would prefer to be married.

In passing we should mention that financial independence was not seen as a great boon. A majority of the single mothers in the sample drew multiple benefits but none of them celebrated this as a sign of freedom. Reliance on their own-right entitlements from the state did not leave them feeling more confident, and most were hoping to get off benefits as soon as they could. Some were using their time as state dependants to prepare for work – which *was* seen as offering greater independence. But in practice most were seeking more security through marriage.

Thus the state of cohabitee, frequently held up as a modern alternative to marriage, shows up in our study as a stage along the road to marriage itself. For example, Lisa Oakley was a single mother with one child when we first made contact with her. By the time of our second interview she had acquired a fresh baby – together with its father as a co-resident partner. She seemed to be in the process of constructing a more conventional, more public relationship with this partner. This was more than just a one-to-one bond as it gave her a network of additional 'in-laws'. She visited her partner's mother in north London more often than he did himself, and had struck up a firm friendship with his sister. Her brother's partner was also close to her. She had more frequent contact with these women than with the men who linked her with them – for example every few months with her brother compared with every week or so for his partner.

Lisa appeared to enjoy these affinal ties, as they would have been called when kinship relations were more formal, and regaled us with a number of conventional, 'married' views – such as that men these days were allowed too easily to avoid commitment and responsibilities: 'People get out of relationships too easily. People, especially the men, are so insecure that they can't handle the responsibility.' An intriguing aspect of this slide back towards conventionality was a tendency to draw attention to differences between men and women. She had a sister living round the corner, and saw her frequently. 'I speak to her even more on the phone – nearly every day. She's handy for borrowing things.' But of her brother she said, 'Because he's a brother I don't see him.' This was not because of the sex difference. Her current partner had a brother too, and of them she said, 'They're lucky if they bump into each other at Christmas.' (Though, as a woman, she was clearly assuming that they would actually regard this as lucky.)

Her attitudes were also less than tolerant of gays – another group that has flourished as traditional family ties have declined. 'We had a big gay festival in the park last summer. I didn't see why it had to be in a residential area. I walked around and I had never known there were so many people with chips on their shoulders.'

Many others fell into this pattern. Josephine Kennedy, a single mother at the first interview, had a resident partner (but not a new baby) by the second, and was already leaving her children with her present 'mother-in-law' for long periods at weekends. Sharon Thomas, on the other hand, had been separated from her husband when we first made contact with her, and was living as a single mother. Three years later her husband was back with her.

The gulf we found between mothers and childless women also coincided quite closely with the division between the old working class and the incoming, transient middle-class young women, often working in the City and yet to become mothers. Many of the latter were very comfortable with current family lifestyles, which they often recognised as an extension of the life-stage of adult independence which occurs between childhood and parenthood. Our informant Sandra Collimore, for instance, a childless cohabiting personnel manager in her early twenties, staked a firm claim for regarding cohabitation as responsible, and mainstream:

> I don't think people's opinion of marriage and family has gone down that much; it is a timing question. People are not seeing the necessity of just getting married and having children. They want to do these things in the order that suits their circumstances. People tend to remarry after divorce, which tends to indicate that they do like to reorganise into family units and basically still have got faith in marriage and family units. There is just less pressure on people today to conform – that is to get married at eighteen, have kids at twenty, and grow old gracefully. There is more freedom now. There is a tendency for people to remain single while they want to, without pressure from family and friends to conform to a pattern of living.

So life for most people still seems to follow broadly the same path as it always has, that is from childhood, through a period of independence, on to parenthood and the interdependence between adults characteristic of married life. What has changed is, firstly, that many (middle-class) women now wait longer before becoming parents and, secondly, that public attitudes and policy are geared to their sentiments, rather than those of mothers and older women. Since our fieldwork was completed there seems to have been a slight national movement back towards high valuation of motherhood within a private, family context.* But there is still a general lack of interest among policymakers in how women, especially working-class women, change when they become mothers.

Once women *do* have children, serious choice flies out of the window. The chances for them to enjoy Anthony Giddens' 'pure relationships' – that is relationships based on free personal choices, unconstrained by institutional prescriptions[15] – are decimated or worse. When you have children to look after you are either tied down directly by them, or have to negotiate with other people – partners, parents, relatives and friends – to help you out. No one with children dependent on them can be independent of others. As they realise this, the mothers in our study rediscover that conventional families offer wide and durable networks, and are an effective basis for securing support. And it is at this point too that they understand, irrespective of whether they enjoy such support themselves, how weak the place of mothers has become in a community where families are no longer at the centre.

Women in the Community

We found a sense of loss among older women who could remember how things used to be regarding their place in the local community. Up to the fifties and sixties working-class neighbourhoods were manifestly organised around overlapping extended families. Through kin, one had a territorial base and many other ties too. But since then, increased (and often enforced) mobility has taken a heavy toll.

This decline is partly a continuation of the processes explained in *Family and Kinship*. At that time Mum's domain was already starting to be diminished by housing relocations, following the war and local redevelopments, which scattered family members and reduced ease and therefore frequency of contact. The effects of these waves of dispersal were noted by several of our new respondents:

> There are a lot of lonely old people around here who don't see a soul. A lot of old people moved out with the GLC. They had the chance of a one-bedroom flat come up. And their children have moved as well, so the family breaks up.

---

*This observation is based on our recent analyses of *British Social Attitudes* data, which we hope to publish later.

The dispersal of East End families has been in progress throughout the twentieth century, with particularly heavy movement during and after the war. And as the welfare state has relieved poverty, so too have more people been willing (and able) to leave:

> My brothers and sisters moved out, so I don't see so much of them now. They've bought their own houses and they've moved out, but if we need help they're here straight away. It's not as it used to be. People were much closer years ago. When people were poor they kept closer together. People are moving away from the area, so families are bound to break up.

What seems to have become increasingly common in the latter part of the twentieth century, though, is that younger family members have been obliged to move out simply because of shortages – which many link with immigration – in social housing.

> My son, he's had to buy his own house, the council would not house him though he's born and bred here. He had to move out of the borough altogether.
> Younger people are moving away because they can't get placed here. Years ago you lived with your parents when you got married, then eventually you got a place of your own. Today the children can't get a council place here so they have to move out of the area away from their families.

This has serious consequences for the operation of extended families. People can and do still keep in touch with relatives – by phone and regular visits – but families are not so ineluctably bound up with community any more. Mum's role at the intersection of neighbourhood and kinship, which was the mainspring of East End matriarchy, is much less significant. One of the remaining Bethnal Green Mums lamented it:

> I'm lucky that my immediate family is close. There are too many youngsters leaving home now. There isn't a grandmother or auntie for children to fall back on now. So they just disappear.

Families, accordingly, have become much narrower and more private in their compass, and much less influential in neighbourhood affairs, and this is arguably a great loss to local communities in terms of available experience and socialising influences on the young. It may also contribute to the weakening of conjugal relations, and reinforce tendencies towards single-lineage kin groups. *Family and Kinship* recorded that after marriage men tended to see more of their mothers-in-law than their mothers. But there were still patriarchal legal principles embodied in marriage – such as obligations to provide material support with corresponding social expectations – which helped to counteract the stronger emotional and practical ties running along the maternal line. These days the combined effect of more casual relationships with physical dispersal of kinship groups is that many older women have little contact with grandchildren through sons, and may not even know of their existence.

All this adds up to a considerable further decline, since *Family and Kinship*, in the role of Mum in the community, even for women blessed with daughters. The lesser importance of marriage and the male line means that cross-cutting networks of descent play a smaller part in organising relationships in the neighbourhood. Family ties no longer give access to people controlling valued local resources, such as jobs and flats. Nor do family alliances offer so much opportunity for building local business links or political power. Being Mum has been confined to a private, domestic context, and the public influence formerly available to most women through their families has been reduced.

What seems to have happened is that the welfare state has appropriated the role which older women used to play. The growth of a national family – the nanny state in some accounts – has created an additional system of public care and support which now goes beyond helping ordinary families and is instead taking power and meaning away from them. This was on the horizon in the 1950s. *Family and Kinship* pointed out that, with the shifting of housing ownership from private landlord to the council, Mum was starting to lose power to the state over tenancy rights. But in personal services she was resisting the challenge:

> The state has established a welfare service of doctors, clinics, and health visitors, which has an advisory as well as purely medical function. But the arrival of the expert has not led to the banishment of the grandmother. She has an advantage over the men of the service in that she is a woman, and over its female members, who are often unmarried, in that she has been a mother herself. The daughter's very existence demonstrates that she knows what she is talking about. When the wife gets contradictory advice from the welfare clinics and from her Mum, she usually listens to the person she trusts most.[16]

Since then Mum has lost ground steadily and comprehensively. An army of social workers now organises her children's and grandchildren's lives, often around moral principles and child-rearing practices with which she disagrees. And in public housing the formal rules governing allocations mean that she has little influence on proceedings. Even more insidiously, those cracks and loopholes which do allow local people to secure tenancies against the incoming mass of needy newcomers tend to be hostile to traditional family values and structures. Thus, local people stand a better chance of social housing when their families have broken or cannot cope.

As we see later (in chapter 8) this is regarded by many white residents as weakening traditional family groups. Similarly, housing and other social policies are regarded by many as promoting single-parenting:

> There are so many one-parent families around here nowadays, as these are encouraged by social services. They claim and just get new equipment, several times over. They soon learn to play the system. There is no justice any more, when you've always paid your way. Youngsters leave home and then claim on the state; they have babies to get a house. Older people are just not like that. East Enders are hard-working and proud. These people nowadays have no pride. The government has taken away their self-respect.

So we found many quite aggrieved older women, who sense that the welfare state which was designed to help them has in the event taken their children and their role away from them. They are no longer at the centre of community life. That place is now occupied (as we explore further in the next chapter) by professionals, for whom it is just a job. The outcome of bringing family care into the public realm has not been, as Eleanor Rathbone proposed, to raise the status of motherhood. Instead mothers and older women have had their authority usurped by social workers – often young and relatively inexperienced in 'life'. The vital link between women's power and family life has been severely disrupted.

Bangladeshis moving into the East End have not yet been fully subjected to these influences themselves. The nature of migrant status, involving interests both here and in the homeland, plus the connection between the large size of their families and UK welfare measures of need, combine to give family ties an overwhelmingly positive value for them. But as time passes those who stay poor here should expect to find that the operation of the contemporary welfare state increasingly comes into conflict for them too with the maintenance of an active and fulfilling and supportive family life.

Market trading and small shops are a vital part of the local economy and the weekend markets attract people from all over London.

Chapter 6

Work and Family

After 1970, the secure post-war world of the white East End working class suddenly began to crumble around them, as they saw their docking, factory and warehouse jobs disappear in the great de-industrialisation of the 1970s and 1980s, only to be replaced with a new economy for which they were not prepared. Traditionally they had taken little active interest in education. Typically, they left school at the first possible moment, with minimal qualifications, and got a local job through family connections. East End school leavers and their parents now watched as Bangladeshis gained qualifications and moved on to high-status jobs in the newly dominant knowledge economy. Others found themselves dependent on state benefits, and in the same welfare queues as their new Bangladeshi neighbours – whom they saw as benefitting from the system at the expense of old-timers.

So at the very time that they were becoming open to competition from Bangladeshi newcomers, the overriding experience of white Bethnal Greeners was of not being able to compete. The Bangladeshis had come to Britain to do manual jobs similar to those traditionally done by the white working class. Initially there was no direct conflict of interests, as many white jobs involved some degree of skill acquired not through formal education but on the job, while the Bangladeshis were content to occupy the least skilled and least prestigious positions that no one else wanted. The economic restructuring which struck with such force after 1970 affected these menial jobs as much as those held by the white working class. However, Bangladeshi family life seems to have been better than its white counterpart at helping its members to cope with the new world, and to achieve a better accommodation with the state.

The New Economy

During the lifetime of our oldest cohort of informants the local economy has been transformed beyond recognition. Rapid change started with the Second World War. Both then and in the following decade the razing of large areas in the borough, and reduction in the population, hit some local trades such as garment-making heavily.

However, the nature of the locality did not change that much: in relation to the rest of London the proportion of local workers in the docks, related distributive trades and small clothing and furniture workshops stayed high. In many respects the traditional pattern of local economic activity was intact, if scaled down, and remained so for the next twenty years.

Manufacturing was in decline right across the country in the 1970s and 1980s, but the impact was felt early in Tower Hamlets because of the collapse of the docks and connected local industries. Local economic activity virtually stagnated until the 1980s, when the rebuilding of Docklands set off a wider commercial regeneration. This rebirth has created a largely new economy, however, rather than reviving the old. To the anger of many local residents, even the actual construction work, to which locals could have contributed, was largely done by workers brought in from outside. The white-collar jobs that resulted went at first almost entirely to people who lived in other areas and later, as new housing was completed, to people moving in from other areas. In the last part of the twentieth century the class composition of residents in the borough caught up with the rest of the country, and now approaches that of London generally.* However this has not been – as in Britain generally – through an upgrading of the existing community, so much as by its replacement with newcomers.

Since the original study of Bethnal Green there has been a gradual convergence between the industrial profiles of Tower Hamlets and of London generally. Although the shift from docks to Docklands has been especially intense, it embodies and reflects longer-term nationwide changes. The industries most characteristic of the East End have declined within it faster than in London as a whole. For example, the proportion of woodworkers was much higher in Tower Hamlets vis-à-vis London in 1951, but by 1991 had reached a level that was nearer the average for Greater London. The local survival of the clothing business as a niche activity is closely linked with the arrival of Bangladeshi migrants. Among clothing workers, men have retained their high profile but are mostly now Bangladeshi men working for Bangladeshi businesses. The white women workers who were part of the foundation of the rag trade have now abandoned this occupation and have been replaced by Bangladeshi women, often working informally at home as piece-workers.

In most non-manufacturing work, Tower Hamlets was poorly represented in the fifties but across the board has now moved close to London averages. For clerical work, the employment rate in the borough for both men and women has converged with that for London generally by rising while the rate in the rest of London has fallen; for professional occupations, rates in Tower Hamlets have increased while those for London overall have fluctuated; and for administrative/managerial work (former clerical work

---

*Between the censuses of 1971 and 1991, the most rapid period of change, the proportion of non-manual workers in Tower Hamlets increased from 27 to 53 per cent, compared with an increase from 51 to 65 per cent in London as a whole.

upgraded) the borough rate has converged with that of London by increasing even more rapidly and from a lower base than London's as a whole.

Joining the Mainstream

Another aspect of convergence is that work is no longer so local. The inward-looking East End was remarkable for the extent to which people lived near their jobs. But the creation of a new City, reliant on commuters, has rapidly tilted the balance. More workers now commute, especially from neighbouring Essex, and there is less overlap between working and resident populations. Again, however, the Bangladeshi community has slowed this trend because of the localised nature of their work in clothing and catering.

The build-up of a commuting workforce has been most marked in the occupations serving the financial and communications industries. The creation of new work may also be accelerating a change in the local resident class structure, as it is the higher paid workers who can afford to move into the new housing being developed alongside the new commercial premises. Continuing change in the composition of the borough was evident during the period of restudy fieldwork, with the building of much more middle-class housing in Docklands itself and further gentrification of existing dwellings.

An important aspect of this changing economy is that work is both less rooted in local community and has a different relationship with family. In the 1950s kinship networks were closely tied to economic life in that they underwrote people's material security and helped them to find employment or assured small family businesses of some custom. Families still looked after their own, and in particular this meant giving priority to getting young men into work. The original *Family and Kinship* study found that small local businesses were already in decline, and many of the traditional craft-based family firms which had flourished in Bethnal Green in earlier decades no longer existed. More of the jobs were in larger enterprises, which were often located outside Bethnal Green itself. However, relatives could still help each other. Families were grapevines with tendrils in large companies, constantly tapping into job opportunities:

> [My father] recommended me to go for it and said it was a good job if you're prepared to work hard. I went to see the Personnel Officer at Head Office and he said 'nothing doing'. I said then I'd come because my father asked me to call. He said, 'Oh yes. Who's that, your father?' and I said, 'Mr Meadows.' He said, 'Oh yes, I know Mr Meadows. He used to work here, didn't he? Hang on a minute.' He went out and in a few minutes he came back and said, 'Yes, Meadows, we can fix you up.'[1]

Such practices constituted part of a well-tried kinship system for recruiting workers, fully endorsed by such unions as the TGWU for dockers and for porters in the big

London food markets, and by printing unions in Fleet Street. The result was a high rate of father–son succession in these industries, and where this took place it helped to bind men more closely into family life. But this link was not so highly valued as it had been before the war. There was very low unemployment in the fifties. People had more choice, and already this seemed to be reducing men's commitment to family ties:

> Now that men can get jobs of their own choosing without being introduced by relatives, it is becoming more rare for sons to follow a family tradition. Less than a quarter of our husbands (as we saw) had the same occupation as their fathers. But all our wives had the same work as their mothers.[2]

When the traditional economy collapsed, this pattern of male employment was an early casualty, and during the 1970s and 1980s growing numbers of the white male population remained out of work. The picture for women was rather different. This was partly because the new economy was producing more service jobs which they were interested in doing. However, a more important factor has been the rise of social services within the welfare state. This has created a great deal of new work in community-based occupations, including education and work with children. Among the incoming, middle-class women the ICS survey also found a sizeable contingent of self-employed workers in the personal-service sector, including a wide range of alternative therapists offering private healthcare. This can be seen as part of the movement of women into family-*type*, caring occupations, which are now part of the public realm. Appreciating what is happening here is vital to a real understanding of the changes that have taken place in local community life.

Working for the National Family

Commentaries on women's work in modern Britain over the last couple of generations tend to portray them as breaking into male domains of work. There is, however, an under-analysed class dimension to this, and it may be a misleading interpretation of changes in the East End. Among women in earlier generations, going out to work did indeed mean venturing into a world dominated by men, but for most women family life remained their main concern. Once they were married with children, they fitted paid work around family life, and older women tended to retire from the labour market to look after grandchildren when they were born. In part this was so that their daughters, who had higher earning power, could continue to work, but also because they saw home as both central and important.

For most, work entailed labouring in a world of material production and distribution. The bulk of working women in the East End were employed as clothing machinists or in the paper, printing and even furniture industries, which made up the bulk of manufacturing jobs in the area. Some of these women will have been homeworkers, using their own machines. And some will have been employed in traditionally female roles within the factories – as cooks in the canteen for example. But the majority worked alongside men, making things, and formed quite high proportions of the productive workers in these industries.

Among working women respondents in the restudy there was no longer much sense of working in a male world, mainly because work now referred to different sorts of activities. Its character had changed. Far from moving into a male world, women had taken many of their own traditional female activities – once carried out informally as part of family and community life – into the public domain. This may even have increased the occupational segregation of men and women. Older women in the sample had, or had had, jobs in light industry as machinists, clothing workers, factory cleaners. Some worked in sales, again next to men. Only a few had undertaken specifically 'female' work, usually in domestic service – a job market that went into steep decline after the war.

By contrast many of the women under 35 worked as nursery assistants, in local government departments, or as office workers in service industries. Quite a large number had professional jobs in teaching, medicine and a variety of personal services. None was a machinist, or wanted to be, and those young women who talked about their career aspirations invariably listed teaching and the caring professions as their ideal. They wanted to work 'with people' – and often specifically with children. New women's work is solidly grounded in *human relations* activities, and consists almost entirely of teaching, advising, caring, managing and communicating. Traditional domestic jobs have also seen a recovery, but largely within state social services, rather than the private sector.

The motor of this shift may well have been the expansion of the post-war welfare state, which gave a new national family dimension to citizenship. This has altered the state fundamentally by putting the personal well-being of people at the centre of state policy; it is this which, by pulling much of women's time and labour into the public sector, has made women's work more visible and created a direct voice for them in the state.

The opening up of new areas of work for women in the public domain has also enabled many to improve their status in it. Mandy Charlton is an interesting case here, as her own progression involved not only social betterment and economic independence, but also embraced a loosening of her previous family relationships.

Mandy's parents, parents-in-law and husband all had traditional local working-class employment, as dockers, cleaners and drivers. We do not know how she felt about this earlier in her life, especially when she married. But by the first interview, when she had just started part-time work, it was evidently a source of irritation and conflict. The job which she had found was in a local social-services multi-cultural playgroup project, which she felt promoted good relations between children of different ethnic groups in the borough. This was national family work par excellence – and entailed organising the distribution of support and resources between competing contestants, rather than the 'production of things' which characterised the old East End economy. Doing it soon made her conscious that her husband held many views with which she disagreed. She valued tolerance greatly, and admitted to having been less tolerant herself when young – for example when she had been hostile to a friend's 'coloured' boyfriend. Her work with minority groups had clearly made her believe in a more inclusive, public family.

> We get funding for multi-cultural toys. When it comes to toys most children don't notice. They will take up black dolls the same as they would white dolls. Some dislike boy dolls, others don't. People from different ethnic groups play with them differently, though. One good toy is a vegetable pack which has sweetcorn and yams and things like that in it. It can give people an idea about what other people eat. There can be jigsaw puzzles, too, with Asians in them as well as whites. Also different dressing-up clothes which include saris, and a black rider on a horse. Then there are cooking sets which have things in them like a Chinese wok. The children all just get on with it as though it was nothing special.

Mandy still saw a lot of her parents and siblings, but had become her own person, in control of her life and able to follow her own conscience rather than somebody else's. Significantly, she said that she welcomed living as a single parent because it made her freer to form her own opinions and to be an autonomous citizen. It was, moreover, her growing commitment to this new public morality and social vision – together, no doubt, with the fact that this project was paying her wages, while her husband had become unemployed – which gave her the strength to detach herself from the person-alised support system of her family and set up as an independent, working woman.

It is significant too that Mandy Charlton's transformation, from mainly being a wife and mother into a care worker who had children, also seems to have triggered her de-velopment into a local community activist. Since moving into her new home she had, on top of her paid work, become street representative on a number of neighbourhood committees. Her qualification for this, apart from her enthusiasm and personal charm, was the experience and contacts which she made as a council employee. This reflects how local power for women in the community is now based less on a network of kinship ties and more on paid work in the welfare state. And, in turn, this also means that women who are keen to exercise influence in the community, including on behalf of their families, now find that having this sort of work can help them to do so.

The Family Business

So there are new types of connection between family and locality which are developing – even if they are not available to so many women as in the past. But the old links are not entirely dead either. In our own interviewing we were intrigued to find a small number of extended families continuing classic Bethnal Green lifestyles. Kristin O'Keefe's kin were a good example, who would not have seemed out of place in the fifties. This pattern included having a cluster of family households within walking distance of each other, and engaging in regular mutual support and socialising. It was notable that this clearly embraced in-laws, as the intertwining of lines of descent both pulls families together and knits them at the same time into a wider local community.

Such a pattern is the exception now. But what stands out, most intriguingly, from our case studies is how often, where it *has* survived, this tends to be in those families with their own small businesses – in some cases family firms that have operated for generations. Families that work together, and have shared economic interests, are the ones that stay together. Not just this, they are often the ones that have managed to keep their male members working and involved.

Kristin provided a vivid example of all this. Her husband, Patrick – a self-employed builder – had shared his business with his own father. Patrick was never actually around during any of the interviews but was nevertheless felt as present, as their flat hummed constantly with family references and activities. Kristin herself was a full-time house-wife with six children under 14. She was close not only to her own mother, but to her mother-in-law (whose house is the focus of family life) and sisters-in-law as well. This group of women often took their holidays together, with all of the children, and commonly left their husbands behind. Kristin seemed quite comfortable with this division of labour. She sensed that men were inclined to see family activities as obligations, and noted that, 'when women made family visits they would do it with their children, whereas men would just pop round as briefly as they could by themselves'. This segregated model of family life, although no longer conventional, did seem to work well for her, possibly because of the way that family businesses give men a clear role in family affairs. Kristin's father too had a small business, which was still operating in the Bow area even though he and most of the rest of the family now lived in Essex. Her 12-year-old son, Gary, already spent a lot of time at her father's business, where he was sometimes allowed to drive a fork-lift truck, and had decided that he wanted to work there when he finished school.

What comes over suggestively in those family businesses based around male succession is that where men have economic interests that make it in their interests to cultivate local ties, they seem to remain strongly embedded in the community through their families – even if many of the actual social links are themselves chiefly maintained by female members within those families. Secondly, and following on from this, the interweaving of male and female descent lines that this sexual division of labour produces seems then to generate a much wider extended family network, with more points of contact in the community, and helps to retain the pertinence of local family ties. So the general loosening of men's involvement in family life which emerged in the new survey may be tied up in a number of ways with the increasing detachment of family life from locality.

We did indeed notice that, unlike in the 1950s survey, none of the men interviewed in the 1990s provided us with personal accounts of old Bethnal Green family life. There is a possible imbalance developing here: contrast this with the way that many white women continue to show strong commitment to families while also being directly involved in economic affairs. Nora Gerrard, for example, was an active grandmother, with a grandson living in her flat because his parental home (one of her daughters') is too crowded. Nora's own mother, through whom she acquired her flat in the old days under a mother–daughter scheme whereby daughters could apply for housing near their mothers, lived nearby and was seen frequently. Her oldest daughter had a job in a Bethnal Green shop that she had inherited from Nora, and which Nora before her had inherited from her own mother. As if this were not enough, Nora now ran a home-sales business that involved her daughters and one of her sisters. The female line in this family had production and consumption elements intertwined all along it. There were, accordingly, signs of it being more self-sufficient, and possibly somewhat inward-looking, because of this.

Bangladeshis in the Labour Market

When it came to work we found the Bangladeshis, yet again, very redolent of 1950s Bethnal Green society, and altogether it struck us that the position they are finding in the east London economy is little different from that of the many groups which arrived before them. Incoming minority groups settling in the East End in the past have generally taken for granted the broad ground rule that the price to pay for being accepted during the early stages of settlement is restraint on ambition. They have had to work their collective passage before achieving full membership of the community and nation. But this expectation became moderated during the period of Bangladeshi arrival by the shift in the UK towards a more centrally regulated society. Ever since the Labour administration of Harold Wilson there have been increasing efforts (by no means always successful) to give state support to the most disadvantaged people in society, among whom recent immigrants figure prominently.

This has changed attitudes. The earliest Bangladeshi arrivals took care to avoid direct competition with white workers, especially in the northern cities, and accepted tacitly the idea of a split labour market – one for whites and another for people like themselves. But their children, especially those who have gone through school alongside white children, are less ready to accept this. And this is already dividing the community along generational lines.

As shown earlier, the first Bangladeshi migrants remained part of the Lascar sea-going community, and lived by servicing that community on land. It was only in the second part of the last century, around the time that the first Bethnal Green study was undertaken, that Bangladeshis started moving out of an 'ethnic' enclave into the mainstream British economy. However, as had been the case in the navy, Bangladeshis were at first confined to the least skilled, most arduous work, on the least popular shifts. And workers were not managed on the same basis as white workers but hired, fired and organised on the shop floor by agents and foremen who belonged to the minority group themselves and acted as go-betweens on their behalf.

Some migrants did settle down straight away in the Tower Hamlets area, taking jobs white workers did not want. Within the East End economy the work which corresponded most closely to the industrial jobs being taken elsewhere in Britain was low-skill labour in the least-profitable sectors of the rag trade. Spitalfields still contained many small clothing factories and workshops, which had for centuries been a source of employment for impoverished migrants. In a process sometimes referred to as 'ethnic succession', a number of existing employers – in particular Jews – no longer able to find enough recruits within their own community took on Bangladeshi workers (like Faruk) and taught them all about the trade.

The most dynamic and positive initiative since the 1970s has, however, been in catering. This is more popular for Bangladeshi entrepreneurs than the rag trade because it imposes less drudgery and offers greater autonomy. There are more young men involved in it, including many of the new arrivals from Bangladesh who are joining British Bangladeshi wives already living in the UK.[3]

Although this niche activity clearly involves seclusion within a non-competing domain it also forms a major success story. The number of Indian restaurants serving the general British public rose dramatically from the 1940s onwards. It has been estimated that by 1960 there were 300[4] and this rose to 2,000 by 1970,[5] 3,000 by 1980[6] and was approaching 10,000 at the start of the twenty-first century. This gives Bangladeshis a firm foothold in the economy, and a source of capital from which they may, like the Chinese before them, now hope to extend outwards commercially. In the meantime it gives migrants like Shohel's father some control over their lives:

> When I was born my father had a factory, a tailoring factory near Aldgate. After that he bought a restaurant as a partnership. It didn't work out; that's when I was about five or six. And then he bought another restaurant, basically because he wanted to own one on his own, because he got fed up with people messing around with him. And he's doing that business even now.

The Indian restaurant business has spread widely in Britain but Brick Lane is still its centre.[7] Because the trade does not directly challenge white jobs it is not a source of great hostility. And as well as serving the City – in classic East End fashion – the local trade also now provides services for the growing middle class of Tower Hamlets itself.

Even so, catering is not seen as highly desirable by many Bangladeshis, and according to commentators like Sam Aaronovitch never really has been. It would not be a respectable occupation in Bangladesh itself, where Londoni who work in restaurants are sometimes jokingly referred to as OCs (onion cutters) and DCs (dish cleaners) by their countrymen.* Our informants also suggested that youths schooled in the UK found it a servile occupation with bad hours and low, unreliable pay. Furthermore, we were told that restaurant managers, in return, considered them rather insolent and fussy:

> Young people who grow up here are quite reluctant to take those jobs, because the conditions are not good money-wise, and the work hours long. And people have a sort of taboo about the boys of Brick Lane, and Tower Hamlets boys. Boys who are growing up here: the restaurant owners are quite reluctant to take them because they would fight; they would end up fighting. And they argue with the customers, and so forth ... There are employment agencies in Brick Lane who mainly cater for the restaurant trade, private restaurants run by Bangladeshi people. One of the governors ... told me the first condition is not to send any boy from Tower Hamlets. Because they are often rude to customers and they do not follow any discipline or whatever in the restaurant, and they want money and so on. There is obviously some talk going on in the market that they are not good as employees.

Faruk shared this view. He had himself come to Britain to put his head down, work hard and earn money – for which eventually he seemed to have paid a price in terms of bad health. So he was critical of the manner and expectations of younger generations:

> Now we say there is no job in this country. I do not believe it. It depends upon one's attitude. We were uneducated, we had no choice. Now our kids, they have some education, so they want chair-table [white-collar] jobs. In this country, that kind of job is hard to get; it was so always. They do not need educated people, they have enough. They let us in to do 'labourer' jobs. Our people do not understand this. If they want 'labourer' jobs there are plenty and money is good. Now the matter is to shake off pride and take them.

This may be a rather one-sided perception of the problem. Ashraf Zaman is a member of the 'half-generation' who arrived (at the age of 12) old enough to have absorbed a good deal of Bengali culture and values beforehand but still young enough to be receptive to local circumstances and the Bangladeshis growing up here. His view was that many young people were choosy about their jobs not because of adoption of British attitudes so much as because they felt the weight of their parents' expectations on them. The parents had been willing to take low-status jobs, and suspend their own aspirations, in order to get their children educated here. Ashraf himself had left school early to help support younger siblings. Now some of these

---

*These expressions were explained to us as follows by a young man recently arrived in Britain: 'They are the OCs and DCs. OC is the big district police head back in Bangladesh and DC is the administrative district commissioner, and here they become OCs and DCs, like onion cutter and dish cleaner.'

children felt that to accept the same menial jobs would be a betrayal of their parents' ambitions for them:

> Our younger generation is growing up in a different situation here. It is Europe and they are seeing things here, and they haven't seen what life is like in Bangladesh. My younger brother came into this country when he was four, and I can feel that there are lots of differences between him and me. Younger people do have a different attitude to work, it is true. They are reluctant to take jobs which my father did or I am doing. If they do not get a decent education, though, how can they get proper jobs? But it is also something to do with parents as well. They expect us to become something big, without considering reality. Say one boy is good as a motor mechanic; he should be encouraged to do that. That is what English parents do. But our parents want all of us to become officers.

The trades being adopted by Bangladeshis may not be lucrative, though they *have* proved compatible with family interests – which are particularly important so long as chains of migration are operating. Looking out for work for each other, putting in a word here and there, 'speaking to the guv'nor' and so on, is as much a part of daily life for Bangladeshis now as it was for previous generations of white Bethnal Greeners. These efforts are even more likely to be successful where the bosses themselves are members of the petitioner's own extended family. One of the great attractions of small businesses owned within the community is that they assure family members of employment. Many of the small clothing factories and restaurants in the Brick Lane area mirror family structures.

Organising work within the framework of the family makes it much easier to keep it informal and out of the gaze of officialdom. It can also minimise the amount of actual money that needs to flow – as moral debts are being created or settled within families all the time – and this can help to keep a business more profitable. There are a number of accounting devices commonly used in small businesses to avoid tax and maintain viability. For example, at the time of our main interviewing, waiters who earned £70 per week or less were not required to pay income tax or national insurance, did not have to have employer's national insurance paid on their behalf, and remained eligible for state benefits. No one should be surprised that we did not come across a single waiter who admitted to earning more than that magic figure, nor that restaurants preferred payment for meals in cash so that they could avoid bank statements betraying unaccountably large turnovers.[8]

Businesses which rely mainly on turnover in cash, and also use non-financial transfers and exchanges, may thereby squeeze a better living for more people out of a small revenue. But the bank account which they do (necessarily) hold may understate their actual turnover. So it is then hard for such firms to get loans to finance expansion. Alicia Herbert (1996) has drawn attention to growing use by Bangladeshis of commercial credit – albeit often through the services of an informal go-between. This is because demand for credit – for purposes of weddings and other consumption as much as for business – has outstripped the supply available within the community itself.

It is therefore family again, and to a lesser extent friends, to whom you normally go for credit. You can trust relatives. You have to, as your interests overlap with theirs. Ironically though, in this situation, trust may be needed not because only a relative would risk investing with you, so much as that a relative is the only person you can trust with the knowledge of the minutiae of your business. However, there may be dangers in relying too much on cash, as there is some evidence of a criminal sub-culture preying on legitimate enterprises.[9]

The Future of Family Businesses

The advantages of family-based enterprises are dependent on the continuation of certain attitudes within the Bangladeshi community which may not be compatible with contemporary social values. The situation is regarded with greater ambivalence by younger members of the community. There is a generation gap here, which the older generation regard with the eyes of migrants and their children look at from the viewpoint of citizens. It depends not on age itself, but on whether life is mainly oriented towards the old homeland or the new.

It is towards the old homeland for those who have been intent on sending remittances there. The migrant workers who ground out a living in grim northern mills have been presented by most analysts as victims of our industrial system, cruelly held down by racism. What this account leaves out is that even small remittances sent back to Bangladesh can help families to flourish. Even some migrants now wholly dependent on benefits still seem to be able to send back enough money to buy extra land to augment family property, raise family status and provide material and medical support for elderly or frail relatives. The sending of remittances, along with acceptance of a life of relative poverty in Britain, have to be seen for this generation as part of a culture in which family ties and work are different sides of the same coin, whereby the economic realm is regarded as serving private family ends.

Remittances do pay off, with varying levels of success, for many migrants. They represent a fruitful investment of their labour. Those families with migrant workers in the UK, the Londoni families, are easily recognisable in Sylhet by their larger landholdings, their new and superior houses, their consumer goods and their enhanced standing in the community.* A man whose remittances have helped to bring this about will enjoy influence in his family there and prestige in the wider community. Our informants supplied many examples of this type of family advancement, of which the following is just one example.

Tawfiq Amin arrived in 1963 via PIA (Pakistan International Airlines) with a labour

---

*We are tempted to call this sector of the population a 'remitocracy'.

voucher. He was 30 years old at the time, and came quite casually, to try his luck. He went by cab to his wife's elder brother's restaurant in Edgware. After a few days he went to Bradford where he had a *mama* (maternal uncle). At first he was unable to find a job and was looked after by his uncle. After four weeks living in Bradford, a cousin introduced him to a job in a wool factory in Preston where he worked for twelve weeks. After this a village friend took him to work as a fitter in a metalworking factory in Leeds; this job lasted for three months. During this time Tawfiq lived in a hostel with other Sylhetis, sharing food costs and rent. He was earning £18 per week in Leeds and spending £3 per week on living expenses. 'Rest of the income was saved, sent to Bangladesh to buy land. My wife used to write to me for money to buy land. If I hadn't enough then I used to borrow from friends to buy. A *kare* [nearly one third of an acre] of agricultural land was £50.' In 1967 he went back to Sylhet for eighteen months. On his return he moved to London and worked in garment factories in Spitalfields. In 1976 he performed *hajj* and then returned to Sylhet again, this time for two years, before coming back to tailoring in the same factory. Later, in 1985, 'I went to Bangladesh to bring my family here. They arrived in 1986 and since then I am unemployed.'

In the eyes of English observers this may look like a disorganised and unrewarding life. But this ignores the extent to which the orientations of an old-timer like this are still rooted in homeland concerns. And in these terms many migrants undoubtedly have success stories; of family debts repaid many times over, and honour achieved. Low status within British society is of little consequence to them by comparison. Indeed, many of them leave Britain when their family circumstances allow, and retire with the added bonus of their UK state pensions to enjoy their property and prestige in Sylhet.

Remittances on a large scale have, however, caused problems at both ends. In Bangladesh they have promoted inflation and social division, with the development of the new Londoni aristocracy driving up the price of land. In London itself they may have impeded investment in local family businesses – through which migrants might have carved out a larger local economic niche. One young man, Salim, whom we interviewed when he was aged 31 and married with two children, was regularly sending part of his salary to his family in Sylhet to maintain 'family prestige' (his words). He had only come to the UK aged 12, and he was working as a machinist in a small clothing factory. He explicitly expressed regret that the obligations to his family in Bangladesh prevented him from saving money in the UK to use in setting up his own factory. His obligations towards his kin were inhibiting his entrepreneurial instincts.

Later generations, however, have new interests, new problems to solve and new possibilities. There are ideological pressures on them here to be ambitious and become high-flyers. But the circumstances of ordinary life continue to make family business a valuable and realistic option. Since the opening up of British society a number of talented young white East Enders may indeed have become absorbed into high status occupations. Similarly, some Bangladeshi children going through schools recently have achieved much more prestigious occupations than those of their parents. But the more general of these processes now looks increasingly like a one-off event, caused by a structural expansion of knowledge-based occupations rather than any long-term increase in social mobility.[10] And the more specific process does not look as though it will touch more than a small number of the newly arrived Bangladeshi community. Few of them can expect to be syphoned up into higher echelons of the class system.

Ten years after our main period of interviewing the career trajectories of young Bangladeshis still diverge between the successful, who are increasingly entering City occupations and professions requiring graduate-level qualifications, and who constitute one of the many immigration success stories of this part of London, and the unsuccessful, who leave school with few or no qualifications and who are unemployed or sink into crime.

A few years after the bulk of our interviewing, the writer Tarquin Hall spent a year or so living on Brick Lane and talking to local people. Whether the quotations used in his book[11] are directly transcribed from interviews or are amalgamations of various conversations, they are all reminiscent of our interviews of between five and ten years earlier, with a few exceptions. When we were interviewing there was little mention of drugs, either the problem of growing numbers of addicts, or the burgeoning local drug market, now cited by many as one of the major problems for the local council and local law enforcement. Our own informants were concerned with public disorder, but this took the form of inter-ethnic fights and turf wars rather than competition in the free market of local drug supply. The tragedy for these young people and their families is that some of them seem doomed to join the state-dependent losers in the meritocratic race, living only a few hundred metres from the richest part of the nation and yet with the potential to be unemployed throughout their lives.

We should not be misled by differences in the way that Bangladeshis have been received by the governing class who were, after all, quite content to see them settle in the East End, which is the traditional waiting area for admission into British society. In the long run, the Bangladeshis will probably fare much as previous waves of newcomers have had to, by finding for themselves their own collective niche here. Behind apparent change there may be powerful continuities. This suggestion, however, requires a look at the education system, the subject matter of the next chapter.

Typical primary school in Bethnal Green of 1876.

Chapter 7

Education and Segregation

In the 1970s and 1980s, white East Enders found themselves baffled victims of the great transition to the knowledge economy. Education played a key role in this process. In a place like the East End, where people are accustomed to being subject to authority rather than exercising it, schools represent a centralising state presence which can help to pull residents into wider citizenship but always threatens to discount local values, ties and concerns. The spirit of meritocracy has evolved within the state education system, and local culture has long adopted a wary attitude towards it. In this sense, the aspirations of the Bangladeshi newcomers have been more compatible with the establishment than have those of much of the white population. In consequence, some at least of the migrants' children are overtaking those of the host community in the move into the new local economy.

Tower Hamlets at the time of writing has over seventy primary schools, many of them built by the School Board of London after the revolutionary (for Britain) Education Act of 1870. Dubbed the Forster Act after its architect, William Forster MP, this was the legislation that enabled a national system of state education that for the first time was open to all. 'They stand, closest to where the need is greatest, each one like a tall sentinel at his post, keeping watch and ward over the generation that is to replace our own,' said Charles Booth. For reasons of space and of image, the Board decided to build high: three storeys, towering over the humble dwelling houses and defended by high walls. As Booth went on to say, they were 'uniformly handsome, commodious, and for the most part substantial and well arranged'.[1] The buildings started in a Gothic style and ended in the secular red brick, white windows and gables of the Queen Anne style. The marker stones inscribed in the art nouveau style of that time, with an arabesque logo incorporating the School Board initials, SBL, are too large and solid for anyone to have removed them since. Likewise the buildings themselves: they are, along with the pubs and such churches as have not been turned into flats, some of the oldest and certainly the most substantial buildings in the borough. Internally they have a delightfully generous pattern, with larger classrooms than present building budgets allow and big, high-ceilinged, multi-purpose halls on every floor.

When the 1870 Act began to deprive parents of their children's wages there had been protests, and indifference to the benefits of education persists to this day among some

English working-class families. Manual workers lived by their strength, toughness and acquired dexterity, and the wit which went with these virtues. The class that was created by the demands of the industry of the time was *the* class of Bethnal Green in the 1950s, in the docks and the industries dependent on the docks, which were at the core of the local economy, and in the more skilled textile and furniture industries which served the great consumer market in the wealthier areas to the west.

Most traditional jobs for East End boys and men were manual jobs found through family or personal connections. It was not a question of who you knew mattering more than what you knew, but of what you knew mattering hardly at all. So schools were much less important in the 1950s than they are now. At that time the general attitude was much the same as it had been thirty years before when Major Stern, the chairman of the Brady Street Boys' Club, opening a new building for the club in 1925, said that it was founded in order to give people the opportunity 'to display such qualities as unselfishness, determination, pluck, grit and fair play through the enjoyment of sports and games, all qualities which were well worth having but more difficult to obtain from books'.[2]

In those days, what children learned beyond reading and writing was of little use to them. It mattered more for boys to be good at boxing or to get a certificate for swimming fifty yards, which entitled them to apply for a job in the docks or on the river. Such attitudes persisted: a Tower Hamlets teacher told us that as late as 1975 a pupil's mother said that all she wanted to get out of his schooling was a swimming certificate.

Such indifference to education has been reinforced in its effect lately by two other influences. In the 1950s divorce, separation and cohabitation were as rare amongst white families in Bethnal Green as they are now amongst Bangladeshis. Nowadays every school has to cope with a stream of the victims of family breakdown. A number of teachers we interviewed said that it is as rare for a Bangladeshi boy or girl to suffer from this kind of emotional disturbance as it is common for a white child, though some Bangladeshi children do suffer as a result of the ill-health of their parents, including a relatively high incidence of depression and mental problems among Bangladeshi women.[3]

The second influence hindering potential educational achievement is simply the presence of Bangladeshi and other ethnic minority children in the classroom who do not share white children's lack of interest in education but who are not fluent in English. So a complex spirit of rivalry and resentment within the classroom is now widespread. White parents can resent the special attention the Bangladeshi children get in their early years at school before their English is fluent, and this is made worse by the fact that the academic results of older Bangladeshi children are better than those of white children. This can reinforce antagonism to Bangladeshis and to the teachers who support them, and move the parents' attitudes from indifference (as it was in the 1950s) to outright hostility. To understand this range of feelings we need to look at the *positive* value of the school system to the Bangladeshis.

Education and Adaptation

Bangladeshi children's experience of schooling is totally different from that of white pupils. For immigrants arriving from a different way of life – essentially a rural peasant existence, where education is largely paid for privately – and with a distinct cultural heritage that inhibits full participation in British society, the school system here provides a welcome fast-track to the understanding of and preparation for life in Britain. Bangladeshi parents may have some misgivings about certain aspects of British society in general, but they would not have brought their children here if they did not want them to be British educated and domiciled. Very few parents now believe that their Londoni children have any kind of realistic future in rural Sylhet, even as retirees.

The pace of entry of Bangladeshi children into Tower Hamlets schools has been dramatic, even by East End standards. Bangladeshi children hardly figured in the 1971 census, and began to arrive en masse only during the 1970s. By 1981 32 per cent of pupils in primary schools in Tower Hamlets were Bangladeshis, and 18 per cent of those in secondary schools. Ten years later these figures were up again, to 48 and 46 per cent. By 1998 54 per cent of pupils *overall* in Tower Hamlets schools were Bangladeshi, since when the rate of increase has slowed a little, although as the numbers in primary schools have continued to rise (see table 7.3 on p. 147), we can assume that overall numbers will continue to grow for a while.[4]

Clearly such a sharp influx of so many children into one London Education Authority area will have created some problems. It has necessitated the re-opening of some schools long since closed and the building of new ones. Newly arrived Bangladeshi children face many practical difficulties in switching to school in Britain, of which the most immediate is language. Even those born here usually start primary school at some disadvantage. Before they can learn anything of significance in the classroom, they first have to learn the language of their teachers. A teacher in a secondary school, where the difficulties for newly arrived pupils are more extreme than for younger children, said:

> One of the basic tactics you tend to use if you've got a new non-English speaker in the class, hopefully one of the other kids will translate for you. You sort of try and build up that sort of relationship. To some extent that is cheating, because you are using some of the kids as teachers. There's an argument that this is a good thing as well – like they are more likely to listen to their friends than they are to you.

The teachers have been helped by the financial support given for English language teaching by Section 11 of the 1966 Local Government Act, the purpose of which was to help schools support pupils who do not speak English as a first language.[5] At one stage, one Tower Hamlets secondary school had twenty-five Section 11 teachers whose purpose was to teach English to their pupils.

Despite such assistance, Bangladeshis themselves concede the burdens that language acquisition has put on schools. Naveen said to us:

I think as we get more and more Asians living here, the teachers have more to cope with. Whereas when we first came [in the early eighties], there were fewer Asian people, you know, very few, not as many as you get now. And they had more time to concentrate on individual cases. Whereas now they've got classes full with Asian kids and they're – I don't think it would be fair to say that it's their fault, because it isn't …

However, these special language teachers were seen to be provided for Bangladeshis, not at all for whites. The white parents did not see why the incomers should be so privileged, and felt this all the more when the Bangladeshi children began to outdo their own in examinations.*

Academic progress among Bangladeshi children might have been even faster had not some families continued the custom, established by the first male migrants when living alone in Britain, of making regular visits to Bangladesh. Children might be taken out of school for several weeks, or even months, and find it hard to catch up on their return. A report from the local authority in 1997 found that 27 per cent of Bangladeshi pupils had taken extended leave during school term-time in the previous two years.[6] Schools have tried to reduce the incidence and duration of these trips by being tougher about keeping open school places in the event of long absences. This has been successful, especially in popular and over-subscribed schools: Bangladeshi parents are unwilling to jeopardise their children's education in this way.

Poor housing has also had a detrimental effect on Bangladeshi children's education. Despite all the council has done to give priority to those in the greatest need, Bangladeshi families are still the worst off for housing. Their households are, above all, the most overcrowded – often extremely so. Mrs Flynn, an elderly lady in our main sample, said her Bangladeshi neighbour had fifteen beds in five bedrooms with two jammed together for all the young children. One of our informants, Farzana, described the bedroom she shared with three sisters. It contained four single beds and a small table, leaving no floor space. Whichever girl got home first used the table for homework; the others had to work on their beds. At the same time their youngest sister, aged two at the time, demanded play and entertainment from them. In such circumstances there may barely be room for boys to do anything. They often prefer, and are sometimes encouraged, to go outside to be with friends, especially in those neighbourhoods which are considered safe.

Despite their handicaps when it comes to language and housing, however, and their difficult start in education, Bangladeshi pupils have made considerable progress. This is a tribute to the efforts of the teachers and the LEA but it is in no small measure also due to the simple fact that Bangladeshi parents value education so highly. Many people

---

*A factor which has changed the situation since we carried out our main field study is that as a result of the arrival of eastern European asylum seekers there is now an increasing number of *white* non-English speaking children in the schools.

in Sylhet itself want to get away from complete dependence on agriculture if they can, and education offers the best route to other kinds of work. Children who do well at school in either country are on the way to doing well in adult life. Bangladeshi parents are external supporters of the teachers; their children are better disciplined and more biddable, and this is reflected in their academic results, above all of the girls. Peter Dawkins, who teaches at an all-girls secondary school, put it quite explicitly:

> [The girls] value education. I think they see it as a way of improving their life chances. They see that quite early on. And they work very, very hard. They are well behaved in the classroom and that allows teachers to teach well. You know, I don't think we are a brilliant set of teachers, but teachers have to be allowed to do a good job and because of their attitudes we are able to do a better job than we would if we were chasing up various disciplinary problems.

In this respect Bangladeshis are like earlier immigrants to the East End described by Charles Booth in 1902: 'Jewish children, encouraged in every way at home, often progress with astonishing rapidity, and seldom fail to reward the ambition of their parents by a substantial advance on their original condition.'[7]

School Success of Bangladeshi Pupils

Measured in terms of examination success, Tower Hamlets schools improved greatly during the 1990s, and in 2003 Tower Hamlets had four secondary schools in the national top ten achievers in terms of added value, which can be considered a triumph for the teachers of the borough.[8] Bangladeshi children have been in the vanguard of this improvement, and have overtaken the other main ethnic categories in the borough – ESW (white English, Scottish and Welsh) and Black Caribbean – during this period. Table 7.1 charts this improvement, which shows the GCSE results for the borough approaching the national average steadily, even if still falling short of matching it. During the nineties pupils in all groups improved their score, but Bangladeshis improved most of all.

Because of their numbers, Bangladeshi pupils are playing the main role in raising the average GCSE score for the borough, but it should not be overlooked that other, smaller minorities have also done well. When the relative performance of groups is compared, it becomes evident that this is as much a matter of ESW and Black Caribbean pupils performing badly as of Bangladeshis performing outstandingly well.[9] There is also a sex dimension to this, with girls in all groups outperforming boys – though possibly less so in the case of Bangladeshis. Table 7.2 uses the data for three years between 1994 and 2002 to illustrate this differential: girls outperform boys in both of the largest groups, with Bangladeshi girls in the lead.

Table 7.1 **Percentages achieving 5 GCSE passes at grades A+ to C, 1990–2002**[a]

Ethnic category	1990	1994	1998	2002
Bangladeshi	9[b]	21	33	46
Black Caribbean	11[b]	16	18	24
English, Scottish, Welsh[c]	10[b]	16	21	30
All Tower Hamlets	10	19	28	42
National average	35	43	46	51

a All figures rounded to nearest whole number.
b Ethnic breakdown by this measure is not available for 1990; figures derived from ethnic breakdown for 'Average Performance Scores'.
c Also includes Irish in 1990.
Source: London Borough of Tower Hamlets: Reports of Education Strategy Group, and Minutes of Education Committee, Education and Community Services Committee, and Scrutiny Panel for Learning, Achievement and Leisure.

Table 7.2 **Percentages achieving 5 GCSE passes at grades A+ to C, by ethnicity and sex, 1994–2002**

Ethnic category	1994		1998		2002	
	Boys	Girls	Boys	Girls	Boys	Girls
Bangladeshi	19	23	30	37	43	49
English, Scottish, Welsh	15	18	18	25	25	36
All Tower Hamlets		19		28		42
National average		43		46		51

Source: as for Table 7.1.

White Demoralisation and Flight

The relative academic success of Bangladeshi children creates a difficult situation for white parents, though we have to remember that this is not a new phenomenon in the area. The 1950s study found that some of the Jewish respondents commented that whereas people in their own families had seen education as a means of climbing out of the area, local non-Jewish working-class people made it hard for their own children to take up opportunities:

> We were Jewish immigrants and so we had no class really. It was different for us. The English working class had a fear of being thought snobs. I can remember two girls who won scholarships but did not take them up and I am sure that it was not on account of the money, they could have afforded it, but they thought it was above their station to go to grammar school.[10]

Some white parents, however, tell themselves that rapid progress by immigrants' children is not simply due to the industry of those children themselves and support of their families, but also reflects the solicitude of school staff, to the disadvantage of white children. White parents have started to question the priorities of teachers, which some expressed as virtually requiring white children to fail in order for schools to be seen as doing their job of helping the children of minority groups. Parents like Mandy Charlton, who are well disposed towards Bangladeshis, try to avoid feeling resentful by making it clear that any problems are the result of government actions – in presiding over the concentration of minorities in the area and then pumping in extra resources specifically earmarked for helping these children:

> I know that schools get Section 11 support for Bengalis. The heads get more money for Bengali families so they're prepared to take them in coming from longer distances. A white family can't get in unless they're more local, as not so much money comes with them. That sort of thing is down to the government really, not to the schools.

But displacing blame like this from Bangladeshis themselves does not solve the problem for white families, and it is significant that Mandy, a local East Ender who has come up in the world, is sending her own children to secondary schools outside the borough, in west London in fact. Others are quick to blame the Bangladeshis themselves. Gerry Green, a cabby (another prominent local business), compared the preference that he saw Bangladeshis getting with the lack of help given to earlier immigrants such as the Jews:

> It doesn't matter where these people come from, they're lowering the standard of education. I resent living in an English-speaking country with Urdu signs in the hospitals and housing estates. This used to be a Jewish area and you never had signs in Hebrew. I resent never having had a proper education in east London. Like most cab drivers, we're smart but not educated. I resent that the immigrants are seeing that this generation of east Londoners doesn't have an education either.*

There is considerable ambivalence among white parents. On one hand there is the local tradition of not attaching great significance to education, and of resenting its interference in family life. On the other hand, if there are prizes to be won, and teachers are helping local children to get a leg up, then it grates if the benefits go to newcomers who have not been long on the scene. Those white parents who are ambitious for their children are the ones most likely to experience mixed feelings, and this prompts 'white flight' and the desire to settle in an area where they feel the schools will be more responsive to them. Thus for many, like Kristin O'Keefe, at least part of the appeal of

---

*This respondent is wrong though about signs being in 'Urdu', and from his age obviously would have gone through the school system himself during its post-war golden age. We note too that for him 'immigrants' are not 'east Londoners'.

moving out from Tower Hamlets is to avoid the conflicts of interest they have with local Bangladeshis so long as they stay here. The family business could still be based here, as that is where its contacts are, but family life and consumption can be exported to a more congenial setting. Kristin believes that the lack of attention of teachers to white children, as she sees it, means that parents have to spend much more time giving help themselves. She reckons that she has to do a lot of extra reading and spelling practice when her children get home from school, and feels that it is getting too much.

The flight out of the area which often results typically takes place at the end of a child's primary schooling. People who had already left to live further out in east London or Essex or Hertfordshire could not tell us about what they had already done: they were not in our sample. But some still in the locality were eager to depart. Alice Roe was one of these. She made her position quite clear when she answered a question we put to everyone in the informal interviews to find out if they knew the location of Bangladesh. Her answer was, 'Just around the corner.' She is desperate to get away, partly for her son's sake:

> I've brought him up to be respectful, not a thug. He gets no support from the school. A mother went into the playground and assaulted him at lunchtime. So I've told my son that if anyone pushes him, or grabs hold of his clothes, he's got to hit back, show he won't accept it. He hates doing it – he's a member of Greenpeace, doesn't want to hurt anything – and I hate telling him to. And the secondary school is worse. The school they allocated to my son only had four white children in it. He didn't get into my first-choice [primary] school, they allocated him to Bangabandhu – only thirteen children there spoke English. A brand-new school and that's what they named it. It's one of the best-resourced schools in the borough. We're the ethnic minority in Tower Hamlets.

The desire of white parents to avoid schools with more than a few Bangladeshis has led to a polarisation in their ethnic composition, with some schools being mainly white and others mainly Bangladeshi. Few primary schools have a balance between ethnic groups which reflects properly the local population, of which 58 per cent of those aged 0–17 were Bangladeshi at the time of the 2001 census. In 2002 seventeen had over 90 per cent Bangladeshi pupils and another nine (all denominational) had fewer than 10 per cent. Out of sixteen secondary schools in 2002, four denominational schools (three Roman Catholic) had 3 per cent or fewer Bangladeshi pupils, while nearby three non-denominational schools had in excess of 90 per cent – with a further one over 80 per cent.[11] Half of the secondary schools were therefore very segregated and did not reflect the balance of their local population. These observations are made not in order to suggest that the schools with large Bangladeshi populations are in any sense 'Muslim' schools, as sociologist Tariq Modood has criticised others for doing,[12] but to emphasise the ease with which children can pass through the education system without encountering many pupils from the other main ethnic group living in the same place as they do themselves. This has implications for the persistence of rumour and prejudice.

It is not hard to work out why schools do not mirror closely the distribution of population in their local areas. There is a degree of parental choice available and this would in itself account in large part for the ethnic polarisation in the schools. Bangladeshi parents have different priorities: some of them want schools with many white children so that their children will be able to improve their English more quickly; many more want above all single-sex education, especially for their girls. The white parents, when asked, have less complicated views. Most can perceive no advantage to them in a racially mixed school. With a few exceptions they do their best to avoid schools dominated in numbers by Bangladeshis.

What both parents and pupils can do is limited by the selection systems in place. In theory, parents have a free choice of schools wherever they live, and if preferences were the only consideration then schools might be even more largely white or Bangladeshi than they already are. This is what happens in youth clubs, whose members can exercise a completely free choice. In the 1990s there were no mixed youth clubs in the borough.

Tactics of White Parents

White parents have three main tactics open to them. They can try to get their children to white, or whiter, schools within the borough. They can move their children out of the borough without changing residence themselves. Or the family as a whole can move elsewhere.

The white citadels are the Roman Catholic schools. Like other church schools, they represent an earlier form of community organisation flourishing before secular state schools became the norm after a long campaign by the educational reform lobby of the nineteenth century for the provision of universal education. The Catholic schools are picking up a new kind of support from people who remain secular in many ways but attach themselves expediently to the church as a haven for protecting them from newcomers.

This is paradoxical in the eyes of many. Father Reilly, whose family has been in the East End since 1848 when his ancestors fled from the Irish potato famine, and who had himself spent a lifetime in the church here, argued that East Enders were not essentially racist. The lines of division were cultural, including religious. And this showed in the way that churches were racially integrative. Throughout east London many Black Caribbeans could be found in Catholic churches, and in parts such as East Ham where there were Indian Catholics from Goa, they were actively involved too. The problem in Tower Hamlets was that the Asians were almost all Muslims. It was the difference of religion that isolated them: 'There are many mixed-race children in the church, too. White and West Indian, and a few white with Asian; though no West Indian with Asian.'

This may be the case. But the fact that Asians in Tower Hamlets *were* Muslim did mean that the denominational schools had become refuges for white families there, and school procedures helped to enable this. Their governors are allowed to determine their selection system and they can select according to a child's religion. Since Bangladeshis are Muslims, the consequence is that few of them get into Catholic schools.

All around the borough stories abound of people who have had their children baptised in a Catholic church in order to make sure of getting entry to a Catholic school later on. The church is the anteroom to the school. Baptism 'puts children's names down' for a particular school long before the time when they will actually go there.

Joy Jarvis exemplifies the general motivation: 'I've got [my daughter] down for a Catholic school. I mean, one consideration is that they don't really take Indians 'cos they're not the same faith!' Parents who are trying to get a place in a denominational school believe a note from a member of the clergy could be helpful. Nora Gerrard asked her Methodist minister for a letter to prove that her grandson goes to church: 'It's for Raine's School, where he hopes to go. It helps a bit because it's a Christian school.' Melissa Terry told us, 'I've had to go to church for three years to get a church school where there's half whites.'

Parents' freedom of choice extends outside the borough. Since the famous *Greenwich* judgment which followed on the 1980 Act, it has been illegal for any admission policy to discriminate against pupils from outside an LEA's own area.* This does not stop schools giving a preference to local children, but it does mean that parents have a better chance of getting their children into schools which are just over the border of Tower Hamlets where another LEA has the same rules about proximity. Hackney does, and every year a sizeable number of local girls, some of them Bangladeshi, are enrolled in a girls' secondary school in Hackney, it being their nearest school. It also means that parents can successfully select Catholic schools which do not have a strong neighbourhood preference. In 1994, for example, out of the 210 pupils whose preference was for an out-of-borough secondary school, 50 per cent came from Catholic primary schools within the borough and went to Catholic secondary schools outside it.[13]

The third strategy some white families pursue, of family movement out of the area, is likely to prove numerically the most important, and there is some evidence to show its effects. The education authorities have kept records of pupil ethnicity for over twenty years. Table 7.3 shows the rapid changes in proportions of Bangladeshi and English, Scottish, Welsh and Irish children over the period.[14]

Dramatic as these percentages are, they do not tell us anything directly about white flight. For that we have to look at the actual *numbers* of children on school rolls. What then becomes noteworthy is the difference between primary and secondary schools. In the primary sector, an increase among Bangladeshi pupils has taken place along-

---

* The House of Lords *Greenwich* judgment of 1989 established that LEA-maintained schools may not give priority to children simply on the grounds that they live in the authority's administrative area.

Table 7.3 **Changing ethnic balance in Tower Hamlets schools, 1981–2004 (by percentage)**

	Primary schools		Secondary schools	
	Bangladeshi	ESW/I[a]	Bangladeshi	ESW/I[a]
1981	32	52	18	62
1986[b]	42	41	36	45
1991	48	36	46	37
1996	51	32	56	27
2001	56	30	55	28
2004[c]	62	18	54	21

a English, Scottish, Welsh and Irish. Those who described themselves as white Irish (2 per cent of Tower Hamlets' total population in 2001) were removed from this category in school roll figures after 1990.
b No survey in 1986. Figures given are averages for 1985 plus 1987.
c Most recent figures available.

side a more gently declining ESW/I figure. This is why several additional schools have been needed during this period, to meet rising overall demand. In the secondary sector, however, the absolute number of white pupils declined rapidly between 1980 and the mid-1990s, so that there was hardly any increase in total numbers. According to figures supplied by the LEA, approximate numbers of 'white' secondary school pupils dropped from just over 7,000 in 1981 to 3,200 ESW/I pupils in 1996 and to 2,960 in 2004. This presumably reflects the fact that it is often at the point of transfer to secondary school that white pupils and their families move out of the borough.

One of our interviewees, Erica Upton, moved out to Billericay in Essex between interviews when her son progressed to secondary school. We went to see her in her new home. Although she is not Catholic herself, her husband is an Irish Catholic with a strong family base in the county – all having moved there some time ago from the East End – and their son was on this basis able to gain entry to her husband's former school. Before moving she had lived all her life in Bethnal Green. But she was happy to get away from the schools.

> All the schools in Bethnal Green now have too many Asians. The children have to eat Asian food at school,* and many of the lessons revolve around the Asian way of life. I think they are trying to take over. When I go back to visit my parents I feel that they are all looking at me and thinking that I should not be there.

---

*Schools do not impose Asian food on children. See, for example, the description of Mary Matthews below.

Resolving Conflict

In these circumstances the schools and teachers of Tower Hamlets are left with a demanding role, promoting a common British culture and identity against a backdrop of considerable racial hostility. Schools are in principle a place where community spirit is generated, as parents are brought together by the shared work of bringing up the next generation, and forge ties outside their family which turn into valuable friendships. Even in the fraught atmosphere of Bethnal Green this sort of thing does happen. One of our white interviewees, Kath Holden, was herself a sort of immigrant, coming from outside London, and this made her more sensitive to the feelings of Bangladeshis. She suspected that Bangladeshis thought that all whites were out to get them: '[They think] we believe that they are second-class citizens. Unfortunately it's true of a lot of our people. They do think that.' This made her more aware of the value of school-gate contacts, and she had built a number of friendships as a result. 'Fatima is a good friend; she has twins the same age as Kevin ... She's a single parent now. She had the father deported to Pakistan; there was a lot of family pressure and she went back to try to make it work but it didn't. So she's back now.' Kath was a strong believer that mixing between groups would overcome racial hostilities. 'Thirty years ago we were full of prejudice about the West Indians. That's gone now. More and more of our children will go in for mixed marriages. Nature will take its course.'

This is encouraging, but it is inside the schools that most of the work is done. Much staff time and energy goes into keeping a peace, between not just pupils but also parents and other groups in the local community, before ordinary teaching itself can even begin. Inevitably the bulk of this conflict management has been directed towards white people, as it is they who are objecting to state educational policies, and who feel aggrieved. And inevitably the sympathies of most teachers lie with the Bangladeshis, as the main victims of hostility. But it is not as simple as that: it is probably among teachers that there is greatest experience and understanding of community relations locally, and of the shifts in them, and of their complexities and diverse implications. It is teachers who occupy the front line of wider multi-cultural citizenship building here on behalf of the state. Sometimes this means they get caught up in the hostilities, even when they are off duty. Tony Hicks was refereeing a weekend game of football when some of the white boys started beating up one of the black boys. Tony tried to intervene and found himself getting beaten up too. He finds himself avoiding gangs of young men since then.

It is not just the teaching staff, however, who play a role here. We carried out some direct observations of schools and we found that, in primary schools in particular, the ancillary staff of dinnerladies and others played a key role. They often served as intermediary figures linking the local community and the professional teaching staff, and provided a human warmth that would otherwise be lacking. Many had been on the staff of their schools for a good deal longer than most of the teachers, knew children's parents and grandparents and lived within a short walk of the school.

Mary Matthews at Pankhurst Junior School was a good example. She lived just opposite the school, and her two daughters had been pupils there. Her official title is Senior Meals Supervisor and she moves on from the midday meal to the Playcentre, where she works from 3.15 to 5.15 every afternoon. She has been working at the school for eighteen years. She is a link with the district, how it is and how it used to be.

Mary is most in evidence in the dinner hour. On the day we met her, only three out of 350 children were going home for dinner. The rest tucked in to their shepherd's pie or fishcake, mashed potato, mixed veg, salad and pudding. The children were getting a decent meal (with the poor ones getting it free) and learning social skills at the same time. What they heard from Mary as she walked up and down was, 'Use your knife *and* fork, Darren,' or 'Sit nicely, Charlotte' or 'Eat up, come on, it's playtime soon.'

As she puts on her second hat and walks out into the concrete playground she is swamped by small hands tugging for attention, crying, laughing, telling stories. Dipping into her pocket, she pulls out a wad of tissues always handy for wiping crying eyes or dirty hands. One little girl is in tears after a fall. Mary tries to reassure her that she is uninjured but the girl will have none of it and continues to grip Mary's hand. Trying again, Mary asks her to fetch a jacket from a corner of the playground. The girl trots off merrily but affects a limp as she sees Mary again. Mary says that many of the children spend more time with her and her team than with their own parents. She and the colleague who was in charge of the Playcentre, and other local people doing similar jobs, either paid or as volunteers, do their bit for race relations by treating the children all in the same motherly way.

Several schools have developed a 'code of conduct' to which pupils should subscribe. They accord with Pankhurst's head teacher's vision of a good primary school. She told us that, 'Primary schools are very moral places.' At Pankhurst there is a specific mention of respect for other people's 'race', and disrespect of that aspect is taken especially seriously. Offenders are referred to the head or deputy head, and if there is a repetition a misconduct form is sent to the parents. The parents, their child and the teacher then meet to work out what can be done to avoid or change such behaviour. The result of the policy did seem to be that children of different racial groups behaved well to each other, at least while they were on school premises.

Nothing the school could do would avoid there being some bigoted parents, but with the children it was different. One parent, Mrs Barber, told us: 'Paul's friends at school are mostly Asians. He says the white boys are too naughty. You'll see a black boy, a white boy and an Asian boy playing together but you don't see the adults together.'

Many children find it hard to act and talk in one manner in school and in another at home. One little white boy of six put his fingers in his ears whenever the word 'Islam' was mentioned at school, as though he would be under an evil spell if he did not keep the word at bay. His parents had told him this was what he should always do. His teacher persuaded him otherwise, but how could the little boy not be puzzled by being given two such different instructions? Who was he to believe? It is not uncommon to find family and school divided and white children caught in the middle, between the values of their parents and the values of their teachers. Steve Cummings, a secondary-school teacher, gave an example of a boy in his class who was like that:

> That poor kid has all the pressure he is getting from his father at home – and his father is a classic: the crew cut, the jeans, the bovver boots, the lot. He's getting all the hassle and pressure from me from the other side. Plus he does happen to like a couple of Bangladeshi boys. Now imagine the emotional and sensory pressures. He's getting it from three or four directions at once. At the age of 14 or 15 he is trying to make his own mind up, and he's bound to blow up now and again.

When it comes to religion the teachers at most schools make great efforts to be even-handed, but there were still complaints from both camps. Kosira Khatun, a student in a local college, felt quite strongly about this:

> Our festivals are not given the same value as their festivals. A very good example would be during the Christmas festival; there are holidays for all people. But during Eid employers refuse to give holidays, even if it's only for a day. Even schools with a large majority of Bangladeshi students and other Muslim minorities are expected to attend school, even though they are aware that it's a very special occasion for Muslims. Students who fail to attend are marked down as absent.

There were also grouses the other way round. Mrs Roe said that at her son's school 'they did not want to have Christmas' because it would upset the great majority of Asians. From outside we can only sympathise with the teachers, who have to struggle to keep everybody content.

The Value of Leadership

At secondary-school level the formal structures become more important, and the difference that can be made by dedicated and charismatic leadership is great. Kendal is a large secondary school in a new building and strategically placed between the largely Bangladeshi west of the borough and the largely white east. Some of the staff could remember the day, some ten years before our visit in the mid-1990s, when the first Bangladeshi boy appeared in the school. That boy now runs an Indian restaurant in North Wales but keeps in touch with one of the teachers.

In the early 1990s the school was plagued by racial violence. The Metropolitan Police were sending heads of all secondary schools in the borough a weekly fax recording the major incidents, especially racial incidents, of the previous week. Trouble could run from one school to another and from those faxes heads could predict what might face them the following week. At the worst times Kendal figured prominently. The danger was exacerbated by people from the BNP who stood outside the gates peddling 'Rights for Whites' leaflets. The staff manned the gates to encourage pupils to put the leaflets into a bin, but the tension in the school grew and the corridors became potential battlefields for tit-for-tat exchanges. Pupils brought knives with them to school. The staff were often tipped off by worried children and the teachers would have to conduct a weapons search of the suspects. One of the worst incidents was when a group of Bangladeshi boys arrived in a van armed with baseball bats and crates of bottles which were used as weapons in a street fight against a white–black alliance.

Such violence was an outcome of the non-Asian reaction to the growing Bangladeshi presence in the school, and the reaction of Bangladeshis to predominantly white anger. Why us? Why this school? asked white parents. Their children were having to put up with more and more pupils with limited English. It wasn't just Bangladeshis, they said, and not just the language issue: one Somali boy had never seen scissors and had to be taught how to use them. However, we were told by teachers that the Bangladeshi and Somali and Turkish children were, despite all they had to learn, on the whole much easier to have in the classroom than the white pupils.

The recovery of Kendal school can be traced back to the arrival of a new head, Roger Dewey. His first task was to reduce the level of violence. A ban on knives was strictly enforced, and any pupil found in possession of one faced automatic expulsion. The perimeters of the school building were made more secure, cameras set up at the gates, holes in the boundary fence mended, parents' help sought. This last was easier said than done: at parents' meetings everything he and other teachers said had to be interpreted in Sylheti, which was both tedious and inflammatory to many white parents, so a system of segregated meetings had been implemented. One positive outcome from the above-mentioned street fight was that the hastily arranged all-parents' meeting that followed went some way towards relieving the tension. The parents' desire not to see their children injured surpassed ethnic considerations.

Results among the pupils were less immediate, but the mood gradually began to change. Children began to converse in small groups. Some began searching for ways to tackle conflict. A school youth centre was opened as a lunchtime meeting place. Youth councils were set up. School trips were arranged to a mountaineering centre in Scotland. Pupils got on better when they were away from the school and some inter-ethnic friendships sprang up. Slowly, confidence began to rise. The school was helped by a fruitful relationship with one of the City of London banks, which provided volunteer help with homework, finance for teaching resources and holiday funding.

People we met in the school were ready, without any prompting, to pay tribute to Roger Dewey. A dinnerlady said, 'To be honest, when Mr Dewey took over, in regards to fights, we used to get a lot of gangs hanging about, but he had a tough job on his hands when he first took over. He's done marvellous. I speak very highly of him.' A 14-year-old Bangladeshi girl thought that, 'The school is making a better impression now. Before, people used to think it was a bad school and it's quite changed. I think it's got to do with a new headmaster and everything, and rules and regulations, uniform and everything. There's less violence as well.' We gathered that the greater level of discipline was much appreciated by Bangladeshi parents.

Perhaps the greatest asset of the head is that he knows it is impossible to solve deep-seated social problems quickly, if ever. The problem is a recurring one and continuous action is required to cope with it. Another teacher said that, 'Roger has also become quite well known in the district around the school. He has been to scores of community meetings and tenants' meetings. At times he has had to take a lot of flak. People vent their anger on the school. But he's going on tirelessly, meeting with councillors and local groups.' Significantly, in the early years of the new century, this secondary school was one of the very few whose population matched reasonably closely the ethnic make-up of its surrounding area; the head has successfully avoided the segregated nature of too many of Tower Hamlet's schools.

Roger Dewey's school is an outstanding example, but the local education authority as a whole seems to have had considerable success in adapting to its changing populations of pupils, in helping to contain conflict and in promoting better relationships and common citizenship. The main beneficiaries, however, over the last twenty years seem to have been the Bangladeshis. They have established themselves in the system and achieved significant academic success. But we must not assume that this is how things will carry on. There is a feeling among young Bangladeshis like Naveen Mannan that the main period of Bangladeshi school success may in fact already be over, and may have been rooted in the mid-1980s. For the cohort entering primary schools then were the first to enter so young – and with such a long period of schooling before them – and also the last (for a while, at any rate) to enter a system in which the majority of their peers were already English speakers. Many who have come after them will still go to school in the first instance with little English, since their parents may not speak it at home, but they will find a large majority of other children there not speaking it either.

We do not know what the long-term effect of this will be but it may be the case that while Bangladeshi top performers continue to forge ahead, the relative rate of increase for *average* Bangladeshi attainment may slow down. It is still too soon to say whether this is the start of a new trend. It may, however, be significant that the group who were influencing national Bangladeshi examination success around the mid-1990s contains many like Naveen, whose school experience was different from that of both her younger and older siblings. Naveen came with her mother to join her father in England in the early 1980s. Neither of her parents spoke English at home, so she had to learn it at school. She went to primary school at five and, looking back on it, could congratulate herself on her good fortune, not only because of the good grounding she got in English. It is less easy for others:

> From what I learned when I was in primary school, or first year and second year at sec-
> ondary school, now it's very difficult to get a young child in Tower Hamlets to give them
> a good education. It's virtually impossible. I mean, school-wise, a lot of good primary

schools are usually Church of England or Roman Catholic and don't take non-Christian kids in, and that's a problem.

Naveen was wrong about the Church of England primary schools, some of which have high proportions of Bangladeshi Muslim pupils. Nevertheless, she is perhaps right to fear that none of her siblings will have as good a chance as she did. Her older sister and brother were already 14 and 13 when they first went to an English school, and their English never became good enough for them to get on well. Her three younger siblings were British born, but by the time they went to school too the schools had 'filled up' with Bangladeshis, so to learn English was more difficult for them too.

Already, then, there is a sense that the best of the opportunities may be slipping away, at least for rapid advancement. What has been achieved over the last generation is considerable. But what follows may be bound to represent a slowing down and something of a disappointment.

Part of the Teviot Estate being demolished in 2004.

Chapter 8

Whose Home?

There was yet another matter about which the white East End working class found itself baffled and resentful. We have already seen that many lost their traditional jobs, to be reduced again to the welfare dependence they believed they had shaken off for ever, and that their children often failed to make the critical jump into the knowledge economy and the meritocratic society. On top of this, they found their traditional paths to housing blocked by new obstacles, which seemed to them systematically to favour the newcomers over themselves.

Shelter is, after food, the most elemental of scarce goods and the fate of newcomers depends in part upon whether and where they can get a roof to put over the heads of their families. It is under a roof that people can have control over their lives; they work out their relationships with each other, contribute to an intimate domestic economy and enjoy such leisure as their work allows them. It is housing, as E. J. B. Rose noted in the classic *Colour and Citizenship*,[1] which is 'by common consent the one which acts as the crucial determinant of the newcomer's future in the country and that of his family'. The right to housing is a central tenet of modern citizenship, and constitutes one of the most valuable forms of property that citizens can possess.

It is the access of Bangladeshis to housing, in particular public housing, in Tower Hamlets that has enabled their rapid settlement here. The way in which housing is acquired and transmitted has changed greatly since the 1950s. At the time of the original Bethnal Green study much housing belonged to private landlords, but tenancies were often owned informally, supported in local custom, by families, as it suited landlords and established residents alike to give priority to kith and kin. As the state has taken over welfare services and placed greater emphasis on individual entitlement, families have lost influence over the transmission of tenancies. So for many people changes in family life have taken place alongside, and as part of, changes in both the administration and the nature of public housing.

These trends have been national but in the East End, because of the high levels of poverty and deprivation there,[2] the involvement of the state has been greater than almost anywhere else in the country. Combined with Bangladeshi settlement, the consequences for the housing rights of white Bethnal Greeners have been overwhelming.

But even without the arrival of these migrants the shifts in housing would have had profound effects on people's lives.

Housing conditions in the East End were improving gradually throughout the first half of the twentieth century, not least because of the steady decline in the birth rate. But what really speeded up this process was the Second World War. During the war numerous overcrowded dwellings were destroyed and many families were evacuated who never returned. The population of the borough fell dramatically, mainly among the overcrowded. Between 1931 and 1951, census figures show a significant reduction in the proportions of large households and overcrowding in the boroughs that would later make up Tower Hamlets – an improvement in comparison with London as a whole, but an improvement that was not sustained.

What has happened since the war indirectly reflects the declining significance of family ties in East End life. When the original study was carried out in the 1950s, family was, as it always had been, an important organising principle for housing. Peter Sanders' grandparents were helped at the beginning of the century: '[My grandmother's] parents lived next door, and no doubt her mother had recommended or "spoken for" them to the rent collector for the Portals Trust, which owned the whole terrace of twenty houses on that side of the road.'[3] Although overcrowding was far less evident than before the war, young couples still often spent the first few years of marriage living with their parents – usually the wife's. And when they did move out family frequently played a part in helping them to find their own housing and family members could and usually chose to live near each other.

The result of the system was that marriage did not break the relationship of a lifetime with the family of origin but could even strengthen it. The newlyweds would find accommodation within a few minutes' walk and the landlords' vacant properties could be filled easily and quickly with reliable tenants, without any fuss or advertisement. The 'speaking-for' system meant that new and localised extended families were continuously being created.

During the 1950s interview the Bartons described how the local landlords allocated their houses.[4] When they were married in the last year of the war, they had started off living with Mrs Barton's parents. Later Mrs Barton's widowed grandfather moved into a home and her mother asked the rent collector if they could take over the grandfather's tenancy. They did, and there they still were, fairly content. This kind of thing happened often. Private ownership was friendly to the family in those days.

As Mr Trimble said in 1956: 'Around here it's all a family affair – mothers speak for daughters and mothers speak for sons and all that kind of thing.'[5] The custom of speaking for relatives was not regarded as nepotism but was thoroughly approved of by a body of sentiment in each street and tenement block owned by one of the big housing charities.

In the 1990s we interviewed some elderly people living in the Outer London new town studied in the 1950s. One of them, Stanley Green, reminisced about his childhood in Bethnal Green:

We never used to lock the door. If my mother wasn't in and I wanted a cup of water I would just go next door. If somebody had a baby, they, the neighbours, would look after her, do all the errands, the washing. It was nice family life. You could say it was a great big family with lots of mums and dads.

Mr Green might almost have revised for his interview by reading *Family and Kinship in East London*.

Among Bangladeshis, kinship ties had a wider instrumental reach amongst the better off – that is of the kind who might have migrant members in England or other countries – than they did amongst landless people. The reason was that they had property to pass on from one generation to another, which was 'owned' not so much by an individual as by a family. A family can identify with a plot of farmland and, indeed, needs to if the fertility of the land is to be under the care of people looking beyond one generation. People can easily learn to love it. It represents permanence.

It may seem inappropriate to compare a ramshackle little cottage in the middle of a modern city in the 1950s with a *bari* in Sylhet in the 1990s. But the comparison is not so far-fetched. The influence that East End matriarchs had over vacant houses gave them a property right which was used, as much property is used, to reflect and influence kinship by binding extended families together.

The principal conclusion of *Family and Kinship* was that housing designed for poor people should continue to be governed in the time-honoured manner, though under new auspices when matriarchs ceased to be the housing authority:

> In a three-generation family the burden of caring for the young as well, though bound to fall primarily on the mothers, can be lightened by being shared with the grandmothers. The three generations complement each other. Once prise out two of them, and the wives are left without the help of grandmothers, the old without the comfort of children and grandchildren. The question for the authorities is whether they should do more than they are at present to meet the preferences of people who would not willingly forgo these advantages, rather than insisting that thousands more should migrate beyond the city.[6]

As we will see, preference for sons and daughters of residents has remained an issue in Tower Hamlets. But during the 1960s and 70s it came into conflict with the modernising influences of the post-war welfare state. And it was at this point that the local character of the area was seriously challenged.

The Impact of the State

In the 1950s, when the state was beginning to replace private landlords and rehousing still mainly took the form of moving people out to estates beyond the edge of London, local public housing was not yet a significant factor. As rebuilding schemes bore fruit, however, the share of properties owned municipally – by the GLC or constituent boroughs – soared, taking Tower Hamlets well above the level of other Inner London boroughs.

During the 1970s and 80s housing in Tower Hamlets was dominated by local authority provision, and this is why the housing market was able to respond so quickly to state political concerns. Since then the profile has become more complex, but during the critical period of Bangladeshi settlement the levels of public ownership were high. By the end of the 1980s this municipalisation had produced a different balance of housing stock from elsewhere, in which the bulk consisted of purpose-built flats, some 82 per cent of housing stock in Tower Hamlets in 1991 compared with 48 per cent in Inner London as a whole.

This municipal revolution saw a decisive shift away from family succession of tenancies. In Tower Hamlets, as in many other local authorities, to begin with the main principle used for rationing scarce housing resources was a waiting list, whereby prospective tenants were treated according to how long they had been waiting. This effectively gave priority to local families, while removing the direct involvement of (or indeed any reference to) family ties. But this was then replaced in the early seventies by use of housing *need* as the sovereign principle. The force of the new principle – that vacancies in public housing should be allotted to those in the greatest need – is as undeniable as it is in the National Health Service. Many people would now argue that need should not have been allowed to outweigh other considerations as heavily as it did, and that the effect was to produce 'sink estates'.[7] But morally the case seemed undeniable at the time.

Shifts in housing policy and practice also reflected and responded to other changes that were occurring within British family life. People, especially younger people, wanted more personal freedom. The new system of making individuals' needs paramount helped to provide it. In the process it has arguably created perverse incentives for weakening of family ties generally. Marion Daly's marriage, for example, was going through a rough patch at the time when the Dalys were decanted from their flat for refurbishment. Both she and her husband were unemployed, and they had other problems too, so they insisted that their temporary housing was in separate units while sending the children to stay with Mrs Daly's mother near by. The process has since become more complicated because the housing department has passed the tenancy of their old flat to a Bangladeshi family, and the Dalys are jointly suing the council (with legal aid) and hoping to get it back for Mrs Daly to live in with the children. In the meantime the family are scattered. Marion lives in a run-down flat next door to a Bangladeshi family (whose flat, according to a council repair worker, has ten beds in it) and she has had iron gates put across the front door. She has a pet Rottweiler which goes everywhere with her, to fend off unwelcome company. She is still on reasonable terms with her husband but they find that living apart enables them to apply for all manner of benefits and have no plans to reunite.

Paradoxically, a regime that suited white citizens looking for greater individual freedom could also be worked to suit the needs of immigrant family units. For if young adults could claim housing on grounds of being new households in need of their own accommodation, how much more compelling was the case that could be made by Bangladeshi households containing large numbers of residents, spread across several generations, and willing to make the most efficient usage of space available? The arrival of Bangladeshi families, desperate to be reunited and prepared to put up with overcrowding in poor housing in Britain for as long as might be necessary, effectively created two different housing markets in Tower Hamlets. By the early eighties the white and Bangladeshi communities had clearly opposed interests over housing.

This can be shown from data collected in the 1991 and 2001 censuses, which provide figures for ethnic groups. The enormous divergence in housing experience which had been reached by 1991 highlights the nature of housing competition in the borough. Table 8.1 summarises some relevant measures.

Table 8.1 **Housing tenure, 1991 and 2001 (rounded percentage of households)**

Tenure type	*1991*			*2001*		
	Tower Hamlets: whites	*Tower Hamlets: Bangladeshis*	*Greater London: all groups*	*Tower Hamlets: Whites*	*Tower Hamlets: Bangladeshis*	*Greater London: all groups*
Owner-occupied	26	7	57	36	13	57
Privately rented	8	4	12	17	5	17
Housing association	9	12	6	14	20	9
Local authority	55	77	23	33	62	17

Source: UK census data; Willmott, 1994.

We can see that, compared with the rest of London, residents of Tower Hamlets were heavily reliant on local authority housing in both 1991 and 2001. This is particularly true of the Bangladeshis – and we should remember that even those listed as owner-occupiers had mostly become so under specific local authority right-to-buy initiatives.

On overcrowding Bangladeshi households scored startlingly higher densities than other groups. Table 8.2 shows that in 1991 not only were Bangladeshi households much the most likely to be overcrowded, but also that over a third were very severely overcrowded. We should remember that this means that considerably more than a third of Bangladeshi *individuals* were living in overcrowded conditions, because the overcrowded households are also likely to be the largest households. The 2001 figures show the persisting severity of Bangladeshi overcrowding compared with other groups, even where a less harsh measure of overcrowding is applied. However, the 2001 data also show that there has been some convergence with other groups, as new migrants like Black Africans are approaching them. Nationally, Bangladeshis still

Table 8.2 **Overcrowding, 1991–2001ᵃ (rounded percentage of households)**

Ethnic group	1991 – Tower Hamlets only			2001		
	1–1.5 ppr	1.5+ ppr	All 1.0+	T. Hamlets	London	England
White Britishᵇ	2	1	3	17	11	5
White Irishᵇ				21	16	10
Pakistani	22	11	33	46	37	26
Bangladeshi	32	35	67	64	53	44
Black Caribbean	5	2	7	28	23	19
Black African	13	8	21	50	47	42
All households	6	5	11	29	17	7

a 1991, overcrowding defined as households with more than one person per room; 2001, overcrowding measured in terms of deficit of rooms needed – i.e. households needing additional room(s).
b Category 'white' not subdivided in 1991.
Source: UK census data.

suffer the highest rates of overcrowding, but in Tower Hamlets the rate is particularly high.

These housing conditions mean that under the state allocation system it has been easier for Bangladeshis to demonstrate housing need than for others. This has been a powerful factor for the Bangladeshi community at the national level in arguing for help, but locally it has constituted a serious grievance in the eyes of white residents, and a reason for many of them to oppose the new allocation rules. Virtually all of our white respondents made some reference to conflicts over housing, critical of the current procedures, though there was variation in whom they blamed. Arthur Petwick, an elderly childless man living alone, spoke most indignantly:

> The Asians definitely get a lot of preference here. We've got people who've lived in this borough all their lives, and they can't get a place. But when the Asians come here they get something quickly. The council say they're homeless; but they should discourage them from coming here. They're fanning the flames of racial unrest. They're coming round to families with a two- or three-bedroom house and offering them £1,000 to move out because they want it for an Asian family.

Ellen Morgan, a young granny whose offspring now all lived outside London, took a similar line.

> I don't see why [they] are put into a house just because they come into Tower Hamlets, whereas I had to wait twenty-five years on the housing list before I got this place. I read in the last *East London Advertiser* about a Bangladeshi who has two wives and has two homes here. Why should they come from abroad and just get two homes like that? They just go to the Housing Department, tell them they have no place to live, and just get them.

Kristin O'Keefe, on the other hand, recognised that she had played her own cards badly – and her case is unusual. When we interviewed her, her family of eight was crammed into a small converted two-bedroom flat. She and her husband had bought it from the council under the right-to-buy scheme when they had fewer children, but now this was holding them back from getting something larger. They could not afford to buy a bigger place and would be considered intentionally homeless if they tried to get back on the council waiting list. So it was tough for her to see newcomers getting large flats:

> My Bangladeshi neighbours were in the country for less than two years, and then were given the whole of the house next door. There were six of them – five now that one has moved out. The house is three storeys, with five bedrooms. I don't hold it against them, as they're good as gold. But it does seem a bit unfair when you see other people waiting for years.

Much more typical was the experience of Joyce Darty when she tried to help her daughter to find a flat. Joyce is not hostile to Bangladeshis themselves, as we saw in relation to her workmates. And she gets on with those in her flats too:

> We've got Pakistani people upstairs and you don't know they're there. The mother doesn't speak or nothing, but the father will come down and say good morning and that ... One of them is always putting her arm round me, and we get on very well together.

So it is all the more telling that she got angry with the housing office.

> I did get angry with them once. When my daughter got married she couldn't get a place and had to live with her mother-in-law for a while. Then her mother-in-law found some empty rooms above a grocery store near Roman Road, and my husband and his dad and my daughter's husband worked hard on it to make it look lovely for them. Jennifer was as happy as a sandboy, and everything seemed fine until Mr Cohen, the owner of the shop, died and his wife said that they would have to sell it. She said, 'I'm sorry, Jennifer, but I'll try my hardest to keep you in the flat whoever takes it over.' But the betting shop took over and wanted the flat for offices.
> Jennifer did not know what to do. She said, 'Will you come up the housing place with me, Mum?' and we went up and told them what happened. They said, 'We can put you in a bed and breakfast but not your husband.' I said, 'She was born and bred here, and all these foreigners have just been given a place to live. What's wrong with her? If she coloured her face, then would you give her a place then?' The woman said, 'If you say that again I'll have the law onto you.' I said to her, 'It's you who makes me prejudiced.' It is those people that do, not the foreigners. Anyway, they didn't give her a place, but Mrs Cohen did give her longer to get out of the flat ...
> If any place round here gets vacant you know who's going to get it. And that makes people prejudiced. It isn't people, it is the government and those big-hearted ones who've got their own big houses and make these rules which make people like us prejudiced. It's a terrible thing.
> The place upstairs went free because this old man died and this girl I knew had three

little babies and she asked me if anywhere was going around me. She was on the housing list, but when we tried to find out about the flat they said it's already gone. The next thing you know it was Bengalis who got it. Same as those houses over there; every one has got Bengali people in it now. None of them are working, so why couldn't they let that girl with the babies have something? That makes me prejudiced if anything does. It's not the people, it's all those goody two shoes, those housing people who do it.

The two communities are making different types of demand on the housing department. Bangladeshis mainly need large units for large families and extended family households. Whites, on the other hand, rarely need large flats, and under the rules do not often need additional housing at all. What they would often like to have, though, and feel entitled to expect, is something near to where they have grown up.

Yet another pressure is from yuppies. One of the problems for the East End is that, as the image of Tower Hamlets has changed, it has become for the first time a desirable area for those with money.[8] These contrasting desires have generated a multiple market in housing; and this has become fundamental to the political structure and processes of the borough.

Census data from 1991 show that over 80 per cent of Bangladeshi households contained at least two adults plus children, compared with just 13 per cent of white households. Similarly, the average number of dependent children in a Bangladeshi household was, at 3, more than seven times the figure for whites (0.4). Some detail can be added to these contrasts by looking at the relationships between co-residents. The ICS survey in 1992 listed all people in households according to their kinship tie with the survey respondent. Table 8.3 sorts responses according to whether the respondents were white, Bangladeshi or black, and shows the proportion of respondents in each category who had a specified relative living in their household. (Non-kin household members are not included here.) The figures confirm that Bangladeshi households contain a rich variety of kin – with more than one in five containing in-laws. The black group, containing a number of refugees and recent migrants, showed more children than white households, and fewer extended family members than among Bangladeshis, but also recorded a shortage of spouses.

The tight concentration of Bangladeshi families in large households is partly a matter of cultural preference, but there is also a strategic aspect to it, relating to the demands of the migration process and the need for family help and solidarity, which may help to sustain the preference. Applicants for entry visas, and for residence rights, are required to show that they will have somewhere to live. Bangladeshis already resident in Britain may as a result find themselves putting up newcomers until they have found places of their own, or are entitled to apply for them. While newcomers are unable to seek public support for a year, households will tolerate or conceal overcrowding. But when this probationary period is completed the new arrivals are free to declare themselves technically homeless. Naveen's Aunt Sultana had recently done this:

Table 8.3 **Relatives in household: 1992 (percentage households containing residents in specified relationship to subject)**

Relationship to subject	White	Bangladeshi	Black[a]
Husband	21	37	14
Wife	19	33	16
Spouse total	*40*	*70*	*30*
Daughter	16	57	26
Son	21	69	40
Brother	4	23	5
Sister	2	16	7
Father	5	16	7
Mother	7	23	16
Grandson	1	4	2
Granddaughter	2	8	–
An 'in-law'[b]	1	22	–
Number of households surveyed	535	171	43

a Half Black Caribbean one third Black African.
b Mainly sister-in-law, daughter-in-law, mother-in-law.

When Sultana came back married from Bangladesh, with her husband Helal, they moved in with our family. Helal is my mother's younger brother. But this made us very overcrowded; there must have been a dozen people in a three-bedroom flat. So as soon as they could they declared themselves homeless, and were moved to a hotel near Euston station. Helal worked in an Indian restaurant near King's Cross, from about 11 to 3 for lunchtime, and then again from about 6 until midnight. So it was quite convenient. The day after their baby was born they got the offer of a flat in a tower block in Bow, and so they were soon living back near us again.

The crowded Bangladeshi household does not just mean that household members are more likely to have a strong case for securing available public housing. Family ties remain useful to those who are establishing their citizenship rights in the UK in a way that does not apply to existing citizens. Thus the strong family commitments of Bangladeshis, including ties to relations still in Bangladesh, enhance in various ways their ability to demonstrate objective need for public housing, and help to intensify competition and conflict with the white community.

The divergent character of their housing needs also means that the two communities adopt different arguments to back up their respective claims, and to inform their grievances. Bangladeshis can decisively out-score whites in terms of overall need. But the existing housing stock is mainly geared towards small household units. So points have not always converted into allocations, and Bangladeshis have often felt annoyed that their particular requirements have been ignored. They have also been resentful for a while, and with some justification, that they tend to be offered older, more run-down properties.[9] For their part many whites, especially old-timers, resist the idea that levels of measurable need (including homelessness – however defined) should be the ruling principle. Even though it is embedded in central government policy, and has been now for over a generation, white East Enders feel that the idea of need should not completely override local and community connections in the allocation of housing.

Sometimes sheer persistence works. Paul Driscoll found that constant badgering of the housing office was the thing to do. He got his present flat in the block where he had grown up:

> The housing office was just a few yards from where I was living. I sent them three or four letters a day, and phoned them the same amount until, eventually, they gave me my maisonette ... When I was growing up it used to be sons and daughters. Sons and daughters kept the community spirit as they knew one another. It has slowly died, though. To me it's more racist to chuck out sons and daughters than to keep sons and daughters.

Right from the beginning of Bangladeshi family settlement in Tower Hamlets there has, therefore, been a contest for housing in which both groups feel badly treated. Bangladeshis are overcrowded, and many feel that the promises made by the official points system are not honoured. Whites are hard pressed to make any case at all under current procedures, and may be inclined to try to subvert the system to get what they want.

Mavis Browning was one of many who felt that she had been put in an impossible position by the housing department. When she tried to get a flat locally for her daughter, to avoid her having to leave the area, she was advised that the best thing to do would be to stop treating her as a daughter, by turning her out and making her homeless:*

> The community here isn't as close as it used to be. It has broken down. Our children have to move out because there are no flats for them, so the children have to move away. There are a lot of old people here with no one to look after them. If there are any houses going, they go to people with the most children. My daughter was living with me and my father, who has since died, and my son. My daughter and I had to share a bedroom. But when she applied for a council flat they said she wasn't high enough up on the list. She didn't have enough points to get a place. The social worker told me she would get a place if I turned her and her daughter out onto the streets. But I couldn't do that. So in the end she and her present boyfriend managed to buy a flat in Chingford. They can't really afford it, but there's no alternative.

By refusing to accommodate to the new rules, Mrs Browning lost out. Her position

---

*Perverse incentives such as these have now largely been removed from the administration of social housing.

is echoed by many other respondents, who find council actions, particularly in relation to homelessness, hostile to ordinary family life. Pat Friday said:

> I would lay part of the blame for family break-up on council housing. In days gone by, children used to live with the parents even after they got married. Now that is not accepted at all. The parents get left in Inner London, places like Hackney and Tower Hamlets, while the children have to go out to Essex, and vote Tory.

Rita Baron, a single mother who told us that she had had to move out of Bethnal Green, and at the second interview was living in a nearby borough, complained:

> These days housing is not for those who live in the borough, it's for outsiders. I've had to come out of my borough and into another borough even though I'm under the sons and daughters act. It's a well known thing. I had to declare myself homeless.

Many whites would argue that the sort of strategy recommended to Mrs Browning is justified on the grounds that the system has been rigged to enable Bangladeshis to leap-frog them into available accommodation. There is a battle here between principles and different sectors of the poor. From the outset this has produced a serious dilemma for the strongly Labour council in Tower Hamlets. It soon resulted in a sharper split between New and Old Labour than found anywhere else in the country.

The LibDems and White Resistance

Divisions within Labour were exploited effectively by Liberals[10] (later Liberal Democrats) in Tower Hamlets. They became prominent in the borough by operating as a protest party and proved adept at listening to the grievances of local white people about the housing and social services provided by the Labour council. Without openly articulating anti-immigrant sentiments, they indicated sympathy for the idea of promoting local interests and solutions, if necessary opposing national policy, including a housing policy embracing sons and daughters. They started to develop a model of decentralised administration which would permit these interests to express and defend themselves.

From a single Liberal seat in the 1978 local election, the Liberal/SDP vote grew quickly while the Labour Party became more and more divided between the interests of Bangladeshis and its traditional white supporters: New Labour and Old. Many white people were angry.[11] A Liberal/SDP alliance swept through the white north-eastern wards of the borough to take overall control of the council in 1986. Between 1986 and 1994 they pursued a range of new strategies. These may not have been explicitly designed to restrain Bangladeshi demands for a larger share of council housing (especially in the Brick Lane area), but they certainly had that effect.

Their key strategy was the decentralisation of Tower Hamlets into seven 'neighbour-hoods'. Although four of these had a Labour Party majority, the devolution of admin-istrative functions to the neighbourhoods weakened the hand of (centralising) Labour and had the effect of allowing the greater expression of white interests in the borough. More importantly, the implementation of local control and democratic accountability effectively split the Bangladeshi heartland between the tips of the three western neigh-bourhoods of Wapping, Stepney and Bethnal Green. Bangladeshis no longer formed a majority in any of them. With the abolition of the GLC in 1985, Tower Hamlets had inherited a massive GLC housing stock, which gave it control of between 80 and 90 per cent of all residential accommodation in the borough. The scheme for the allocation of tenancies which was implemented within the new decentralised framework made it harder for Bangladeshis to pursue their interests effectively. They could be constrained within the neighbourhood in which they lived, and their choices were limited too.

Under the new devolved system, neighbourhoods became entitled to set their own priorities for housing, while being required to reserve some places for homeless families, including those registered in other neighbourhoods. A borough-wide survey carried out by the LibDems shortly after they took power showed that a large majority of tenants were in favour of preference being given to sons and daughters of existing tenants; and several of the neighbourhoods – including Bethnal Green, with a high proportion of Bangladeshi applicants and a history of National Front voting before the first Liberal was elected in 1978 – adopted policies which gave lower priority to homelessness and made a beginning in housing small numbers of white sons and daughters.

The biggest challenge to the LibDems was what to do about the homeless. Under the 1977 Homeless Persons Act a local authority was obliged to find accommodation for homeless people. But what *was* a homeless family? And how did it affect the growing numbers of Bangladeshis? One might have supposed that to qualify people would have to be actually homeless, living on the streets, but this was not so. The definition, as it emerged in subsequent treatment and debates, went wider than that, to cover people who were potentially or 'invisibly' homeless, as they were described, by being over-crowded in their present residence. The policy was meant to be preventative as well as dealing with people who really were without a home of any kind. Most of the incoming Bangladeshi families were by this time finding accommodation with their relatives in council housing, exacerbating the already severe overcrowding.

The fact that the Bangladeshi homeless were invisible, albeit desperately over-crowded, gave white residents another source of resentment, as invisible homeless Bangladeshis gained preference over their own kin on the housing waiting list, while the thirty-one rough sleepers counted in Tower Hamlets at the time were all white, and all too visible. All local politicians became concerned about such an inflammatory issue.

It was possible for councillors and staff to drag their feet on homelessness by provid-ing short-term bed-and-breakfast 'hotels' well outside Tower Hamlets, the most dismal of temporary homes for families with young children. Another strategy pursued by

Tower Hamlets council was to declare the large number of the families recently arrived from Sylhet to be 'intentionally homeless' because they had voluntarily left homes in Bangladesh, and therefore legally did not need to be rehoused. Alternatively, housing staff could offer them flats in the worst estates and, when the offer was refused, then declare the household intentionally homeless. The High Court upheld the council's view that they had no duty to house such families and in June 1988 the first families affected by this judgment were evicted from such council accommodation as they had and were rehoused in church halls.

Another component of the LibDem strategy was to promote the sale of council housing more vigorously. Selling off stock and reducing the pool of public housing put more restraints on Bangladeshi expansion. Even so, many white residents were disappointed with what had been done to protect their interests, and were looking for something stronger. The BNP took advantage of the situation and in 1993 they won a local by-election in Millwall on the Isle of Dogs, where the council had built a small estate of new dwellings which were much more attractive than most of the council housing around them. The BNP candidate successfully aroused white hostility in the ward by grossly exaggerating the number of these new properties which were to be allocated to Bangladeshi families.[12] In the event both the BNP candidate and the LibDem council were ousted in the subsequent 1994 local elections by a Labour Party reflecting more confidently the deal made twenty years earlier in Spitalfields – though still divided internally over how strongly to emphasise anti-racist strategies.[13]

The Return of Labour

The Labour Party which retook control of the council in 1994 was not the same party as the one voted out in 1986. The holiday from power paved the way for a new realism about what was actually possible in the borough.

Two demographic changes underlie the shift in mood. In the first place Docklands had become established as an important and expanding part of the municipal equation. The presence of a new, highly profitable economic sector, at the cutting edge of globalisation and supporting a strong private housing market, put the cosmopolitan elite in decisive control for the first time. This had a restraining effect on conflict between the white and Asian poor. Political conflicts in the borough acquired an increasingly triangular aspect, with the balance of power firmly held by incoming middle classes. Old Bethnal Green was history.

At the same time, the Bangladeshi community had moved from anxious defence of their heartland towards a much more confident position in the borough as a whole. Those hostile to them had left the borough in large numbers for outer east London and Essex. The BNP stand at Millwall on the Isle of Dogs had brought down the full fury and contempt of the national political class on the local white community, without producing any concessions for them. Street power too was shifting, with organised Asian resistance to white harassment raising Asian self-confidence.

When poor members of a national majority play a national card which fails to mobilise the national elite they risk becoming seen as an 'honorary minority' themselves:[14] that is, a sectarian, petulant group that no longer shares in a progressive national destiny. In a way, the crushing of the BNP at Millwall seems to have turned stubborn white East Enders into just such a group. Parts of the white working class felt they had become voiceless and invisible. The new locals were the Bangladeshi migrants and their children.

This last point has been extremely important for the evolution of housing policy. During the 1990s significant numbers of second- and third-generation Bangladeshis were entering the housing market. A large number of those who have grown up here do not want to live any longer in large, three-generation family groups. Some will be keen to move out of the area entirely, especially those who have done well and wish to become home-owners. Some will be able to expand a little into the spaces vacated by elderly white residents as they die, but overall there are likely to be many more young Bangladeshis who want to stay living locally than will be able to find places.

So during the 1990s convergence grew between white and Bangladeshi communities on the desirability of housing allocation policies that reflected family ties.[15] As an interest in local transmission of tenancies cut increasingly across both of these communities, it was easier for the housing authorities to be more sympathetic to those criteria – which probably appealed to the white community more, as they were the ones who had felt the system to be rigged against them.

However, the shift under New Labour to a more market-oriented social housing regime, around 'choice-based lettings',* has changed the game yet again, and it is unclear how this will impact on these two communities. As in other aspects of local life, it may well be the Bangladeshis who in practice now start to feel a sharp deceleration in their access to national goods. For many migrant families, the first decade or so here has been marked by rapid settlement, eased by official acceptance as needy newcomers. But there is not the space, either physically or socially, for this progress to continue at the same pace. Over the next decade or so we can perhaps expect a greater sharing with the remaining white residents of the sense of collective exclusion and neglect that have been the lot of East Enders for centuries.

---

*This is a new system of allocation in which vacancies are advertised publicly and can be applied for by anyone, with no guarantee of success. See recent Young Foundation analysis in Abbott, 2005.

An uncompromising name for a Tower Hamlets housing estate.

Chapter 9

Hostility to New Communities

A White Laager

At the time of the original study, Bethnal Green had a warmth and conviviality which did much to compensate for its material privations. In a later edition, the authors of *Family and Kinship* noted that:

> Poor, Bethnal Greeners may have been ... but ... their poverty was accompanied by a generosity towards others *like themselves*, by a wide range of attachments, by pride in themselves, their community and their country and by an overflowing vitality.[1]

Today this generosity of spirit is much harder to find. The golden age is no more. When we began the new wave of research in 1992 we designed the initial study mainly to repeat the 1950s project. The emphasis would still be on family life, but with a few general questions added, to elicit opinion about how the area had changed. In their answers all groups revealed at least some hostility towards others, but of the white respondents (who comprised two- thirds of the total sample) a majority expressed an often bitterly negative attitude towards foreign immigrants, and particularly towards to Bangladeshis. Just asking a few preliminary open questions tapped into a great pool of public resentment, and produced a deluge of complaints.*

The mass outpouring of bitterness we elicited is shown clearly in the examples presented below. It is important to report such sentiment. In our view, too many studies have swept 'popular' feelings on race under the carpet, rather than recognising their existence and attempting to understand them.† Our own study began around the time that the BNP was active in the borough, and it is this chauvinism which is now widely

---

*Most of the quotations which follow here are drawn from this preliminary survey, rather than from intensive interviews. So we have given brief descriptions of the respondents rather than names, unless they are informants mentioned by name elsewhere. (See appendix for explanation of research design.)

†A more highly structured study than ours, carried out in Spitalfields around the same time (Erens, 1993), which asked direct questions about almost everything except racial conflict, unsurprisingly failed to discover or report any hostility.

seen by outsiders as the defining quality of real-life East Enders. Another side of their character has revealed itself in these overtly hostile, sometimes inaccurate and often rumour-based perceptions.

This is not to say that the white people we interviewed were implacably resentful. One of the more revealing and human features of the findings lay in the complexity of people's feelings. Most white subjects, including some among the most explicitly hostile to Bangladeshis, admitted that while they resented the immigrants and what they felt their presence was doing to the area, they somehow managed to get on with them, or even to like them:

> I get on well with everyone, I suppose. Although I talk a lot about the Pakis it was the bloke from the paper shop who sent me a card when I was in hospital. (*Elderly man living alone*)

> I do not have much dealing with them [Bangladeshis]. Some live next door to me but I do not see them much. An Asian neighbour took me to the hospital: he was all right to me. If they are all right to me I am all right to them. (*Widower, with children abroad*)

> I get on well with anyone if they leave me alone and don't bother me. Some Pakistani children moved in below last year and sent me a Christmas card. (*Middle-aged divorcee, with child in Essex*)

Behind a critical demeanour, or quirky manner, some were tolerant:

> People drop dead all the time so you should not make a fuss about each one. God left us to live in peace. We are all the same flesh and blood. All God's children are eaten by the same worms when we go. (*Elderly widow living with one of her daughters*)

Besides this common goodwill and sympathy towards Bangladeshis, quite a number of white people were positively anti-racist, and tended to adopt the immigrants' side against whites. A simple assertion that, 'I am totally non-racist and I get on with everyone' (*Middle-aged childless man*), cropped up several times. One or two respondents would substantiate this further, as in, 'I have been to Bangladesh and my children have best friends who are Asian and I am quite proud of that' (*Married housewife with four sons*).

Elsie Plant, an elderly woman who remembered hostility to Jews in the 1930s, summed up that feeling, declaring:

> I get on with most people, and I think that some white people get under my skin at times – always blaming other people for what they think they should have. They're very well off – apart from the homeless. There's no need to grumble. The world is for everybody. Everyone is born the same and should have a roof over their heads. I can't bear all this trouble that goes on, it hurts me. When we were growing up we had a lot of Jewish children around, we lived surrounded by Jewish people, and later on I looked after Jewish children.

Having noted all that, however, we must admit that the overwhelming balance of opinions expressed was negative, sometimes violently so. Many of the respondents who said most about Bangladeshis threw in some extremely offensive remarks about them. A good few of the remarks covering different aspects of everyday life seemed to be based on wild hearsay and popular myth. One old lady reeled off a veritable catalogue of complaints in one breath:

> You have to lock your door where you never used to. My partner ran a local pub for fifty years. You relied on people in the street and doors were open and people sat on doorsteps until late at night. The neighbours are not like they were – but mine are good! There are too many stinks of foreign cooking. You can say I'm racist if you like. The lifts are filthy because of their spitting and urine, and they leave rubbish everywhere. They put it in bags in the grounds, and won't use the chutes at the end of the balcony. The flats used to be beautiful, and the windows clean. It's heartbreaking really now as it's so filthy ... There's too much noise now all night – with their shouting and running about. The kids run amok in the park and tread on plants. (*Granny, with sons in Essex*)

The perception of Bangladeshi food as malodorous was common:

> The smell of their cooking is awful sometimes and it comes right through the air vents. (*Grandfather with son's family in Kent*)

> There's a Pakistani moved in. You get the smell of curry all the time. (*Retired factory worker, with adult child in north London*)

Nearly as many declared that Bangladeshi cooking practices had led to infestations of vermin in their flats:

> The Bengalis they are infecting everyone with their cockroaches. (*Grandfather with many local offspring*)

> The Bengali families have altered it a lot. We are running alive with cockroaches here. There must be a reason for it and you don't like to blame them but it makes you wonder. It upsets me to think that it's getting ruined. It used to be so much cleaner. (*Separated mother with adult children*)

> Bulk food storage in the flats by Bangladeshis brings in the cockroaches. (*Single mother with three children*)

> There are too many Bangladeshis over here, and when Big Daddy goes back to Bangladesh he brings more over here, and food with rice beetles. The house down the road was infested with rice beetles. My sister has been treated for TB and she caught it off the Bengalis. (*Widower, with son out of London*)

> The police had a purge on the shops and found maggots and stuff, which is really disgusting. (*Elderly childless husband*)

We should point out here that our own observations of Bangladeshis' flats were that they were almost invariably clean, neat and well cared-for, despite often being in the most run-down buildings. The two exceptions we noted were family flats in which one of the parents was suffering from mental illness and the whole family was in considerable disarray. However, it is true that there is typically a lot of home cooking done in Bangladeshi households, using fresh (and cheap) ingredients and no doubt contributing to the smells about which some neighbours complained.

Several objected to Bangladeshi personal habits and hygiene, which was sometimes linked to statements about a lack of cleanliness in public places:

> The Bangladeshi people are very dirty and throw sanitary towels and dirty nappies out of the windows. (*Young single mother*)

> In the middle of the night they seem to move in and suddenly they are there. They used to throw their rubbish over the balconies in front of my Mum's flat. Not many of them speak English and that makes it more difficult. (Mrs O'Gara)

> The young Bangladeshis are walking about with an attitude problem. I do not like the way they spit on the floor and spit on the windows. (*Young childless man*)

> The Asians think we are against them. They've got a chip on their shoulder and give you funny looks. They spit in the basket in the laundry: it has to be stopped. (*Middle-aged wife with three grown-up resident sons*)

> Pakis put out their rubbish from their shops onto the street, other shop-keepers never did that. There's no white shops here now, it's all Pakis. Whitechapel – it should be called Blackchapel! (*Widow of market trader*)

Many of these complaints are imaginary or exaggerated, but a few may point to actual differences in lifestyle. Shohel – one of the Bangladeshi informants whom we found most willing to discuss sensitive issues with us – himself recognised that rubbish was a problem:

> I tried to explain to my (English) wife that most of the people in Tower Hamlets are Sylheti village people. They have no social etiquette and no particular material needs other than those they brought with them from home. They live as they'd done there. This accounts for their throwing rubbish out of their flat windows and balconies. There is no refuse collecting in Bangladesh. There it is thrown into the street or into the nearest pit. You just dump it. In Sylheti town it's a bit different. In some of the rich areas there is refuse collection for those rich enough to pay for it ... I'm forever going on about it ... We're only here for one thing, to earn, to send money back, you see. [So we] can be really quite dirty at times, with rubbish being littered outside front doors. That really is a problem and it really is a continuation [of old ways].

A Sense of Foreign Invasion

Fears are entertained that the locality is being taken over, with Bethnal Green becoming

Bangla Green. Few white informants seemed aware that at the time of the interviews Bangladeshis as a whole comprised barely a quarter of the Tower Hamlets population and a very much smaller percentage of the East End as a whole. However, as there were already more Bangladeshi school pupils in Tower Hamlets than white, it is not surprising that our white informants talked as though they as a group were already the minority:

> They have taken over everything, from schools to shops and houses. (*Widower, with family in Essex*)

> I do think too many Bengalis are trying to take over here. (*Middle-aged cabbie*)

> I just resent the large numbers of immigrants with large families who have taken over. (*Young mother with two infants*)

> Bangladeshi people have taken over the shops, though they are usually very nice people. They stay open later, so you can get milk anytime. (*Nurse living in flatshare*)

> Brick Lane – I remember it before Asians took it over the way they have. (Lisa Oakley)

All of this raised the spectre for many of being captured and incorporated into an alien world.

> People come from overseas and get housed straight away. In another forty years this will be like New Delhi. I've got to go into debt and buy a place because I can't get a council flat at all. But all the immigrants around here get all the council places. (*Designer with partner but no children*)

> We are being saturated with immigrants. It worries me because they all have so many children and this area can't cope with all these people. It is overcrowded as it is. (*Single mother with teenage daughter*)

Because the nature of the area was changing, people were leaving, and the more people left, the more it changed:

> When people move out they seem to be replaced by Asians. I've noticed a lot of people seem to want to move away because of this. (*Elderly spinster*)

> I feel threatened when I go out ... they are driving people away from the East End. (*Young separated mother with two children*)

Such images raise the question in some informants' minds of whose country it now is. Bangladeshis, many whites argued, just wanted to do things their own way:

> The Bangladeshis have made a country within a country. They have all their own rules and society and they do not mix in. They do not want anything to do with us. (*Shopkeeper with wife and one child*)

> They all stick together and they look after each other. I suppose it's because they all live in the same house. (*Young man living in shared flat*)

Bangladeshi people are a very close-knit community and they do not want to share any-thing with outsiders. (*Elderly childless man*)

The Asians seem to want everything their own way. You can't help offending them. All the schools are full of Paki children. They seem to have funny ways and are very cliquey and touchy. (*Irish woman with husband but no children*)

The Bangladeshi community was also perceived as insular:

My kids play with other kids but Bangladeshi people tend to shut their kids away. (*Mother with three children*)

They live in their own world, and are not here to mix. If they came prepared to join in with our ways in regard with living standards and religion [it would be different]. We don't really have anything to do with them. They live in a world of their own, which is their choosing not ours. (*Middle-aged man with local children and grandchild*)

The Pakistanis seem to be going around in groups more now than they used to. It is a bit frightening to go out by myself. (*Widow, living with sister*)

The Pakistanis make trouble when they are all together, but if they live separately [i.e. dispersed] they are all right. (*Computer analyst living alone*)

Some whites, however, also recognised that such Bangladeshi grouping was a pos-sible manifestation of immigrants' own apprehension about living in an alien world:

Bangladeshis and Pakistanis are the most hostile and unfriendly groups around here, although I sometimes think they are frightened of us. (*Publican's wife*)

It's amazing, we're surrounded by Indians but we have no talking with them. They're getting more brighter now; but they're frightened or shy – and a lot of them don't speak English. (*Shop assistant living with husband and teenage son*)

Others regarded Bangladeshis as wanting to impose their lifestyle or culture on everyone else. White schoolchildren were commonly portrayed as being drawn into a Bangladeshi world, in both culinary as well as an academic sense.

Things have changed since the immigrants moved in. You can't walk around, as groups of Pakis approach you. Schooling is different. My nephews are being fed curry and rice every day, and learning to speak Bengali. The teachers are Bengali – but we are supposed to be English-speaking. (*Care-worker living with boyfriend*)

We found very little to support the implications in the above comments when we discussed official LEA policy with teachers, dinnerladies or parents. Many children (white and Bangladeshi) like to eat curry sometimes, Bengali is offered at schools at GCSE and A level, and a small but growing number of (English-speaking) teachers are Bengali. However, the changes believed to be happening were seen as a lowering of standards. Mrs O'Gara said:

It's my kids I think of. I said to my daughter, 'Don't stay here. It would be the finish for your children.' Schools have gone down. Janice went to playschool in Margate Street when she was three. It was lovely. Now I'm told there are so many Asian children you have to put your name down as soon as your child is born and then you may not get in. I wouldn't advise anyone living here to have any children unless they know they can move away to somewhere where they'd have a better chance.

Mrs Shelley wanted to move out of Bethnal Green to the suburbs because, 'There's not too many Asians there. The kids would get a better schooling.' And there is un-neighbourly behaviour : 'I used to find it hard living upstairs with them downstairs because they never seemed to come alive until after 11.00 pm.'

The issue of Bangladeshi children ignoring or not understanding what was appropriate behaviour in public, such as not picking the flowers in the park, cropped up regularly:

> My old home has been knocked down and now it is the park. I like to sit and read my paper out there on a Sunday, and recently I watched the Bangladeshi kids pulling up the flowers. I told them off. (*Widow with child in south London*)

> The kids run riot and pull up plants [in the park]. I can't say anything because I would be called a racist. (*Retired union official*)

> If you say anything about picking the flowers, if you say, 'That's not nice,' then they just say something back in their own language. (*Postman living with wife and grown-up son*)

Claims on the Welfare State

By far the largest number of complaints arose, however, in relation to Bangladeshi claims on the welfare state. A majority of white respondents questioned Bangladeshi rights and entitlements, or expressed resentment at the level of demands which they placed on the system. Listening to these litanies, it became obvious that a large number of the accusations made were thoroughly implausible, or involved serious ignorance about how welfare procedures operated. Many just recycled popular myth as fact or personal experience. Few white respondents seemed aware that many Bangladeshi men had worked for decades in Tower Hamlets or in grim northern factories before moving to London. They had earned their pensions and other rights just like anyone else. But in many such cases the facts of the matter were probably irrelevant. Opposition was categorical. Many whites were objecting not to specific abuses of the welfare system, but to the more fundamental fact that Bangladeshis had *any* right to benefits at all. This belief coloured their interpretation of any information which came their way, and made them reckless of accuracy.

One recurring theme was that Bangladeshis were very 'pushy':

It's always been a mixture of races here but this is the only race in east London that is always demanding things, it demands and demands and it's drained us dry. (Mr Barry)

Bangladeshi people do not speak English. But if they want something from you they do speak English. If they have a new nursery school they do not want anyone else to use it. (*Dental receptionist living with mother*)

The Bengalis can be a bit of a pain, especially at the clinic because they push in and do not queue up at all. (*Housewife with two young children*)

The Bangladeshis are getting a bit aggressive now because they want everything done for them. (*Middle-aged housewife*)

I don't get on with Bangladeshi people. There are a lot of them around here, and they like to push their weight around. (*Painter/decorator with young family*)

Frequently this sentiment was linked openly to criticism of large Bangladeshi families, which most whites see as giving Bangladeshis an unfair advantage when it comes to housing allocation and choosing schools for their children:

Well, you never see them working. They just live in their houses, lots of them, and you never see them go to work and they do have large families. They get family allowances and all the help. They seem to know what to do and where to go. They all look after one another. (*Retired shopkeeper*)

They give preference to people with children, and the Bengalis have three to every one child we have. (*Unemployed single mother with one child*)

The Pakis have huge families and the council seems to give them all the best housing. As soon as something is free they get in first. Some new places have just been built and they move in. We have been on the council list for ages but are getting nowhere. We live in one room with a small toddler. It's just not fair. (*Young mother*)

One man took his two daughters home to Bangladesh and was away so long from his council flat that people complained. So he came back, with the daughters. Each daughter came with a baby but no husband. (*Middle-aged man living with friend*)

My lone parent benefit has been cut. No one has ever addressed the fact that their religion promotes breeding. The burden is now on the taxpayer. Once the Bengali man with ten kids gets one in school they'll all get a place. That keeps my son out. (Alice Roe)

The point about fertility came up so frequently that we asked Shohel what the feeling about this was inside the Bangladeshi community. He explained that it was a real problem with the first-generation and recent migrants:

Contraception is practised by the more educated, wealthier people; but in many ways it is a taboo subject. No one talks about it. It's one of those things you keep behind closed doors ... You do get leaflets – Bengali-language pamphlets in mother-and-children centres and doctors' surgeries – but I don't think people take any notice of them whatsoever ... I think that's a major problem the community needs to encounter; it's a real obstacle if we are to get out of this cycle of poverty ... In many ways it's quite crude to say this but many families seem to be sprouting children every other year, and it's something we need to get across. But its going to be a very difficult job, whoever does it, because whenever there's any criticism of their way of life or their culture they immediately tend to think, 'Ah, no, these people are trying to ruin our way of life. Let's put up the walls, the barriers. These people are trying to destroy us.' So it's difficult. You can't even be constructively critical because it's seen as being offensive. It's a very difficult subject; very, very difficult subject.

For most whites, though, having large families just meant that Bangladeshis were adept at getting more out of the welfare system than they were:

Definitely the Asians get everything that is going, from the largest houses to all the benefits they want. (*Young single man living with parents*)

I do feel that all this race relations is one way, because a coloured family can get all the benefits going while white families have to wait. (*Mother with two children*)

Actually, I've noticed that in the chemist they never seem to pay for any of their medicines. They just sign for it. They seem to get a lot of benefit things free whereas if you are in work you don't get nothing. When at work you have to pay for everything. There is an estate along Vallance Road especially for them. If a house becomes vacant in a row of houses they put an Asian family in it. On this estate Asian people have kicked up a fuss and complained if Asians are not housed on the estate. These Asians are supposed to be homeless, but when they move in they have all their new furniture because you see it going in. (*Elderly woman living alone*)

Queuing up in the post office, they draw hundreds while we get a pittance. They push you around and insult you. (*Pensioner with disabled husband*)

You see Asians getting so many hundreds over the counter, when so many get nothing. (*Mother, with three children*)

There are enough arguments at the post office when they're all getting their benefits, withdrawing £150 next to the little old lady with her £60. (*Bus driver with wife and one child*)

Bangladeshis were perceived as getting both quicker and better treatment from the authorities:

All the new houses are for immigrants. Big houses for big Pakistani families. They're officially not working so they don't pay the rent ... They're moving in everywhere. They come to take advantage of our social security. (*Childless woman living with parents*)

There's a lot more Asians living on this estate and it never used to be that bad. I've noticed that they seem to get parks and play areas built near their homes. (*Widow with daughter living nearby*)

The Bangladeshis get the best homes, the largest homes, and make them like the mud huts like where they come from. (*Builder with wife and four children*)

When it came to use of the NHS, Kristin O'Keefe felt that Bangladeshis made no attempt to look after themselves before going to the hospital, or even to a doctor:

> Last Saturday my youngest, Karen, had a very high temperature and I was worried about meningitis, so in the afternoon I took her to the Children's Hospital in Hackney Road, which is very near. We had been to the doctor in the morning, but it had got worse during the day. But we had to wait six hours before anyone saw her. There were lots of Asians in there, and it makes going to the hospital murder. In my experience if their children are ill they don't try things like Calpol first, or even take them to the doctor. They just take them straight to the hospital.

Joyce Darty – who, as we have seen, held several Bangladeshi work colleagues in high regard – made it clear that her quarrel was with the way that Bangladeshis tended to live off the state. She felt that what fuelled prejudice was when some received benefits that others wanted but could not get:

> You find that most people who lived in Bethnal Green have moved out. They're not getting anything like a fair deal. Me and my husband don't get a farthing off anyone. We only get our pension ... We pay poll tax and get 25 per cent off; other than that we don't get anything. But I was in a post office the other day. It was packed in there and most of them was Bengali. They wasn't just going up with one book but with eight or nine books and they were sending the money back to their country. And of course it caused a riot. People were saying, 'Look at this so-and-so; I bet he hasn't done a day's work here. I bet if there was a war here they'd all go back to their own country.' It makes people say it. It do make people say it. I know I'm a bit of a softy, and I think of what it must have been like in their own country. And then I tell myself, 'Well, you've got to think of your own country!'

As stressed before, remarks about Bangladeshis living in squalor are not borne out by our own observations: quite the reverse. However, it is true that there are a number of large Bangladeshi families containing elderly males who do not work because they are ill or retired, and some of these men will be those who arouse resentment as they collect state benefits at the post office, despite possibly having worked for decades in gruelling conditions in the UK. The fact that so many Bangladeshis manage to live adequately in Britain on relatively low incomes[2] and still send money to family in Bangladesh can, of course, also be seen as an impressive demonstration of efficient domestic economics. Arguments about appropriate levels of public support are endless. What we saw was that Bangladeshis prioritise the interests of family, including family in Bangladesh, above some of the material 'necessities' of life in Britain. For example we noticed the relative (though not total) absence of lavish modern technology, such as computers and expensive audio-visual systems, in comparison with homes occupied by white families. Yet some of their white neighbours perceive them to be managing well, too well even, on what they receive from the state.

The Roots of Hostility

Although white subjects often accused Bangladeshis of playing the welfare system, there was also a widespread feeling that it was the system itself, rather than the players, that was mainly at fault. The rules seemed slanted to respond preferentially to Bangladeshi needs. And there was some feeling that mechanisms for government funding of local councils probably encouraged such councils to accommodate more immigrants than their boroughs could cope with:

> We have fifty thousand immigrants here now, and our council gets paid from the government to take them in ... It's our country, but everything goes to the immigrants. (*Retired British Rail worker, with daughter in Essex*)

> The council bends over backwards to please people in the ethnic minorities. That applies in all things with the council, in all services. It's not the people's fault, and even people from ethnic minorities themselves agree that I'm right. (*Office worker with wife and one child*)

As a result of this apparent preference, Bangladeshis could leapfrog whites to the front of the queue:

> They'd come over from Heathrow immigration and straight away they'd be housed. Our children couldn't afford to buy around here, so they had to move out. (*Elderly woman with several children/grandchildren*)

> When I left home and tried to get a flat I sat for over an hour [in the housing office] waiting to see someone. An Asian came in with his suitcase and said 'family just come – need a flat', and he got sorted out straight away. All the improved and new places are given to Asians and people with no connection to the East End. (*Childless woman in shared flat*)

> Empty flats are not given to white people, locals. They are kept for foreigners, Asians, who have not even arrived here yet. (*Late middle-aged separated woman living alone*)

Such success was resented, despite the number of Bangladeshis living in far from luxurious conditions. But what hurt most was the idea that Bangladeshis had been served with entitlements on what seemed a far more generous basis than whites, and were getting goods that really belonged to whites. There is more than a faint echo here of the sentiments expressed by members of 'cargo cults': movements reported in Pacific islands by anthropologists working in the early twentieth century which regard well-off outsiders as having stolen wealth which local people feel must surely have been intended by the ancestral gods for their own consumption and enjoyment.[3] For 'gods' we can substitute 'founding fathers of the welfare state'.

We get shovelled aside. A man I know went into a rights office,* but they didn't want to know him because he's white. (*Separated woman living with friend*)

We've got too many Bangladeshis and Asians here ... They're all living rent free. There are only two of them in this block – one right above us. But sometimes we can't breathe in here. The stink from what they're cooking and we've got the air-freshener out and everything! What annoys me most is what they're getting free. And do you know what *we're* paying for? We're paying full poll-tax and everything. And do you know why? Because me and my husband worked hard, so we have to pay for everything. (Mrs Phillips)

We could fill a volume with such complaints, and will draw on a few more in the next chapter when we look in detail at the political battles that have resulted from this inter-group tension. But before that we must first look at *who* in the white community feels the greatest resentment towards incoming Bangladeshis. This is highly germane to understanding what is going on.

Understanding Hostility

Antagonism towards minorities often revolves around particular stereotypes. Jews in the East End have been portrayed as illegal or dishonest traders; the Irish were variously seen as lazy and as undercutting general wage levels; the Maltese were sexual predators, and so on. The stereotype of the Bangladeshi migrant which emerges in our data is of someone with a large family out to plunder the welfare system. To understand the roots of this image fully, and the anxieties it reflects, we will need to look at how post-war Britain and its class structure have developed during the lifetime of our respondents, at how those changes have coincided with Bangladeshi settlement, and why migrants may be picking up the blame. When we consider how hostility to Bangladeshis was distributed among our respondents, the pattern suggests that these other changes have been underestimated as causes of tension.

We put white responses into four main categories. The largest, into which 41 per cent of white respondents fitted, expressed almost entirely **hostile** opinions. A further 18 per cent registered mainly resentment at Bangladeshi settlement and behaviour, while qualifying their hostility with comments making it clear that they did not necessarily blame the Bangladeshis themselves for what was happening in the area. These we refer to as **mixed** in their response. Only a small proportion (11 per cent) were mainly **positive** in their comments about Bangladeshis, and tended to take their side on specific issues of conflict arising in the interview. Finally 30 per cent of white respondents

---

*A One Stop Shop (of which there are several in the borough) which deals with all enquiries regarding council services.

were classified by us as **indifferent**. This was either because they said explicitly that they were just not interested in Bangladeshis, and that Bangladeshis 'did not bother them', or, perhaps slightly in the majority of these cases, because they refused or failed to say enough to allow us to make a clear judgment about their response.

When we explore the social characteristics which tend to be associated with these positions it becomes easier to understand how and why certain people take such apparently irrational stances in relation to Bangladeshis. The orthodox view in academic circles seems to be that expression of racial hostility is misguided and reveals personal inadequacy.[4] This view is reflected in a book by social policy expert Danny Burns and two colleagues which looks at community issues in Tower Hamlets in the 1980s.[5] The authors acknowledge, rather grudgingly, that racial hostility may reflect the politics of the 'defended community', where a group is losing its stake in an area. But they go on to qualify this by defining such communities as 'imagined', and to explain why some people are more inclined towards hostility than others in terms of their personal psychology. This is, for example, how they account for the fact that tenants' organisers in Tower Hamlets, who have led the white resistance to Bangladeshi settlement, are often pensioners:

> Clearly, such people are more likely to have the time [to get involved], and they may also have the length of experience as a local resident which gives them a certain legitimacy. It is also likely that they are at the stage in the life-cycle to experience a strong internal need to preserve things from 'decline' irrespective of whether this refers to the physical body, the body of the family or of the community.[6]

The sentiments expressed here are similar to the line developed by the Labour Party since regaining office in 1997 – as explored here by sociologist Frank Furedi:

> The New Labour political elite is wholly committed to this world-view, and genuinely believes that the older generations in particular are more or less incurable racists. In April 2000, Clive Soley, chairman of the Parliamentary Labour Party, told a party strategy meeting that old age pensioners were 'predominantly Conservative' and 'often racist'. Other Labour MPs echoed Soley's sentiments – one Labour MP, cited in *The Sunday Times* (London), condemned pensioners for being 'like Alf Garnett', the racist and reactionary television character. For New Labour, race represents an opportunity to claim a moral advantage over its opponents.[7]

We would certainly agree that older people are more likely to display racist attitudes. This comes out strongly in our own findings.[8] The expression of hostility towards Bangladeshis is consistently associated with age, with nearly half of white over-55s recording generally hostile opinions (compared with a quarter of the under-35s) and few holding positive views. But this does not require a psychological interpretation. It makes adequate sense (and is rational) when linked not simply to such respondents' own personal decline but also to changes that this generation has experienced – including historical developments in the administration of social services, to which our respondents refer.

Many of the older people interviewed felt bewildered by recent social changes, and considered, for example, that the modern welfare system had lost the important moral sense of reciprocity which originally informed it.

This link between racial hostility and age is at the same time a reflection of local origins and commitment. A majority of the older white people in the survey had either been born in the area, married into it, or spent most of their lives in it. So on top of feeling that society in general is losing its direction, many of these also feel that their own little corner of Britain is changing for the worse, that it is being taken away from people like themselves and given to others. Hence there is also a strong connection between hostile attitudes towards Bangladeshis and being rooted in Bethnal Green (or having a partner so rooted).

Such local commitment has a bearing on one of the crucial common features of racial attitudes, which is the way in which events are seen as taking place between groups rather than among free individuals. Hostile respondents often refer to second-hand experiences of people they know (or commonly, to no more than hearsay) to justify their views, hence the exaggeration and distortion to which we have drawn attention in places. This sort of behaviour is interpreted by psychologists as evidence of the irrationality of their feelings. However, it can also be seen as showing a link between racial (and ethnic) hostilities and group loyalties. When you belong to a group whose members you care about, their suffering or pain becomes your own too.[9] This squares with our own findings. The people who are most put out by Bangladeshi settlement are precisely those with the longest involvement in the community and greatest stake in the area. Conversely, those who mind least about Bangladeshi settlement are those with least local commitment. They have not been there long and are in many cases transient residents who do not plan to stay for long either.

Hence it is among the 'yuppies' that we found the most reliably positive attitudes towards Bangladeshis, commonly tailing off quite quickly into an indifference to the issues, or gentle suggestion that the respondent was above such matters. Jeremy Land, a houseman at the London Hospital, enjoyed the exotic atmosphere that the Bangladeshis provided:

> I felt I wanted a complete change of environment after Cambridge, and the Royal London gave me the opportunity. The type of population here offered some very interesting medicine, with the ethnic mix allowing me an interesting lifestyle too. My grandmother, born and brought up in Kensington, feels that London has become much too foreign. But for me that's the most interesting aspect.

Antonia Andrews, another medic, declared, 'I am totally non-racist; I get on with them all.' Melanie Turner, art therapist, spoke like many other newcomers when she observed, 'I don't think I've got a problem with any person of any colour or culture.' The response of Tristram Williams, investment banker – 'It doesn't make any difference to me' – was short and to the point. And the position taken by Spencer Ratcliff, an advertising copywriter, who said, 'I don't know of any hard evidence that Bangladeshis get favourable treatment,' was not just detached but liable to put an interviewer on the defensive.

This interpretation also provides a further way of looking at the connection between racially positive or indifferent attitudes to Bangladeshis and education. A high level of education is generally taken in discussions of race attitudes as a likely indicator of rationality, and of tolerance based on understanding of difference,[10] and our data do indeed show that there is a strong association between education and positive sentiments towards Bangladeshis. However, there are more mundane considerations which should not be overlooked, for education is also a useful measure of people's capacity to move on easily from one area to another. It is a property distinctive of modern meritocrats and one which widens their choice of locality – because better-educated people can find work over a wider geographical area.

So the attitudes of the younger, more mobile, individualistic, cosmopolitan, 'yuppy' sector of the east London population can reasonably be assumed to be related to their strong position in the modern job market. It is overwhelmingly those with higher qualifications, who can escape whenever they want from the East End, who can take a more impersonal and principled view of the area's problems. For them, the presence of Bangladeshis may even be a bonus as it gives the locality an exotic aspect and cheap, agreeable eating spots – rather like being on a permanent foreign holiday.

Family and Hostility

Another important ingredient in local commitment is family responsibility, which introduces a more intimate level of concern for other people, and of group loyalty. Crucially, our figures showed that people with children – both parents with currently dependent children, and 'family elders' with grown-up children and perhaps grandchildren too – proved more likely to be hostile than the childless. Details are given in the appendix at the end of this book, but what is particularly important here is that the resulting pattern is stronger than that for age by itself. Older people without children to worry about are rather like younger, childless respondents in their views. Gertrude Bohm, for example, an elderly childless woman who had lived all her life in Bethnal Green but had no close relatives left, found the area less pleasant than when she was young. It was dirtier, noisier, and there was now a lot of traffic. But she was not worried by the presence of Bangladeshis: 'I have always been housed and moved; I have never had many problems with housing. So I have nothing to do with them myself.' Maud Flowers, also born in Bethnal Green and now a childless widow, who had been in her block for forty-four years, seemed brimming with optimism on all fronts:

> I think the whole neighbourhood has improved greatly in lots of ways. We used to have to share bathrooms and toilets and cleaning facilities. We used to take turns cleaning the landings and the outside. Now that all comes in with the rent. We've got different people here. We've got a couple of West Indians; overhead we've got a Muslim chap. I think that's good, the variety of people. They bring fresh blood to the place. The places are cleaner, the streets are cleaner, and children are looked after better. It was deplorable how shabby some of the kids were when I went to school. We've got parks around here now. This area is really nice. We've had a few break-ins – you expect that I suppose, especially in a ground-floor flat. It's so quiet now, even when the children are home it's quiet. It used to be very noisy.

Such statements expressing confidence in change, by old-time residents in their late seventies and eighties, suggest that it is not age in itself that determines attitudes, but levels of personal security and, perhaps, whether or not old people have offspring to worry about. For those older people who *do* have children seem different in their orientations. This should perhaps therefore be seen as the manifestation more of social commitment rather than of some inherent disposition – as assumed by the commentators quoted earlier. It may have been in recognition of this that David Pinker, a young architect working in the area, when asked about changes in family life, replied that, 'Family is a miserable institution.'

There are also sex differences involved, which relate to social commitments. More women than men are active parents and grandparents by virtue of becoming a parent earlier in life, living longer as grandparents and having lives which are more caught up in day-to-day family life once they become parents. Among our respondents, many complaints about Bangladeshis took the form of problems encountered at school or with social services by respondents' children. And women were far more forthcoming with such tales. There is accordingly definite overrepresentation of women among those displaying hostile attitudes, again borne out by details given in the appendix. This increases with age, suggesting that the effect of 'parenthood' not only occurs earlier for women, but is also stronger.

The influence of parenting on attitudes seems to apply whether or not children are living locally.[11] However, family ties are almost by definition a crucial basic component of local community sentiments, and it is in those cases where respondents have a wide range of family members living near by, with family and local community overlapping and intertwining, that we find the clearest differences between negative and positive attitudes to Bangladeshis. This emerges when we compare race-attitude data with our 'Local Family Network Density' index (LFND).* Those respondents with dense local

---

*This was a measure which we developed for counting the total numbers (and categories) of relatives which respondents had living locally. For a brief tabulation showing the relationship of various factors (such as local family network density) with racial hostility, see the appendix. Further data appear in the technical report for the ICS study on the Young Foundation website.

kinship networks recorded much more hostile attitudes. Once we had analysed the results, it came as no surprise to us to discover that the respondent who notched up the highest density score had declared himself to be a supporter of the British National Party.

So our measure of local family ties tallies closely with the extent to which respondents expressed hostility to Bangladeshi immigrants. Significantly, it is the strongest predictor of antagonism, and can be taken as the best indicator of the extent to which a subject feels concerned about others in the local community. In practice there, is of course, considerable overlap between age and having a dense kin network, as most of the people who score highly on hostility in this table are themselves locally born older people. But the LFND measure confirms that those older people who do *not* have current close family ties in the area are far more able to ignore the population changes taking place. So long as their immediate personal needs are met, those people with no local kin tend, in spite of age and place of birth, to be less concerned about the future well-being of others and less likely to resent the arrival of Bangladeshis.

Thus the type of person who turned out in the survey to be the most hostile of all to Bangladeshis was, to our initial surprise, the local granny – the archetypal East End 'Mum' and heroine of *Family and Kinship in East London* – with a busy extended family revolving around her. This does, however, make sense if inter-group hostility is the other side of group loyalty. And it all fits in with the pattern of complaints recorded. For it is Mum's life that will be diminished if her offspring do have to move out of the area, or that has become diminished because some of her offspring already have done so. And it is she who listens sympathetically to the stories her children and grandchildren bring home of how Bangladeshis are taking over the borough, who worries for them when they cannot seem to get flats locally, and who tries to put pressure on the housing office on their behalf. Unable to 'speak for' them effectively, Mum is largely confined now to grumbling with them and on their behalf.

So the Mums (and family elders as a whole) are the ones who remember with bitterness the promises made to local people at the end of the Second World War about rebuilding the East End (a better East End it was to be, too, in most people's recollection) for future generations to enjoy. Now they feel themselves strangers in their own land. It may be the memory of broken pledges like this, pledges from leaders to ordinary people who now feel forgotten and forsaken, which, more than personal pathologies, mould the shape of contemporary hostility and conflict.

War memorial in Cyprus Street, Bethnal Green, dressed for Armistice Day 2005.

Chapter 10

Promises and Betrayal

We can understand the hostility of white working-class Bethnal Greeners to Bangladeshis only by reference to their history, both before and after the Second World War, and to the impact of the war itself on their expectations. Throughout its history the East End of London had been at the bottom of the pile, on the margin of British society and excluded from mainstream opportunities.

Local people coped with this exclusion by turning inwards and cultivating a private view of their place in the world. One of the first outputs of the newly formed Institute of Community Studies in the 1950s was an article showing how local people maintained self-respect by inverting conventional ranking of occupations, valuing manual (and productive) labour highly and middle-class professions as unimportant or parasitical. Only the medical profession retained its position as an occupation of high esteem and value.[1] This helped to counter received definitions, which – justifiably or otherwise – saw the East End community as dependent on help from outside which they had neither earned nor deserved. Such enforced dependency helps explain why local political culture has found the idea of charity so distasteful. It abhorred the Poor Law, and wherever possible has emphasised community self-help and independence. Early socialist action around the beginning of the twentieth century by Keir Hardie and his supporters and fellow radicals was built on ideas of the dignity of manual labour and the value of mutual-aid associations.

This moral resistance did not break the cycle, though. What eventually undermined the low national valuation of East Enders most emphatically, and lifted the yoke of collective indebtedness, was the Second World War and the crucial part played by the docks during the war in maintaining the links between the metropolis and the rest of the British Empire, and in supplying forces overseas. So the work done at this time in the East End was not merely important to the nation. It became *critically* so. Traditional polarisations between City and East End, gent and cockney, nation and outcasts, were thrown out of balance by this moment of collective peril and moral unity.

Their Finest Hour

I'm glad that we [Buckingham Palace] have been bombed. It makes me feel I can look the East End in the face. (Queen Elizabeth, 1942)

The significance of the Second World War lay in the way that it gave East Enders the chance to prove their loyalty and worth. Britain had not been invaded for nearly 900 years.[2] There had been threats at times during that period: the Armada; Napoleon; some limited air raids during the First World War. But these were as nothing compared with the war that was to come. The massive requirements of the military machine added to the effects of enemy naval blockades caused enormous disruption to the economy. A German invasion was a real danger and, above all, advances in aerial warfare meant that civilians were now directly in the line of fire and suffered many casualties. Indeed, during the first three years of war there were more British civilians killed than soldiers.[3] In this 'total war' the home front was as important as the field of battle, and the resulting sense of national unity achieved was strong and evident to everyone involved.

One of us wrote a short book early in the war about the bombing and its implications for civil defence and welfare services. The severity of the experience was a powerful factor prompting greater centralisation of public administration:

Cities have been besieged and laid waste in earlier wars ... But never before has a great world centre, whose population runs into many millions, been subjected to destructive bombing raids – by day and by night – over a long period of time ... Never before have so many human beings, living together in a relatively small space, been called upon to adjust their ways of life so fundamentally, in so short a space of time, as the people of Greater London in the winter of 1940 ... The part played by its civil population in the defence of their homes and their workplaces is an expression of a conception of public service which must surely find a permanent place in our national life.[4]

East London was a focal point of this heightened sense of national solidarity. From the outset of British participation in war the docks were the prime target of German aerial bombardment. The first and last German flying-bomb strikes on London were in the docklands. The main force of the Blitz and the heaviest bombing throughout the war as a whole were concentrated within a few miles of the docks. The greatest damage to civilian life and property, wartime displacement of population and, when it came to it, permanent disruption of local community life was sustained in this area, with the population in 1950 less than half that in 1939. This was where national suffering was hardest, and the place that people elsewhere in Britain first thought of when contemplating the effort and the sacrifices being made by civilians.

The lives of all older East Enders were changed by the war, and there are memorials to wartime events throughout the area. These include a prominent plaque at the entrance to the Bethnal Green underground station, a hundred yards from the ICS office, reminding visitors going down the steps where they are.

Site of the worst civilian disaster of the Second World War.
In memory of 173 men, women and children
who lost their lives on the evening of Wednesday 3rd March 1943
descending these steps to Bethnal Green Underground Air Raid Shelter.
Not forgotten.

One of our oldest informants, Leah Brodski, narrowly escaped being part of this toll. Her family was sitting in mourning for her mother, who had died of natural causes a few days earlier, when they heard what she thought was an air-raid warning:

> I said to my sister Sarah, 'What are we going to do?' 'Into the street,' she said, and then 'Let's go to the tube.' 'Come on, then,' I says. We just managed to get a few steps and then the bombs started raining down. I said, 'We'll have to go into the street shelter instead!' We would have had it if we had gone on. We would have been killed. Hundreds of people were trampled to death trying to get into the tube that day.

Joyce Darty was a teenager at the time of the war. She saw many people killed in the Blitz, and lost some close relatives:

> There used to be a building at the top of Turin Street where a lot of market people lived. A land mine fell there and I had some relatives who got killed there. One of my uncles who was down there worked for the Water Board. They only recognised him by his uniform, because he had no head on.

Her future husband, Harry, lost seven relatives in the Bethnal Green tube disaster. But people had to keep going, and learned to live with it:

> You heard the bombs and you used to sit in the shelter and pray that things were going to be all right. We used to take our bedding down and then you came out in the morning and you didn't know if there were any houses left. It was a terrible thing to think you're walking home to see if you have a home *left* ... A lot of people used to feel safe under the staircase and in the coal cupboard, because the stairs was always left standing after a raid ... People used to go under the table, 'n' all ... When my sister was getting married one went off in the afternoon and we all got under the table.

Ordinary family life was impossible:

> My sister got married in March 1940. By six o'clock on the wedding night her husband had gone off to war. He went off in the army and then abroad to Burma. He went off with nice fair hair and came back with grey hair. She never saw him for five years, and while he was gone she was working on the railway driving a horse and cart.

This intense involvement at the front line of national endeavour made the war a mixed experience for east Londoners. They endured great hardship, but to many ordinary people in the area it was their finest hour. For once in their lives they were valued, even heroes. Joyce Darty still remembers how uplifted they all felt when victory was declared:

> We all felt so proud. Most people were just crying, and there were parties everywhere. We all went down to a pub in Hoxton where my husband-to-be's family lived, and everybody at the party was shouting for pink gins.

Local contribution to victory marked a tremendous national enhancement to the reputation of a community accustomed to being bottom of the pile. Only a few years before the onset of war even the local elite of men who were lucky enough to have jobs in the docks had been regarded by the rest of the country as political pariahs and national traitors on account of their part in the General Strike and, later, their support for Oswald Mosley's British Union of Fascists. But with war all that was quickly forgotten. The gatekeepers to imperial trade were transformed into the defenders of Britain's economic lifelines and the ultimate saviours of freedom and civilisation. This was spelt out in the Port of London Authority's monthly magazine towards the end of the war (April 1945), in a feature widely reported and telling local people what they already knew.

Target No. 1 for the Luftwaffe

> German broadcasts during the height of the Battle of Britain ... leave no doubt that the German High Command regarded London in general, and the London docks in particular, as the focal point of attack against the British Empire, then the last barrier between Germany and world domination.

This status as national (and imperial) saviours, and as symbols of resistance to evil, had grown as the war progressed. It was referred to constantly by public speakers in the area. During the war members of the royal family made numerous visits to the East End, and this helped to foster the remarkable degree of patriotism which was later displayed at the Coronation of Elizabeth II in 1953. It was a case of mutual admiration. East Enders admired the royals, and believed that the royals could see their value.* Towards the end of the war this was confirmed by the promptness of the royal visit by George VI and his consort together with the Princesses Elizabeth and Margaret Rose to the survivors of a massive V2 rocket attack which had devastated the bottom end of Vallance Road – the last German air strike before surrender – at which everyone joined in singing 'There'll Always Be an England'.†

---

*The *Evening Standard* noted in 1999, at the unveiling by the Queen Mother at St Paul's Cathedral of a memorial to the London civilians killed in the bombing, that '[The Queen Mother's] many visits to the sites of the worst bombings in the East End won her a special place in the hearts of Londoners.' Langley, 1999.

†This choice of tribute contained some unintentional irony, in view of the East End's historical attitude to the Jews. Of the 130 people killed by the V2 rocket, some 120 were Jewish, including journalist Jonathan Freedland's grandmother (Freedland, 2005).

The Promised Land

Local people therefore saw the Labour victory at the 1945 general election as something that they had achieved and earned for themselves (and their ilk) rather than received from on high as yet more 'charity'. From where they were standing, the welfare state that the Labour government created was a reward for effort during a war in which they had visibly been heroes themselves. Moreover, the agent for securing that just reward, the Labour government, was itself a product of East End will, principles and endeavour. To them, the new regime meant that they were now appreciated. Deputy wartime leader Clement Attlee, speaking in his own Limehouse constituency in the heart of docklands in February 1945, endorsed the pledge by indicating that the 'haves' in the nation were now ready to share their wealth with those who had fought and suffered alongside them.

> Lots of people have come to me and said, 'I have been a Conservative all my life but I am changing now. I have seen the nation come first in war, and I want to see it come first in peace.'[5]

A few years of sacrifice and suffering appeared to have freed East Enders from centuries of moral servitude, and dissolved class barriers. State-managed social security would be a *right*, rather than a gift from superiors carrying the stigma of dependence. War had demonstrated the mutual dependence that all citizens had on each other. The welfare state would carry this over into peace, too. Significantly, there were many promises made that a high priority would be given to reconstruction of the bombed housing stock in east London. This would be as replacement for lost dwellings, and fulfilment of outstanding pre-war housing improvement schemes. But above all it was part of the general building of a better society on the ruins of the old which the British people had a right to expect as the end of the war came into sight.

The initial lowliness of their position, plus their key role in the national effort, encouraged many East Enders to think that a better society really was on the way. They had played a disproportionate part in winning the war, so they could expect something special in return. And, indeed, many of the rewards to the nation, including valuable entitlements to benefits unknown before, were launched in the East End. With hindsight it is easy to see that this was partly to do with easy access to and from Westminster, just a few stops down the District Line from Aldgate East. But it was also symbolic of east London's role, and reflected the high regard in which the nation held it. And it expressed the strong position of East End MPs in the post-war government – no coincidence itself. The member for Limehouse, Attlee, was prime minister, Ernest Bevin, former (and formerly anti-national) leader of the London dockers, was foreign secretary, and the 'Cockney Socialist', Herbert Morrison, who had masterminded the 1945 Labour manifesto, was chief architect for building the post-war welfare state. The place and its party arrived in tandem.

The symbolism shows up clearly in the launching of a new benefit: the family allowance. Wartime coping and suffering by civilian families, predominantly mothers with children, had helped to underline the mutualist case for the state to organise financial support for raising children, and for mothers themselves to receive these funds. Motherhood was specifically mentioned as a valuable contribution to the nation. The principal architect of the welfare state, William Beveridge, spoke about this in the East End while campaigning for the Liberals in the 1945 election, and Eleanor Rathbone, on whose insistence state payments were made to direct to mothers, had worked tirelessly in the East End while formulating her philosophy.*

Thus the first payment of a family allowance was staged in the heart of Stepney. As the doors of Commercial Road Post Office opened the person at the head of the queue, Mrs May Ann Hall, was flattered to be greeted by James Griffiths, Minister of National Insurance, his wife, and a posse of BBC sound engineers and cameramen who were recording the event for overseas broadcasting and posterity. When she received her money, she was invited to make a 'spontaneous' statement on behalf of mothers:

> Speaking as a mother of four, I realise what a very great help this will be to the mothers of the country.

Mr Griffiths duly replied:

> This is an historic day for it is the occasion of the first family pay day in our history. The family allowance represents an investment by the nation in the children of today – the citizens of tomorrow. *It is appropriate we should mark it in this bomb-scarred Stepney, where mothers proved their steadfastness through six years of war.* (emphasis added).[6]

Likewise, special efforts were made to arrange that the first new permanent dwellings to be completed in London after the war were constructed in Stepney. The first block to be erected, West India House, was opened in December 1946 by Attlee, the local MP and PM, who spoke to those attending about local feelings:

> The people in Stepney did not like having to leave the borough. He remembered how, when the bombs were falling, people came to him and said 'This is the third time that I have been bombed out. Hitler has tried to drive me out of Stepney. He is not going to succeed.' That spirit was going to help in the building of the new Stepney.[†]

---

*And is remembered locally in a street named after her on the Keir Hardie estate in West Ham, just outside Tower Hamlets. See also chapter 5 above.

†The link between housing, war and moral reparation had already been made in Poplar before the end of the war, through the use of German prisoners of war to clear land where short-term prefabricated dwellings were to be located, and to help in their erection. Report in *East London Advertiser*, 6 December 1946.

And in the same month the Minister of Transport, Alfred Barnes, opened the Central Line extension from Liverpool Street to Stratford:

> Addressing the gathering, Mr Barnes said that it was gratifying to see the new Tube projection spreading out towards the East, and that the population of East London who suffered in the grim conflict should be some of the first to benefit by the important new transport facilities.[7]

This achievement had been possible only because building work had started before the war. Indeed, the semi-completed Bethnal Green tube station had already played a valuable – if also tragic – wartime role as air-raid shelter. The association added to the sense that building the new society was a return on the war effort of the working class. Although poorly regarded and shabbily treated in the thirties, they had shown their loyalty and grit in the dark days when it mattered.

After the war Britain rewarded itself with a settlement which bridged ancient divisions and offered the prospect of sustained social justice. As historian Peter Hennessy has noted, war was followed by a period of unprecedented optimism.

> Britain had never – and still hasn't – experienced a progressive phase to match 1945–51. It is largely, though not wholly, the achievement of these years – and the wartime experience, the crucial platform on which those advances were built – that 1951 Britain, certainly compared to the UK of 1931 or any previous decade, was a kinder, gentler and a far, far better place in which to be born, to grow up, to live, love, work and even to die.[8]

Nowhere was the sense of optimism sharper or the reward more warmly appreciated than among East Enders. Having arrived at the party as Cinderella they had left as the princess. There was a widespread conviction locally that the just war against Hitler's total evil, in which east London had played such an important role, had triggered a thorough reconstruction not only of British and European society, but of the whole world order. In the afterglow of victory the East End enjoyed a remarkable lightening of spirit. It was more included in the British nation, and its constituent elements were more united with each other. This was the historical context for the tremendous vitality and local solidarity that was visible in the street parties held on VE Day and a few years later at the coronation, and which was still evident when *Family and Kinship* was written. A few years earlier, Michael Young and Edward Shils had written, 'The central fact is that Britain came into the coronation period with a degree of moral consensus such as few societies have ever manifested.'[9] We would add that this coincided with the period of research for *Family and Kinship* and is reflected in the findings of that book.

What also must be emphasised is that this party time was also a Labour Party time. Because of the war, and not least through the importance of east London's war effort, the political party which was so triumphant in the area was able to upgrade itself into a truly national governing party. This was an important ingredient in local celebration, for now the boot was on a foot that could be trusted. Promises were being made which could be relied on, and the conviction that the just war against Hitler had been the catalyst for a new social order was surely grounded.

Giving the East End a Voice

Post-war East Enders may have overestimated their own contribution to history, and expected too much in return, but if this was a myth it was one in which the Labour Party willingly colluded. Labour had much to gain from identifying itself with its East End constituents and using them as a symbolic representation of the working class. There were mutual benefits to Labour and east Londoners in collaborating to announce the imminent building there of a New Jerusalem. East London needed a Labour government to guarantee that the working class was fully admitted to the nation. But Labour also needed the East End, with its heroic working-class images of war, in order to transform itself into a governing party with a mandate to overhaul British social institutions.

Identifying with east Londoners helped the Labour Party to strengthen a characteristic necessary to overcome suspicions towards it in the country at large: visible patriotism. Until the declaration of war against Hitler, senior figures in the party had often appeared to lack full commitment to the nation.[10] Ramsay MacDonald, who became the first Labour prime minister in 1924, had been widely regarded as an internationalist following a Soviet agenda.[11] Domestically too the party seemed shackled to the sectional interests of the Trades Union Congress. Even its participation in government in the inter-war years had an aura of class co-option to power, in order to help keep the unions in control, rather than of recognition of fitness to lead the country as a whole. This image changed during the war, when 'the patriots became unexpectedly left-wing [and] the left became unexpectedly patriotic'.[12]

The party's tie with the East End was a factor helping it to surmount this limitation – with Clement Attlee, Labour's first non-working-class leader and the party's great pragmatist, presiding quietly over an alliance between socialist principles and popular nationalism. Attlee was an Independent Labour Party idealist when he first settled in Stepney, but as the elected mayor he learned to tap into popular sentiment, and quickly developed a skill in harmonising local interests with universal principles. His personal support for the war against Hitler (initially assisted by internationalist hostility to fascism) made it easy for Churchill to give him a role in the war cabinet as deputy leader. And once installed there his role as domestic leader, while Churchill concentrated on foreign affairs, allowed him to begin stitching together the new welfare state even while the beleaguered population was still earning it.

Throughout the course of the war Attlee delivered frequent speeches in and around his docklands constituency, expressing gratitude to patriotic cockneys. The national legitimacy which east Londoners were accumulating, both in and out of uniform, rubbed off on the Labour Party itself. Long before the end of the war Labour had become the party that ordinary people could rely on not to forget their service to their country. In the 1945 election campaign Dan Frankel, the incumbent Mile End Labour MP, always referred to Mr Attlee as Major Attlee. Labour went on to achieve its first ever overall majority in the Commons, with a good spread of class backgrounds among its MPs, and was effectively freed for the first time from TUC control. It settled into its first period of real power with the East End apparently holding the reins.

This public demonstration of the changing face of Britain encouraged east Londoners to believe all the more in their own heroic destiny, at the point of overlap of all of the progressive interests of the era. Clement Attlee understood this well. He summed up the local feeling the following year when unveiling a memorial in Limehouse to George Lansbury – a local working-class lad who had been party leader before him, when Labour had not enjoyed such broad support in the country as a whole. The chairman of the memorial committee said of Lansbury that he

> was a dear son of the East End of London. He lived and served its people. He believed in the common people and he once wrote that if ever the world was to be redeemed from the curse of war, it would not be by those who claimed superiority of education, but by the myriads who out of their poverty had seen the light of freedom.[13]

Clement Attlee rounded this off by adding that Lansbury 'was a great East Londoner, a great Englishman and a great citizen of the world'.[14] At that moment the interests of east London and the Labour Party seemed universal and indivisible. Symbolically, when Labour began to deliver on its promise to rebuild the East End, the first new estate was named Lansbury.

The Dream Fades

> I think that they will keep on being heroes, but when the war is over they will demand the rewards of heroism: they will expect to get them very soon and no power on earth will be able to rebuild the houses at the speed that will be necessary. (Lord Woolton, speaking in 1940)[15]

High hopes soon led to disappointment. As time passed, it began to dawn on local people that the new government had many other things to do than rebuild the East End. Even if East Enders lived in a promised land, they might not be the chosen people.

Fear surfaced quite early on that the government was more concerned about foreign affairs and alliances than with the needs of ordinary people. In a scenario which almost anticipates contemporary Britain, the foreign secretary Ernest Bevin was portrayed by journalists as a captive of the US and Marshall Plan. Closer to home, MP Alderman C. W. Key, a junior minister, had difficulty as early as 1946 in explaining bread rationing to a meeting of his Bow constituents. 'When Ald. Key asked if there was anyone present who thought it was wrong for us to help the starving people in Europe (by diverting wheat), a woman in the audience jumped up and shouted that it was the British people who should be fed first.' Alderman Key tried to explain that people in depressed parts of Britain were getting more calories than they had before the war. But, 'at this point the interference from people shouting questions to the speaker almost drowned his voice, and the chairman once again called the meeting to order'. Shortly after that the minister had to leave for an important meeting in Westminster.[16]

There was also local impatience with the slow pace of house-building. After completion of a few high-profile projects, construction work slowed down, ostensibly because of shortages in materials. In 1943, the London County Council had published the *County of London Plan*, written by their chief architect-planner, J. H. Forshaw, and Professor Patrick Abercrombie, the most distinguished planner of his day. It opened with an extraordinary frontispiece showing a bombed East End street, the people's sticks of furniture loaded on to a truck. In front, children stare at the camera accusingly. There is a quotation from Churchill:

> Most painful is the number of small houses inhabited by working folk which have been destroyed ... We will rebuild them, more to our credit than some of them were before. London, Liverpool, Manchester, Birmingham may have much more to suffer, but they will rise from their ruins, more healthy, and, I hope, more beautiful ... In all my life I have never been treated with so much kindness as by the people who suffered most.[17]

Plans had been drawn up as early as 1935 to rebuild 700 acres of Stepney, Shoreditch and Bethnal Green, in a corridor a mile and three-quarters long and three-quarters of a mile wide between the London Docks and the Regents Canal.[18] Here the need for slum clearance was exacerbated by extensive war damage. Abercrombie and Forshaw recognised that, 'There is abundant evidence ... that for families with children, houses are preferred to flats. They provide a private garden and yard at the same level as the main rooms of the dwelling, and fit the English temperament.'[19] But the area was too small; if only houses were to be built (and *not* overcrowded), then two-thirds or three-quarters of the people would have to move out. The planners would have liked half houses, half flats, at 100 dwellings to the acre, but even this would have created a major overspill problem. So they compromised at 136 dwellings per acre, putting one-third in houses, two-thirds in eight- and ten-storey flats; half of the families with two or more children would have to go into flats, but even then almost four in ten of those families would have to leave.[20]

All this was embodied into the LCC's statutory development plan in 1951. This showed a huge area of Stepney and Poplar – nearly two square miles – as a comprehensive development area for clearance and rebuilding at the agreed dwelling density of 136 per acre, of which one-third were houses and the rest flats. But because many of the pre-war inhabitants had not returned as anticipated, the scale of the overspill problem was less: 81,000 households would need rehousing, only 71,000 homes were available, so 10,000 would need to go elsewhere. *Family and Kinship*, published a little later, was essentially an attack on this bulldozer approach to planning, with a demand that East Enders be left in the houses and streets they knew. It was an argument that would become all-persuasive a decade or so later, in 1968, when a gas explosion in neighbouring Newham caused the partial collapse of a new high-rise block, Ronan Point, killing four people and injuring more. Soon after, government housing policy shifted to one of rehabilitation. But by then, much of the old East End had gone for ever.

Meanwhile the price that the Labour government was being obliged to pay to secure for Britain an honourable role in the United Nations and new world order involved making commitments that would soon come to be regarded by many ordinary people as compromising national interests.[21] Thus the 1948 British Nationality Act, which was formulated under pressure from the US (see p. 205), could be seen as turning relations within the British Empire upside down. By clarifying and codifying UK residence rights of all citizens of British colonies, it confirmed the entitlement of quite a large chunk of the world's poor to share in the nation's wealth. The metropolitan working class had been struggling for generations to achieve this for itself, and had finally laid claim to it only by enduring the ordeal of the Blitz. Many of them would not be amused when they found that the national club they had fought long and hard to join had been, as it seemed to them, so easily opened up for the benefit of indigent outsiders. The springs of future conflict were being wound up.

End of Empire

Local implications of the changing nature of empire did not start to become apparent until the accelerating tide of immigration was sucked in by labour shortages during the great boom of the late 1950s presided over by Harold Macmillan's Conservative government. This drew public attention to the fact that immigrants popularly regarded as aliens were fully equal to everyone else in law as British citizens. As a result, the politics of race, which have played such a prominent role nationally since the late fifties and sixties, erupted in Britain. But, at least to start with, this was not simply about objections to immigrants because of their race or colour. Essentially it revolved around the right of Commonwealth citizens to live in the UK with full citizenship entitlements. And it was this that the conflicts of the sixties and seventies reworked. The various acts restricting immigration constructed new categories of British citizenship, which graded access to rights of UK residence and state benefits to reflect degrees of connectedness to Britain.

East Enders undoubtedly shared in what the political columnist Polly Toynbee has described as implicit racism,[22] but in the early post-war years before mass migration this sentiment was still compatible with positive attitudes towards imperial and Commonwealth citizens. The front page of the *East London Advertiser* on 21 April 1950 carried a feature (with photograph) which in retrospect seems quite extraordinary: a poignant relic from an age of innocence. It concerns the visit to a Stepney cinema, the Troxy in Commercial Road, of a party of Pakistani nurses during a trip to Britain. The programme of films was interrupted so that they could be taken up onto the stage and presented to the audience, who are reported as warmly applauding the visitors. It is ironic that such early cordiality may have encouraged citizens of the subcontinent to consider migrating here.

Attitudes quickly hardened as the flow of immigrants increased during the fifties, especially in workplaces where white people feared the consequences for wage rates. Resistance to post-war immigration first took to the streets in the late nineteen-fifties. The reaction was particularly strong in east London, around docklands, where after the war popular expectation of rewards from a grateful nation had been so high. Local people assumed that Labour would, or *should*, be on their side, but in reality the Labour Party hierarchy, as the architects of the 1948 British Nationality Act, were strongly opposed to the Conservative proposals to limit the settlement rights of colonial and Commonwealth citizens in the UK.

In parliament Labour opposition to restrictions was weakened by the fact that the most overt hostility towards immigration was found among working-class voters, who still provided the backbone of party support at this time. Several Labour MPs braved the antagonism of their constituents towards immigration (which most had immediately branded as racist and irrational) by speaking against Tory proposals. Then Walter Edwards, MP for Stepney and a former Civil Lord of the Admiralty under Attlee, and still sitting on one of the largest majorities in the Commons, brushed aside the scorn of fellow MPs and came out in favour of restrictions. There were, of course, special local factors that could be cited in east London. Nationalist political sentiments could feed on the history of immigration in the area, and some East End immigrants had been linked with high-profile prostitution rackets. In spite of these specific considerations, Mr Edwards' views were seized on gratefully by the Conservatives as revealing true working-class sentiments in the country. This compromised Labour opposition, and assisted the passage of the first Commonwealth Immigrants Act, 1962, which restricted entry into Britain to those born in Britain, or who held a British passport or labour voucher.[23]

The small amount of post-war immigration which had occurred in the East End was in fact rather different in character from that taking place in most of the country. It revolved around the docks, which for centuries had had an international character, and took the form of colonial seamen using the new welfare rights available under the British Nationality Act to extend their land-based lives and ease their settlement. Activity centred around dockland 'café society' in the Cable Street area of Stepney, where Michael Banton carried out his pioneering work on British race relations.[24] By the end of the 1950s the new social order developing there was attracting interest among different sectors of British society. George Foulser wrote in celebration of the social integration he witnessed in 1960, in an article from which we quote at some length:[25]

> Until a decade ago, Cablestrasse ['as the cognoscenti know it'] was rather a quiet place as waterfronts go. The pubs were pretty lively, of course ... [but] not long after the pubs closed, Cablestrasse would be more or less asleep.
>
> Cablestrasse has acquired a new character nowadays. Almost all the tailors have cleared out. Their shops have become cafes, many of which cater for a particular race, forming a part of present-day Cablestrasse and helping to create the new atmosphere of the district. Cafes which cater for Maltese (from Malta) and cafes which welcome Maltese (from Gozo) are there; cafes for Somalis, Arabs, Indians, Pakistanis, West Africans, West Indians, cafes for whites, cafes for everybody, all-night cafes. I used to frequent one of the all-night cafes with a friend and ship-mate of mine, a Negro Cockney ...
>
> The present-day inhabitants of Cablestrasse are about the most racially mixed crowd of people in Britain, bar the people of Tiger Bay in Cardiff. The exotic new blood began arriving not long after the war. It took a while to settle down. With so many different races in that small area, some friction was inevitable, and for a period Cablestrasse was a dangerous place at night. Fights and murders took place. Seamen were beaten up and robbed almost every night ... [But] There is one thing about present-day Cablestrasse. You will not be molested in any way, as long as you mind your own business ...
>
> There is a team of men, once seamen but now all drinkers of methylated and surgical spirits, in the Cablestrasse area. Some time ago, they solved their housing problem by a pretty unorthodox squatting operation. They entered a derelict churchyard a few hundred yards from Cablestrasse and established squatters' rights in a vault. They tidied the place up by slinging a couple of worm-eaten coffins into the grassy undergrowth outside the vault. Inside five minutes they were settled in, and their house-warming party was in full blast.
>
> They all draw National Assistance. As a homeless person cannot obtain National Assistance an address is necessary. Somehow the Assistance Board accepted the vault as the permanent address.

Local (white) residents objected vociferously to the all-night gambling, and vice.[26] But progressives such as Foulser regarded the lifestyle as a model for the future:

> The Cablestrasse folk are different races, outlooks, upbringing, religion, occupation, and so on. Yet they mix socially as Cablestrasse citizens, with every man amiably disposed towards his neighbour. Even the vault-dwellers are not discriminated against, as long as they are not charged-up and performing. There seems a kind of bond among the people [except between the Maltese from Malta and those from Gozo] ...
>
> Most of Cablestrasse's one-time residents have moved out. The few that have remained have become a part of the new social structure. Usually they are regarded as doyens of the Cablestrasse; as being pioneers in some way or other ...
>
> It's a place with an atmosphere of its own, a combination of British and overseas traditions. From all over the world people have travelled to settle in Cablestrasse; to live and

work together as peaceful fellow-citizens. They are an object-lesson in living for other people everywhere. Long live Cablestrasse.

In retrospect this vision stands out as a clear portent of things to come. The British Empire was coming home, and this was something that could be celebrated in the libertarian sectors of British society. But for the ordinary people living at the point of entry, whose established lives would be directly influenced by settlement, it presented a challenge to their own newly won admission to the nation.

New housing and new offices on the Isle of Dogs.

Chapter 11

Managing Diversity

One way of understanding the overall process of Bangladeshi settlement in the East End, and local reactions to it, is to look at it in the context of Britain's imperial past. Until the Second World War all classes within the metropolitan nation profited together from empire, whether they were aware of it or not. Although East Enders were at the bottom of British society, they were still better off than people in dependent colonies. This gave them a stake in the system and, in some cases, a sense of superiority, which helped to make them loyal British citizens. The generations of East Enders who worked in or near London's docks would have had constant reminders of their position at the heart of the gigantic imperial machine. During the war the idea of defending the whole empire helped unite the classes and nationalities, and in the post-war settlement it was anticipation of sharing more evenly in this national birthright which gave the period such a golden glow.

However, the subsequent transformation of empire soon rendered this compact unsustainable. According to Corelli Barnett's account, one price that the US exacted for its own participation in the war, and for funding post-war reconstruction in Europe, was a dismantling of European external empires and opening up of their possessions to American trade.[1] So in the decades after the war Britain was granting independence to former colonies and at the same time extending to former subjects the right to British citizenship and residence.[2] The immigration which followed brought members of the imperial population to the metropolis, and this represented a loss of position for lower-class indigenous Britons living in the cities. Poor migrants moving into urban localities were not simply competitors but more needy competitors. As the empire was breaking up, the recognition was growing that exploitation was inherent in a centuries-old domination based on an hierarchical administrative structure. At various times social policymakers have appeared to attend particularly to the needs of immigrants, not just as the most needy but as subjects of Britain's long-exploited colonies. In addition to ruling out any claims for special treatment by the indigenous poor, this has entailed steering the development of welfare in ways which do not appear to penalise migrants. Promoting the greater use of means testing, and targeting benefits towards the poorest and most vulnerable, has ensured that the rights of newcomers were strengthened vis-à-vis those of the indigenous poor, so long as the newcomers remained the more needy, as they so often did.

The evolution of this new class and race structure had produced three main social groupings in the East End by the time of our research. Firstly, there are remnants of the old working class which has been displaced from its former supremacy. Locally it used to dominate the area, and still has strong attachments to it. Although in 2001 it still just about constituted the largest sector of the population, it possesses reduced legitimacy for its own specific interests.

Bangladeshi newcomers occupy a contrary position, in that while they are a minority of the adult population, the intensity of their needs has to be given priority, and this may compensate for their lack of numbers. At the same time they still retain strong attachments elsewhere, especially in their country of origin. So their stake in the inner city may not be such a large part of their identity or social capital as it is for white residents.

These two groups are in direct competition for local resources and services, and the existence of a third group holding the balance between them has exacerbated the competition but has also made rapid and extensive Bangladeshi settlement easier. This third group are the middle-class newcomers belonging to a local affluent elite. They do not compete much for local social services, as they tend to be young, often childless and uncommitted to the neighbourhood. Many now live and work locally but pursue leisure activities elsewhere. Others have something of an ideological commitment to the locality and its multi-cultural image. They are more cosmopolitan in their outlook, and it is their political action and intervention – including in support of the migrants – which provides the key to understanding how current East End society operates. The urban elite rules over the other two by standing above both of them to keep the peace. And the strategies they adopt in maintaining balance and control give the emerging social structure within Britain itself a somewhat imperial character.

Conflicting Values

At the level of values, there is an alliance between middle-class newcomers and migrants revolving around commitment to universalist principles of social security, based on need. There is an open disjuncture here with the values of white Bethnal Greeners, certainly of older residents, which reinforces the opposition of the latter to further immigration. Few local whites would, for example, deny that Bangladeshis endure greater real poverty than themselves. What they object to is the way that this need is allowed to override rights and claims arising out of an earlier, more directly *exchange*-based welfare state ethic. It is this which undermines whites' own position, and their trust in government.

As described in chapters 5 and 10, the welfare system built on the post-war class compact was seen as both legitimate and properly respectful of working-class tradition precisely because it incorporated working-class notions of mutual aid within and between families – in which help received when needed is balanced out by that given when it can be afforded. Contributory pensions and national insurance were seen to carry this principle to the state level – and their continuing popularity to this day nationally, especially among older people, still reflects this.[3] New minorities' claims to welfare are, in part at least, resented not because the recipients are black or supposedly inferior per se, but because minorities represent a large and visible part of the something-for-nothing society, in which rights to receive support have manifestly overtaken reciprocal obligations to make contributions. As newcomers, their families cannot have put much into the system, so they should not be expecting yet to take so much out. The old mutualist morality was based on the needs and efforts of families, not just individuals.

Thus a comment often made to us, in one form or another, was that Bangladeshis were not like earlier minorities, who had expected to work their collective passage to full citizenship and its rewards:

> It's hard that they come here and are right away getting these places, handouts, beds delivered to their flats. When the black immigrants came here they had to work for what they got, do all the rough jobs. (*Retired market trader*)

> The older groups of immigrants ran businesses. But the new immigrants are just all spongers. (*Wife of retired book-keeper*)

One Pakistani (a recent immigrant but non-Bangladeshi) informant said that no other groups had been 'mollycoddled' like the Bangladeshis had been. The general moral point here is that Bangladeshis were unlike other minorities in that they had not (yet) contributed much to British society. These remarks are, of course, flawed by a misconception. The original male Bangladeshi migrants did indeed do precisely the same kind of poorly paid and arduous work that other immigrant groups have done, many of them for several decades before bringing their families to the UK. It is an unfortunate consequence of the pattern described earlier of initial male immigration, and their earlier all-but-invisible participation in work and housing, that so few of our white informants realised the extent of Bangladeshi men's long-term contribution to the economy. The sorts of things that respondents said on this issue were:

> [An Asian squatter] moved in with two children. Now he's got six and he's never done a day's work. Why should he when he gets £200 for doing nothing? He was putting in for a car licence when he was up at the Post Office last week. (Mrs Marks)

> They give Asians more preference in this borough than white people who've lived here for years and their sons and daughters ... I don't think the council considers them, especially after their parents have worked in the borough all their lives ... (*Widow with local daughters*)

> They often give the Bangladeshis preference over us who have lived, and our families lived, in this country – whereas what have they ever done for this country that they should be given preference over us? (*School cleaner, with son in Essex*)

I get annoyed with all the coloured groups using our country when they cannot run their own. They get too much help from services compared to us. There are lots of incidents where it's so unfair. Why should we pay for them? They do not contribute to our country at all. (*Retired soldier*)

Effectively, many Bangladeshis appeared to be getting something for nothing, and to 'think that the country owed them a living':

I have no help, no home help, nothing financial or anything else. I worked several days a week all my life for my old age, and I'd have been better off spending it. I'm not benefiting one bit. Ninety per cent of Asians get what they can out of the state. I worked all my life; I didn't work for anything. I don't get anything. They get everything. They put nothing in. (Mrs Marks)

It is essential, though, to notice here that this type of complaint was not directed solely at Bangladeshis. According to many informants, the way in which the government now manages the welfare system means that working people are paying taxes to support others who are happy to do nothing but take. Many such claimants are migrants, and even white people friendly with individual migrants felt that some such entitlements were wrong:

I had an Asian boyfriend – but he came from Essex, from my school, from a different class [from those in Tower Hamlets]. I think it is terrible the way people feel about Asians, but I can see how they feel. It's too easy for people to get benefits who just come into the country. There are people who do a good day's work and they're really annoyed that they're living honestly, and someone else is just getting the benefits. Of course it's not just the Asians, but you see more of it there, there's such a concentration. (*Single young woman working in post office*)

However, most of the respondents hostile to immigrants were no less condemning of white people – especially never-married single mothers, bogus disablement-allowance claimants or long-term able-bodied unemployed and so on – whom they considered to be debasing the welfare system and generally 'living off' it.

So behind the anger at Bangladeshis there was also a more general dismay at the way that British society appeared to be changing. The evolution of the welfare state had turned it from a mutual-aid society writ large, as it seemed at first, into a complex, centralised and bureaucratic system run by middle-class do-gooders who gave generously to those who put nothing into the pot while making ordinary working people who *did* contribute feel like recipients of charity when drawing their own entitlements. Although this has occurred since the arrival of post-war immigrants, few respondents saw the immigrants as being at fault. It was more that the whole moral order had become inverted by the emphasis placed by the state on individual *need*. For if what one gets out of the state is determined by need, rather than by what one has put into it, then dignity has been taken out of citizenship. Dependency is encouraged, the principle of reciprocity has gone, and welfare has simply become a new form of charity. A parody of the Poor Laws was being enacted, with the administration of benefits effectively reminding the lower orders of their dependent place. To these forgotten heroes, it was almost as if they had actually *lost* the war, because the supposed prize of a moral world order has turned to dust.

Modernising the Bangladeshis

This conflict of values between the old working class and the new urban left has often been noted. What is less often appreciated is that many ordinary (that is, non-political) Bangladeshis are in sympathy with the old working-class attitudes. However, the alliance with middle-class patrons (and especially servants of the state) which enabled rapid settlement to take place required a commitment by Bangladeshis to the dominant, universalist view of welfare state provisions. Bangladeshis have collectively accepted this, in order to get the benefits. But it runs against the grain of traditional Bangladeshi morality. Although these values take a more explicitly religious form than those of the old British working class, they are not unlike them in their content – including their focus on the importance of self-reliance and reciprocity. In order to join with the British left in modernising the East End, Bangladeshis have first had to modernise themselves.

As Shohel and others explained to us, in Bangladeshi culture the core of mutual support is provided within the extended family, where moral obligations to give help are seen as overriding, and as not creating any specific debts. A gift or service received creates a moral debt, which if left unpaid produces a relationship of inequality.[4] Within the family such an obligation can be repaid in a variety of ways, including by returning respect to the donor. In Bangladesh larger kin-groupings tend to play the supportive role that neighbours formerly did in Bethnal Green, but apart from that the patterning of support is more similar, with wider community support channelled through charity, organised in Bangladesh through the mosque much in the way that the Poor Law once operated in Britain through the parish structure. And just as Bethnal Greeners did not like accepting charity within the Poor Law, Bangladeshis tried to avoid receiving charitable help, which places the recipients in debt to the donor and puts them into a generalised state of inferiority which can be hard to escape.

Feelings about charity in Bangladesh are written closely into religious ideas about a person's state of grace. As we have already mentioned (p. 94), it is a religious obligation (*farz*) to donate a part of your income as *zakat*, charitable alms. Status in the community depends on it and even unemployed Bangladeshis in Britain will sometimes hand over a portion of their social security benefits in order to meet this obligation.

By the same token, receiving charity is correspondingly avoided where possible, and is regarded as *dis*honourable. Members of better-off families, from which most migrants are drawn, will not have done so, either here or in Bangladesh. As one of our researchers said about the first migrants to Britain:

> Their loyalty to Islam, which placed highest emphasis on *zakat*, made it an obligatory duty on them to earn sufficient *halal* income to provide for their family and give alms to the poor and disadvantaged. A man's contribution towards charities or good causes ensures his, his family members' and his parents' eternal peace in heaven. Yet a large number of families of Bangladeshi origin, which are headed by men, are benefit dependent. They are at the receiving end of the state charity.[5]

Bangladeshi culture defines UK state benefits as *haram* (impure, the opposite of *halal*) in a religious sense. Early migrant workers did try to manage without them and, indeed, many older settlers still think this way. But new attitudes developed when such benefits opened up the possibility of Bangladeshi family settlement here. The end justified the means, and the first important influence of the white urban left lay in persuading Bangladeshis to change their views of welfare benefits. They did this by encouraging them to see themselves as partners in a contract of reciprocity rather than as members of the undeserving poor. One interviewee described this, and the difference between the first and second generations:

> The first generation had the stigma that it was *haram* income. It was not legitimate, or that they did not have an idea that it was their right since they worked and they paid national insurance and so on. First generation often refused it ... But now gradually it is changing. Because of the financial pressure, or maybe their right was explained, that it was their right. But younger people wouldn't bother because it is natural to them, these things, they are so used to it, it is nothing different for them.

The anti-colonial ideology common among left-wing thinkers in the late sixties and early seventies, and prevalent among the squatters, will have helped to overcome Bangladeshi resistance. The modernisers presented themselves as part of a united, internationalist 'working class' movement opposed to all British class greed and oppression. Their ideology asserted that the British state had stolen assets from the empire in order to build up the fortunes of British capitalists. It followed from this that by taking what they were entitled to from the welfare state, immigrants were not (as they might otherwise suppose) receiving charity, but simply claiming what was rightfully theirs. They were facilitating a long-delayed repayment of debt, as well as claiming benefits they deserved as a result of years of work in the UK. Through them the rules of honourable exchange were being fulfilled.

This, then, was the context in which Bangladeshis took decisive action and joined white radicals in building a New Labour party in the borough. Many of the Bangladeshi councillors active during the 1990s (twenty-two out of forty Labour councillors by the end of that period) were involved in the early battles which forged the alliance that has defined local politics ever since. The growth of the settlement has taken place around that *entente*, so that as families arrived, and more traditional interests and sentiments became represented, these had to accept the new, secular power structure and make their accommodations with it. The activists were the ones who had made settlement possible, and planted a new homeland on UK soil. So within the community they soon rivalled, and often were able to displace, the traditional authority of mosque elders.

As settlement has grown, traditional institutions have reasserted themselves and doubts about the morality of the welfare state have revived. Most older settlers, and a growing number of younger, radical Muslims, regard it as a short-term sellout. From our interviews it seems clear that belief in the value of *zakat* (and in the correspondingly polluting effects of *haram* income) is still strong among many Bangladeshis, and not just those educated outside the UK.

It is not clear how many Bangladeshis ever really accepted the proposition that claiming all possible welfare benefits is simply part of the general UK lifestyle. In recent years, however, there has been growing anxiety within the community about possible drift into dependency, or underclass status. This unease betrays lingering uncertainty about the true place of welfare recipients in British society. Reflecting this doubt, Bangladeshis have added some cultural nuances to the status of claimants. An unemployed man on benefits is sometimes called *ranir mehman*, or Queen's guest, and a man who has come from Bangladesh to marry a bride here but has failed to find work and is unemployed may be called *ranir jamai*, or Queen's son-in-law. This is telling, because it translates dependency on the community as a whole into a form of kinship relationship and obligation. The affinal link evoked by the terms may be to an unrealistically high-status person, and so liable to be perceived as asymmetrical, but in principle it places benefits within a system of personalised reciprocity which is capable of paying debts off over time.

An alternative explanation for the allusion – or, given the Bangladeshi delight in metaphor and verbal ambiguity, a *further* dimension to it – may arise from the fact that they also use the Bengali words for 'king' and 'queen' as equivalent to 'do-gooders'. There is awareness among Bangladeshis (as donors of *zakat* themselves) that people dispensing or urging recourse to public benefits may be seeking thereby to increase their own individual moral standing. Thus the choice of royal titles can imply that it is more acceptable to Bangladeshis to receive charity where the donor (or state-agents for donation) are receiving some reward themselves. For in that circumstance no *real* debt may have been created at all.

The Bangladeshis, then, had a real incentive to grasp the new welfare system and ideology. Many may now be regretting it – not simply because of conflict with Islamic values, but also because they see that reliance on benefits may increase the antagonism towards them from other citizens and may even prolong inferior status within British society too. It is, however, still in the community's interest to align with universalistic arguments so long as most members want to keep the service class on their side and, of course, while there is still real hardship in so many Bangladeshi families.

Politics of Race and Anti-racism

> Tower Hamlets [in the early eighties] was a pre-modern local authority ... what existed ... was a highly distinctive local working class culture based upon a latent sense of defended community, a form of community largely lacking formal organisation or effective leadership.[6]

The fact that influential Bangladeshis subscribe to universalist values alongside the urban elite enables the latter to pathologise the old white working class for its more particularistic orientation. So the old Bethnal Greeners have been condemned for their 'irrational' attachment to locality and insistence on exercising housing entitlements there rather than somewhere else. Some useful evidence showing the operation of these racial politics to undermine white resistance can be found in the 1994 study by Burns, Hambleton and Hoggett, which evaluated the Liberal Democratic experiment in municipal decentralisation between 1986 and 1994.

The Burns team appears thoroughly scornful of this experiment. Although Tower Hamlets registered a dramatic increase in voter turnout in local elections over the period 1982–90, more than anywhere else in London, and witnessed a 'reawakening of local political culture',[7] it was seen by them as a populist and regressive manoeuvre:

> One of the distinctive characteristics of Liberal populism in Tower Hamlets has therefore been its introversion. Political energies have been focused upon enemies within – bureaucracy, professionalism, local labourism – rather than upon the more powerful enemies outside. But what of the Bangladeshi community itself? Has this also become a convenient 'enemy within' against which the Liberals have been able to whip up white electoral support by playing the 'race card'? The question has become particularly pertinent since the success of the fascist British National Party (BNP) in the Millwall ward by-election on the Isle of Dogs in September 1993, the first success for a fascist party in a British local government election since the mid-1970s. In the aftermath of this shock victory for the BNP local Liberals stood accused once more of using race scare tactics in their electoral campaign, accusations which led Paddy Ashdown, the leader of the Liberal Party, to order an internal enquiry into the activities of the Tower Hamlets party.[8]

There is a strong assumption here that race is effectively irrelevant to local political issues, and has simply been imported by cheap politicians lacking better ideas to peddle. But in spite of this scepticism, the Burns team do make a number of field observations which help us to see that there has also been an *anti*-racist card played against the white working class. As shown earlier, the main conflicts between white and Bangladeshi residents have concentrated around housing, as this is the public service most firmly bounded by locality. The response of planners to white anxieties has been to dismiss the importance of locality, and to expect people to exercise their housing entitlements elsewhere if necessary. When local white residents have objected, the modernisers have made their assertions of local commitment look unreasonable by suggesting that what they are objecting to really is the fact that the Bangladeshis competing with them are *not white*. Whites resentful of loss of local rights have been discredited politically by being represented as pathological inadequates, not capable of living alongside people different from themselves.*

The Burns study confirms the class dimension to uses of this racist smear. While delegitimising the voice of the working-class residents who feel they are being squeezed out of the area, it also enhances the status of non-resident council officers as good guys who are needed in order to ensure fair play. The polarising effect on the white population was observed during the Burns team's participant observation at a 'tenants advisory forum' held in Stepney to discuss new procedures for tackling racial harassment on council estates. Harassment had been defined by council officers in ways which effectively condoned any behaviour of Bangladeshis as 'defensive', while threatening white tenants with loss of their tenancies, or delays in dealing with their needs. This clearly gave a variety of weapons to officers with which to punish deviant racists. According to the report:

> [A tenant] raised a number of issues. First, he noted from the draft document, those found guilty of racial harassment could have their security of tenure threatened or withdrawn. He clearly felt this to be threatening and questioned its legality. Implying that the introduction of (the drafted policy) would not be without cost he asked, 'Whose repairs are not going to be done?' (loud applause from the audience).[9]

We encountered just such anxieties about municipal victimisation ourselves a few years after this, and these may have prevented a number of our respondents from speaking fully. Some who did not actually express views that were hostile to Bangladeshis (and were mainly coded by us as 'mixed') intimated that there was more they could say about the Bangladeshis, but it was not safe for them to speak out:

> The Asians get flats before anyone else ... But I don't think I should say any more about it, I might get into trouble. (*Middle-aged woman living with adult sons*)

> I think they give priority to the Asians, and if you make any remarks you get hounded as a racist. (*Retired machinist living with wife*)

---

*This sort of thing has happened widely. A pioneer of race research in the East End in the fifties, Michael Banton, has noted (1999) that a common problem which results from over-use of the racism concept is that it eventually leads us to avoid real issues and sets up the idea that there is necessarily something wrong with the people who feel hostile.

You cannot say anything about the injustice because you would be called a racist. (*Retired docker*)

Even some of those who were openly hostile in their declarations to us said that it was better to hold your tongue:

You can't say anything or you're accused of racism ... I don't have a lot to do with the council, but I'm all right so long as I don't say anything. (*Elderly widow*)

The 'advisory' meeting reported by Burns and his colleagues shows vividly the resentment generated among white tenants by what they felt to be attempts to muzzle them. It also reveals the bitterness created by the underlying assumption, never properly aired, that whites could not possibly have a legitimate basis for objecting to heavy settlement by immigrants in 'their' area. The Burns team summed up the monitored tenants' meeting with the following observation:

This meeting demonstrated real racism, a mixture of hatred, aggressive humour, and some honesty ... What was most striking was the class divide. 'The goodies' – the Labour councillor and assorted officers – were all obviously middle-class in dress and language. 'The baddies' were all working-class. We really got the feeling of an almost unbridgeable gulf between two different worlds.[10]

The team nevertheless inclined towards seeing the working-class dissenters as living in a fantasy. In chapter 9 we noted their tendency to classify elderly white tenants as reactionary. In the same way, they treat their perceptions of their environment as a product of ageing, and unreliable, sensibilities. Thus the authors note that local white residents speak as if there had been a golden age in the past when life in the East End was more friendly. What they also note, but fail to latch on to fully when interpreting these perceptions, is the part played in this view of the past by the war and by the period of promises and optimism that followed it, which we feel must indeed have seemed like some sort of a golden age. The main spokesman for the tenants in the recorded meeting came from Siege House (*sic*) on Limehouse Fields estate. This estate, completed soon after the end of the war, clearly had tremendous symbolic value among the local white population. It stood for post-war renewal and reward. Living on it held great meaning:

We conducted a number of detailed interviews with tenants' leaders on the Limehouse Fields estate in Stepney, virtually all of whom were white, and middle-aged or elderly. Most had lived on this estate since it was built just after the Second World War. The estate has suffered from neglect for years and is located on the lower rungs of the ladder of desirable estates in the Stepney area. One could not fail to be struck by the warm feeling that virtually all of those interviewed displayed when asked what it was like in the 'old days'. We were tempted to believe that this was just a romanticisation of a past which was as ordinary and messy as the present, but the tenants were so uniform and so insistent in their pictures of the past that one could not help but wonder whether this was pure nostalgia or actually rooted in a lost reality. According to all of those interviewed, the physical and social environment was far better in the early days of the estate ... Another tenant who had lived on the estate for over twenty years added, 'Look at the grounds, there's lumps and holes everywhere. In the old days, everyone cleaned and took their turn. The people were nicer then. Now, we've got the whole league of nations here.'[11]

The Importance of the War

This reluctance by Burns to credit collective memories of the war period has helped, paradoxically, to show us how central the war is to this whole matter. In the original ICS study of Bethnal Green in the 1950s the authors noted the confident linking of ownership of territory, community loyalty and contribution to the war. Many little turnings were found to have war memorials built on to walls of houses with inscriptions listing the names of people from the street killed in the war. 'Pots and vases of flowers are fixed in a half-circle to the wall; they are renewed regularly by the women of the turning, who make a street collection every Armistice Day.' And in a small court the researchers found, 'on one wall is a proliferation of flowers around a War Memorial, a Union Jack and some faded pictures of the Queen'.[12]

Some of these memorials still exist, but they no longer serve as simple places of proud remembrance, more as points of resistance to the 'invasion' of the area that has since taken place, and symbols of loss and betrayal. This is presumably why our older white working-class informants clung so tenaciously to their memories of the war. It epitomised their sense of injustice and also, very significantly, embodied their attachment – which the welfare state no longer endorses – to a mutualist model of society in which privileges had to be earned. For many of them participation in the war was the main contribution they or their parents had made, and the basis of their sense of losing out. Those who drew most attention to the war were very often the same people who felt that social values had been turned upside down since the arrival of post-war immigrants. In too many ways, service to the community was no longer rewarded:

> We did our war service, and now they do not want to know us. But if you are an immigrant you get the top brick off the chimney. (*Retired driver*)

> I think it is wrong for all these girls [single mothers], and all these foreigners to come into this country and get all this money for children. This should change. Half of these girls are living with these fellas, different people, while poor old people who fought in the war are walking around with nothing and are not able to find places to live. Half of those on the street are because they can't afford to pay rents. In the post office the other day an Indian in front of me collected £200 on one pension book, and an elderly white man behind only collected £57, and he asked the girl behind the counter why the other

collected so much when he had fought for his country and worked all his life. (*Widow, with children in Essex*)

Some respondents noted specifically that the contribution of parents was not being honoured:

Let us have some priorities. *Our parents fought a war for us.* When the Bengalis come here they get full pensions. My wife has just been informed after years of paying full contributions she will only get a £1.59 pension when she retires. Why do they get it when they've contributed nothing? (*Publican*; emphasis added)

Old people now are scrimping and scraping. They don't get half of what they should get. Those who fought in the war would turn in their graves if they knew that Asians were getting everything. Years ago when you had lots of kids you had to support yourself. Now the state keeps you. (*Market trader*)

There was added resentment towards Bangladeshis which figured here, not so much on account of them not being active in the war themselves, but simply because many of them did not seem to know or care about it. They gave it no respect. These feelings were revealed publicly during our study when some unexploded bombs were found near a block of flats in Stepney. Bangladeshi residents could not understand what all the fuss was about, and were very reluctant to move out while the defusing was done. White neighbours interpreted this as an attempt to belittle the dangers, and to devalue the war contribution of local residents.[13]

Ignoring feelings about the war has fuelled hostility. Father Reilly could understand why, in such circumstances, extreme political parties were proving attractive:

The BNP is around: they prey on people's fears. In the Isle of Dogs people felt listened to when the BNP took that seat. When people are dumped on you, people from another part of the world are dumped on you, there isn't enough housing to go around. Local people get called racist because of the lack of housing. We are the back-yard of the richest city in Britain. But we haven't had the resources here.

So you've got people who are angry. There were 13,000 direct bombing raids on this district, they say. The district suffered more than anywhere else in the Blitz. If the proud boast of a country is that it welcomes immigrants, it should not put such a strain on local people that it produces conflict. The English have a sense of being betrayed. There are such wonderful people here. People are nice and good everywhere. But their generosity here is something special. People have time for each other. The other day I asked for volunteers to run a night shelter and I had fifty volunteers in no time.

Race and Class

These findings suggest that conventional attempts to promote racial harmony by at-

tacking 'racism' may not be helping. For such efforts often involve a misrepresenta-
tion of what it is that working-class people are actually trying to say. When they try
to express what they feel they are made to appear bitter, xenophobic and out of touch
with mainstream national opinion. They fear that when they try to defend what they
feel to be their legitimate local interests, they will lose their political voice. They are
then pushed back into deploying brute force – which weakens their case further. In this
respect, perhaps, these remaining fragments of the East End population incorporated
into the nation at the end of the war have become excluded from mainstream society
again. Burns et al. make a similar observation:

> The racist sentiments expressed by those who saw themselves as representatives of the
> interests of local white people had other elements. They clearly felt themselves to be the
> 'silent majority' governed by an officialdom who did not live in the area and therefore
> 'didn't know what it was like'. Moreover, in Stepney under Labour control, these white
> tenants clearly felt that free expression was being denied to them because of the fear
> that those who spoke their mind would be accused of racism ... The paradox is, then,
> that parts of the local white population see themselves in a way that is reminiscent of an
> ethnic minority view – systematically neglected, and faced with an officialdom which
> consists almost entirely of 'outsiders'.[14]

We have quoted at some length here from the Burns study because it was carried out
before our own was started (and when there was more open hostility) by a team of academic researchers who could not remotely be seen as racist, and who make no secret of
their view that local whites were being a touch over-sensitive in their reactions to events.
And yet, in spite of all this, it produces some telling evidence which suggests how class
interests and conflicts may have been aggravating racial tensions in the area.

The Burns picture is congruent with our own studies, some years later, which picked
up a feeling among white East Enders that the outside world was ganging up on them
and was after their territorial assets. Bangladeshis get the wrong end of these feelings,
because they are there and they represent competition. But many of our respondents
saw the real problem as being a bias in the attitude of government and the political
class towards immigrants. This perceived favouring of the interests of newcomers was
regarded as a political mistake, as it invited conflict and confrontation:

> I dislike them all living here and I blame the government for putting them all in one
> place. (*Retired hairdresser living with second husband*)

> The government makes the race problem by just giving them everything and us nothing.
> (*Secretary living with husband and teenage children*)

Some of our respondents seemed to feel that official policy almost set out to provoke
racial hostility:

> I'm not happy with the immigrants. We've got more than our fair share. The housing
> situation will never be solved. All the new houses are for immigrants. Big houses for big
> Pakistani families. They're officially not working, so they don't pay the rent. It is asking

for racist trouble. They're moving in everywhere. They come to take advantage of our social security. They break our laws – with teenagers pregnant by old men, and more than one wife. This is England! I think it will boil over. (*Retired bank messenger*)

The Asians tell us we must not have our Union Jack or our Music Hall at the old Truman's Brewery ... They should stop them coming here as they are fanning the flames of racial unrest. (*Electrician with young family*)

Some whites suspected that the local authority was nervous about resisting the demands of Bangladeshis because of equalities legislation:*

I don't really know, but I think in Tower Hamlets and Hackney they'd be inclined to give preference to ethnic minorities because the race relations would be down on them like a ton of bricks if they didn't. What I do know, jobwise, is that councils are more predisposed to interview you if you tick the ethnic minority box. A friend who is a nurse wasn't getting any interviews, then she ticked the ethnic minority box and started being offered interviews. (*Childless office-worker living in shared flat*)

Others hinted darkly that if the government fails to take note of their interests and concerns then it is inviting people to take matters into their own hands:

There's too many immigrants living in this area. We've got to pay for them and keep them. They don't know what work is. They draw £130–£170 per week, then you see them in the betting shop. It makes my blood boil. There are one or two families here, but we keep them under control in this block. (*Recently retired school dinnerlady*)

Such comments back up the suspicion of some that racism is both being stirred up and projected onto them. Others are more cautious:

We should not really talk about immigrants because it can cause an uprising like back in 1930 when the Blackshirts [the British Union of Fascists] were about. (*Elderly widow with no children*)

Not all reacted in this way, though – certainly not in front of us. They know that such negativity can be and has been turned against them in order that they, who see themselves as the victims of policy, may be blamed for the problems that policy has caused. Insofar as this happens, it represents another way in which the real winners in the tangled interplay of race and class are the new political elite, who grasp the crucial (and honourable) role of keeping peace between warring sectors of the population. As

---

*Our interviewees may have had in mind that the Commission for Racial Equality (CRE) had served a non-discrimination notice under the Race Relations Act in September 1987 against Tower Hamlets council for their discriminatory housing allocation policies, and in 1991 the High Court issued a non-compliance notice against the council (which lapsed in November 1992). See Runnymede Trust, 1993.

mentioned by Burns, one way in which that elite deals with the white working class may be to make them feel that they are really just a minority themselves, possessing only sectional interests.[15]

This seems to extend even to the way that whites are categorised in some municipal records, for example those of the education authorities. As we saw in table 7.3 (p. 147), white children are listed not as 'white', or even 'white British' as would be the case in a national census, for example, but as ESW/Is.

ESW/Is are the four white national *components* of identity in the British Isles – that is English, Scottish, Welsh and Irish – and do not refer to any other white groups. What is significant here is that a title has been found for indigenous whites which, by sub-dividing them in this particular way, manages to turn them into something *less* than fully British and puts them on a par with the last immigrant groups off the plane or most tenuous of hyphenates. This effect is reinforced by the fact that the four constituent identities are never used separately – except for the Irish, who in other contexts are sometimes treated as a distinct group in their own right.[16] What this probably indicates in reality is that they are all redundant references, as the sub-groups they describe do not exist as conscious entities on the ground. They have simply been lumped together as a conglomerate, the better, as some whites would see it, to be collectively diminished. These are the ethnic or national parts making up the borough's population which feel most hard done by over the last few decades, and their belittling compound title captures this loss of position well.

Such a decline of the old working class is no triumph for the Bangladeshis, though. They are all too aware that in many respects it has not made their own lives easier, not least because of the hostility to which they are consequently exposed. Although the new national elite has supported Bangladeshi interests in local conflicts over resources, such backing cannot be relied on in the long run. The British welfare system is sympathetic to new and needy groups, and that is one way it retains its moral legitimacy, but as those groups settle in, and some of their members become incorporated to the ruling class themselves, the solicitude of the elite is liable to move on to more vulnerable groups.

Local – and indeed national – political activists were given something to ponder after the 2005 general election, when the sitting Labour MP for Bethnal Green and Bow lost her seat to the indefatigable George Galloway of the Respect Party. To what extent this was a protest vote at Britain's role in international affairs and to what extent it was a comment on local issues is not clear, but given the number of Bangladeshis who must have voted for Galloway – a vociferous opponent of British involvement in Iraq – the community's alliance with the Labour Party is certainly looking pretty shaky. The ageing first generation are probably still mostly Labour voters, as they always have been, but many of their children and grandchildren have been influenced by global political issues and have looked to Galloway's party to reflect their concern as members of the *ummah* (worldwide community of Muslims).

Class is reasserting itself as the key in British society, albeit in a novel way. This augurs for political instability. Preoccupation with the most vulnerable, which almost invariably is bound to mean the newest arrivals, especially refugees fleeing persecution, means that sooner or later all incoming groups, along with the downgraded national majority, will come to feel that length of residence in the country does not seem to give them a durable or especially valuable stake in it. This constitutes a threat not just to particular groups, but to the whole operation of social democracy. Burns and his team categorised Tower Hamlets as a relic of a pre-modern era. But the alienation of the white working class from government, both local and national, that is evident in the East End could happen in urban Britain more generally. Arguably it is happening already, as shown by the growing – if still limited – support for far-right parties.

Deborah Phillips, a geographer who has herself been very critical of Tower Hamlets' housing policy and, above all, practices, put it very well in 1988; what she wrote then is equally applicable today:

> The East Ender's pride, identity and subculture, born out of a long tradition of poverty and isolation within the capital, are nevertheless still evident amongst the long-established indigenous residents on the council estates. The deeply entrenched white hostility to the Bengali outsiders may represent just one further dimension in the East End's battle for survival in the face of deeply rooted change.[17]

Conclusion: Reclaiming Social Democracy

So what does this all add up to? The Bangladeshis are the first large minority to have settled in east London since the war. Although this is a place with unique features, as we have tried to describe throughout, it is still similar in many ways to other inner-city areas across the country. What this case study shows is that the arrival of minorities has complicated the working of British society.

There have been two important shifts in this period. At the time of the original 1950s study there was a general 'opening up' of British society to greater social mobility following the creation of modern, centralised welfare provisions. Soon afterwards this system was itself adjusted to ensure above all that the poor and needy, including those among incoming minorities, received assistance and enjoyed equal opportunities. These two processes are often assumed to be complementary, but our restudy suggests that they work in contradictory ways, and that provisions which promote well-being and social justice among the most needy groups, including refugees and other recent immigrants, may have the unintended consequence of creating resentment among established citizens, who feel their own 'hard-earned' inclusion is diminished by being shared with others.

The study indicates that racial hostility and community divisions are partly related to questions about perceptions of *fairness* in the allocation of scarce resources within the welfare state. Our informants appear not to be alone; recent research by MORI showed that 45 per cent of their interviewees thought that current welfare systems are 'unfair', and 20 per cent singled out the category 'immigrants/asylum-seekers' as 'major exploiters of the system'.[1] This connection is important. A number of commentators in recent years have linked community tensions in Britain to questions of identity, commitment and culture: there is now widespread lively debate about these issues.[2] Others have looked in general terms at issues of fairness and social justice arising in the contemporary welfare state.[3] But there has not been much discussion yet about the part that the growth of a multi-cultural society itself may have played in shaping these latter issues. Debate on multi-culturalism has tended to be polarised between a generally liberal academia and a generally sceptical and even hostile media, particularly since September 2001.[4] We hope that our study will help to open up this topic for more comprehensive discussion.

The Moral Basis of Immigration

The fundamental issue here as expressed by our white Tower Hamlets informants is that a stable social democracy needs to maintain a fair balance between what citizens put into society and what they get out of it: between their rights and their responsibilities. This is well understood too, if not explicitly, by our Bangladeshi informants, who are all too aware of the necessity of a moral economy based on systems of mutual support, whether for sustainability in Sylhet or for family prosperity in London. However, it may be hard to implement in practice. Establishing a common understanding of reciprocity is a difficult enough challenge within a group that has fixed membership, but it becomes increasingly important to sustain where newcomers are entering the group and need to be integrated into a pre-existing moral economy and loop of mutual support. Maintaining a sense of fairness within a nation during periods of immigration is easiest when a country clearly needs additional workers in order to develop its economy properly. In these circumstances, new immigrants will be seen as agents in creating a larger pot of national wealth, and so will be understood to have legitimacy when receiving benefits from it.

Twenty-first-century Britain does not really fall into this category. For at least two centuries it has been densely populated compared with its neighbours and during the first part of the twentieth century anxieties about the growing population, the capacity of the land to feed it and the threat to the countryside of further development, all prompted outward migration. In the 1950s, however, the Conservative government started to encourage immigration, to prop up declining industries. This was perceived even at the time by some as a capitalist move to keep obsolete factories going by cutting local labour rates, rather than a 'national' good, and it was evaluations such as these which impelled some of the early resistance to Commonwealth immigration.

The argument of economic need for migration has never been compelling in Britain, and has usually remained muted apart from occasional (and current) arguments linked to falling birth rates, the need to secure a future workforce and the immediate shortfall of skilled workers in public services such as the NHS. What has largely sustained the pro-immigration lobby from the mid-1960s onwards, certainly with regard to immigration from outside the EU, has been the political perception that Britain has a moral obligation to share its resources with countries of the former empire, and that this includes a right to settlement in the metropolis. Implicit in this argument is the idea that the rights of immigrants to enjoy the benefits of the current welfare state derive from contributions by their ancestors (albeit involuntary) to the building of the present British economy, which were not properly rewarded within the empire itself. One of Tarquin Hall's academic Bangladeshi informants himself came up with this as an explanation for post-war immigration: 'It strikes me that, having caused such havoc and disruption around the world, you are trying to make amends to those you formerly suppressed.'[5]

This rationale for migration is thus itself largely dependent on the designation of a larger system of exchange, and loop of fairness, of which metropolitan Britain represents only one portion, and which had remained in a chronic state of imbalance throughout empire – which by definition was not a democratic institution. We should bear in mind that against this argument there was always an anti-immigration lobby, whose attitudes provoked increasingly restrictive immigration legislation, until we reached today's situation where migration from ex-colonies is possible only for spouses or for those in one of the categories able to get work permits, which is unlikely in the case of poorly educated Sylhetis. The pro-immigration lobby may have written and spoken forcefully, but the antis have more effectively legislated, especially against ex-imperial subjects.

There was thus at least one moral basis for extending British residence and citizenship rights to the peoples of former imperial possessions. But, although it does employ a language of give and take, this argument has not elicited a sense of fairness among all 'indigenous' Britons, including many of our informants. For a variety of reasons, a chain of reciprocity has not been established in their minds. The first of these is probably that the argument for wider inclusion was introduced retrospectively, so feels to them more like a post-war 'punishment' for empire as opposed to a legitimate argument for sharing British assets more widely. The post-war compact was understood by working-class East Enders as admitting them to full membership of British society. To some extent this itself recognised historical debts by the nation to its lowest orders. Principally, though, it acknowledged the crucial role they played during the war. A further compact made soon afterwards with colonial citizens, especially one not properly discussed within the nation in the way that the creation of the welfare state had been, was felt as a serious diminution, even a snatching back, of their own recent 'reward'.

This might not have been experienced so negatively if the extension of membership to British society was perceived as being on a small scale. It was, however, seen as anything but that. Anti-immigration speeches in the 1960s used inflammatory metaphors of swamping and submersion, and stressed the size of the metropolis relative to the volume of poor people now potentially entitled to settle in it. An already-crowded country containing 50 million was confronted by an ex-empire with many hundreds of millions – most of whom would be able to improve their standard of living substantially by coming here. They argued that national wealth could very quickly become diluted; and while this would still be a marginal improvement for most immigrants, it would be a disproportionate loss for indigenous Britons.

Even in terms of redress for imperial exploitation, it would have been impossible for any government to justify an open-door policy to all immigration. Nor indeed was it the case that a debt to the empire was or is best repaid by taking its most entrepreneurial or educated members as immigrants, as opposed to helping their development *in situ*. On top of this, and as stands out from our own study, the way in which the debt to the rest of empire has been discharged has impinged differentially on various sectors of the indigenous British population. The history of the East End shows that the arrival of new immigrants to the area has often been accompanied by the perception (and sometimes reality) of a downward pressure on the wages of the already lowest-paid. The neediest immigrants have been enabled to settle almost entirely in those localities, such as the East End, inhabited by poor people whose existing social capital is concentrated within them. This has led to intense competition over the resources these locals had once considered their own, or had under their own control, and for state services on which they depended and felt had been designed with them in mind. Their feeling of loss within the system has been enormous, given the failure of the state either to appreciate the degree of change to which they were subject or to support them in the resulting feelings of instability. Some of our Bangladeshi interviewees themselves acknowledged this. Middle-class Britons, on the other hand, have been in a position not just to avoid direct conflict with newcomers but to benefit from them. Much of what the middle classes enjoy in cosmopolitan cities, above all London, are the services and material culture brought to the country by Britain's new communities.

The middle or ruling class has also benefited through a renewal of Britain's leading place in the world. Paradoxically, the post-war immigration enabled the rediscovery and recreation of something which many considered praiseworthy in parts of empire itself – namely the tradition of 'tolerance' which allowed subjects to keep their own customs and religions, and occasionally even rulers. Arrival of a varied assortment of minorities in the metropolis prompted an alliance between the emerging intellectual and political elite and the traditional apologists for empire. This formed around an aspiration to turn Britain into a multi-racial, multi-cultural society which would use liberal and social democratic institutions to govern a diverse population. Looked at this way, the new Britain provided an opportunity to make amends for the sins of previous empire in some style. Thus the creation of such a society soon became an important national goal. It now serves as Britain's distinctive rationale in the current world order, and in many respects can be considered a success.

Confronting the Culture of Entitlement

However, there may be costs – not simply to the old working class but to the nature of British social democracy. One of the unintended and ignored effects on British society of extending citizenship to migrants from former countries of the empire surely lies in the way that it has strengthened the legitimacy of greater emphasis on citizens' rights without working to create a national culture of responsibility, mutuality and solidarity. In the battle for Spitalfields the bitterest complaints by local people did not focus on Bangladeshis as gatecrashers on an original post-war deal. What they were against was the way that giving priority to the housing needs of any and all homeless squatters (*including* Bangladeshis) entailed a demotion of alternative claims based on membership of – and service to – the community. The redundant 'ladder' principle had not seen public housing as a service to which citizens had an automatic entitlement. It was a resource owned by the community, which was to be enjoyed by those in need who had also earned entitlement to it by making an effort to contribute to the common good.

The most obvious beneficiaries in the East End of this change of principles were the Bangladeshis. Through it they had rights confirmed which then formed the basis for the rapid settlement of their local community. This received national approval and endorsement because it clearly helped to assuage considerable hardship, as well as alleviating some post-imperial guilt. But the main ideological beneficiaries of this, and of similar battles being played out across the country which have had wider effects, were the advocates of needs-based public services – such as squatters. It was the indigenous, white squatters in particular, first drawn idealistically to the East End by the vision of Cablestrasse, who then also sensed the strategic advantage to claimants like themselves of bringing poor migrants into their movement, and so anticipated the potential impact of immigration from poor countries on the administration of the welfare state. If many of the most vulnerable and needy claimants are immigrants, it becomes harder to challenge the rights culture or question the spread of means-tested benefits. Opposition to the rhetoric of need, and of rights at the expense of obligations to community, can readily be faced down by the charge that it is motivated by racism. Just as happened in Bethnal Green in the 1970s, those people who press for 'moral' welfare systems, rewarding behaviour which respects community values, are mocked by modernisers as being inadequates who are looking for ways to exclude the strangers they do not know how to live with.

Immigration of impoverished families has thus contributed a powerful, if unintended, effect over the years in smoothing transition towards a more rights-centred culture. In our own findings it is the white community which has been most vocal in its concern about this shift. But this may be partly because the Bangladeshis, who have been collectively very dependent on benefits, have not wanted to speak out against their local representatives. We do know that in private many do articulate reservations about easy rights in the early stages of settlement. The original migrants, like almost all immigrants, arrived expecting to work hard for meagre rewards, in the hope that greater prosperity would follow. We have seen how older Bangladeshis in particular had moral misgivings about unreciprocated 'charity'; one of the achievements of the white liberals was to persuade them that benefits were, in fact, their due following imperial exploitation and after their own years of hard work here.

To date the Bangladeshi settlement in east London, made possible by state support, appears to have been a great success. Between 1971 and 2001 the numbers of Bangladeshis in Tower Hamlets rose from some 4,000 to nearly 66,000, that is from just over 2 per cent of the total borough population to a shade over a third. This is a higher proportion than the Jews represented at the beginning of the twentieth century, and is now the largest concentration of a single minority group in any borough in Britain. None of this would have been conceivable without changes in housing allocation procedures or determined official sanctions against working-class resistance to newcomers. The children of these migrants have gone on, since the mid-1990s, not just to outnumber but also substantially outperform other groups in local schools. Impressive numbers then go on to university, enter into professional careers and disperse to owner-occupation in the boroughs east of Tower Hamlets. The rapidity of this incorporation of successful young Bangladeshis to British life can hardly be overestimated. State promotion of social mobility seems to have delivered notable success in very little time, and to mark a real change from the less interventionist regimes under which earlier waves of migrants arrived.

However, such rapid settlement, and syphoning-off of talented individuals into the new middle class, does not necessarily mean successful accommodation for the group as a whole in the longer term. It may be too individualistic. Meritocratic progress benefits selected individuals, but it may then leave their community less able to make a collective contribution to the nation, on which its more general acceptance and integration hangs. The culture of rights providing personal support for less successful individuals may similarly weaken a group further by devaluing reciprocity within it. For example, Bangladeshis entering employment in the public sector or the City are expected by their colleagues to conform to British working practice and not prioritise the need for work of their own friends and relatives. Some of the Bangladeshi community-based safety nets have developed holes. After a while, the only collective structures retaining any strength may be those oriented to a homeland other than Britain.

So the downside of rapid settlement is that less successful group members, whose lives and work are still largely centred in their ethnic community, will find its strength ebbing away, as it is increasingly populated by people like themselves, the losers in the meritocratic race. Gentle but relentless individualisation – encouraged through universalist welfare support – means that members rarely *need* to make a call on group membership. If and when they try to do so they may find it too atrophied to be of much use. It will not provide the refuge of alternative values and dreams, and identity – even a hyphenated identity – or strong personal ties which might protect them from full exposure to, and the risk of failure in, the meritocratic cauldron of mainstream society. This is the danger for the Bangladeshis, as it was for the working-class Bethnal Greeners originally described in *Family and Kinship in East London*.

A particular hazard here is that if initial achievements come fast, only a slight diminution of pace will *feel* like failure. We found considerably more resentment about aspects of life in Britain among the younger generation of Bangladeshis who have grown up here and had their expectations raised. The lives of the migrant generation are so manifestly improved in material terms by the simple act of coming here that they are inclined to feel satisfied. But among their children there is bound to be some sense of a slowing down of progress, and greater consciousness of obstacles and resistance. There has, in fact, been a good deal of social mobility, and compared with their cousins in distant places such as Oldham, young Bangladeshis in the area have found it possible to achieve a lot in a short time, and many have moved up and out. Early success for some may presage disappointment for many.

A strong community can protect its members from failure to move on. Back in the days when initial settlement took longer, there was plenty of time for an immigrant community to take root and construct a viable collective accommodation to the new homeland, encompassing a range of individual levels of success and integration. This could then dissolve gradually as members scattered and became absorbed into the mainstream. At the time when we were doing our fieldwork the last Jewish shops and organisations in the area, which had operated throughout the twentieth century as a means of adjustment to life in Britain for descendants of nineteenth-century immigrants, were finally closing down. This is how long it had taken that community to leave its base in the East End.

State help has enabled Bangladeshis to settle, and some of them to move on quickly. But not all. Unless a relatively strong and enduring community remains to protect them, many of those who lack qualifications to succeed may be doomed to a place in the nation within, or not far away from, the underclass of citizenry trapped into personal dependence on state support. They will find they have joined, and now share the problems of, the lower reaches of the white population whose own lives have become limited by the rights culture. Already by the middle of 2005 it was becoming obvious how potentially dangerous even a small number of young men could be who feel alienated from and antagonistic to the rest of the country. Too-speedy dissolution of the ethnic community could multiply these risks.

The Problem of Centralism

In this book we have attempted to explain the hostility directed towards Bangladeshis by white East Enders. The main reason we have identified is that the state's reception of newcomers has ridden over the existing local community's assumptions about their ownership of public resources, and that this has precipitated a loss of confidence in the fairness of British social democracy. Analytically, we can link this to the post-war social revolution which created a centralised state committed to maximising individual opportunities and providing personal security for all those who need it. This new system fits the lives and values of the new ruling class itself – by emphasising individual responsibilities and rewards – while also in their view providing acceptable safeguards for more humble sectors of the population. But many ordinary people, especially those who have lived under some other regime, or who are struggling to stay out of the underclass, do not feel that it is compatible with their own understanding of what the good society is like and how it should work.

The conflicts of interest which consequently arise have set white East Enders against political modernisers and the minorities whom they regard as favoured by them. There has been a racial aspect to this division, but it is probable that this will fade as the new-comers settle in and more needy groups arrive and attract prime public concern. Over the last couple of decades, certainly within Tower Hamlets, Black Caribbeans who came (or whose parents came) in the 1950s and 1960s have felt state solicitude slipping away from them to more recent arrivals, the Bangladeshis being a prime example. And this process may now be embracing Bangladeshis too, and helping to feed the alienation of the young and sharpen tensions generated by international events. So the attachment of minorities themselves to a highly centralised and individualised society is likely to become more qualified as time goes on.

The central problem here is, we believe, that by attempting to use state power to create a fairer society, modernisers may be forgetting the importance of informal moral economies in giving ordinary people some power to control their own lives according to their own values: some stake in the system. The rise of public virtue is eclipsing the private realm. It is this which may now be pulling us into an increasingly polarised and unstable society, in which small groups feel powerless to resist the influence of mass, impersonal forces. Most people in all communities believe in the value of informal mutual support in sustaining a decent and humane society. But the over-centralisation of welfare in the name of strict equality is stifling this. Face-to-face relationships carry little weight when confronted by faceless policies from the state.

The incorporation into the nation of previous waves of immigrants to the East End was carried out mainly through informal social processes for providing mutual per-sonal support and assistance in finding housing and work. Though this may have taken longer than centrally sponsored settlement, and entailed some transitional inequali-ties, we do know that in certain key respects it worked. Newcomers had time to adjust, collectively, to their new homeland and to evolve sustainable identities and loyalties. Above all, perhaps, because incorporation required (which it does not now) the forging of active economic and local-political ties with members of the national majority, it in-volved shared recognition by both the host community and newcomers that the latter 'belonged' by virtue of participating conscientiously in the life of the community that was admitting them. The key to this process, as with the settlement of most minorities in other countries, was that needy immigrants needed to make some manifest con-tribution to the host society. An exchange takes place between the national majority and newcomers to the nation, whereby legitimacy to a full share in collective benefits is earned – and felt to be merited – by those groups seen to contribute to the common good.

Some of our informants told us they believe that in Britain in recent years this has been reversed. The rights of immigrants and even of potential immigrants – who have yet to enter the system or even to think about doing so – sometimes seem to them to be given greater moral weight than those of families who have been here for generations. The message that this sends them is that national resources no longer belong in any real sense to them as citizens of the nation, but are in the gift of the ruling class. So instead of feeling that they are at the centre of the nation, they feel more than just not championed by the elite, but actually pushed *away* by it. This is a prescription for mass civic insecurity.

It is also a squandering of those benefits that immigration can deliver. We are often reminded that a great contribution to British society has been made by immigrants in the past. This is true, and the Bangladeshi community's emerging contribution is evident throughout Britain, not least – and not only – in the country's huge national network of Indian restaurants. But as one of us points out elsewhere, such dividends have accrued partly because immigrants in the past had to work hard to gain full admission to the nation.[6] They had a spur. If you take away the need to make an effort, and integrate many newcomers straight into a state-dependent underclass, then nobody wins. For example, looking at contemporary regulations, it surely does not help that newly arrived asylum seekers are kept dependent on (meagre) benefits rather than being allowed, and motivated, to work, and it is surely in everybody's interest that they should be helped to do so. After all, it is well documented that many do in fact work whenever possible; their efforts should be legitimised.

Related to this, we should not neglect here the extent to which the experience of generous state welfare benefits can distort newcomers' view of life in Britain, and their aspirations. In their own countries of origin, there may be few or no public supports available for its own citizens, let alone new migrants. The scale of material help given to them in Britain can lead them to believe that Britain must be enormously rich, which of course, as a nation, it is. However, many of them do not understand that there are many ordinary Britons – above all in their own locality – who do not live well, and may have a rational basis for resenting the competition arising from their arrival. There is still very little social mixing between ordinary members of the Bangladeshi community and white neighbours in Tower Hamlets, not least because of the segregated nature of the local school populations. This allows myths and prejudices to survive unchallenged – including the assumption that most white people are well off and, conversely, that all Bangladeshis are welfare dependent.

The Way Back to Moral Solvency

The culture of entitlement is now deeply entrenched in British society as a whole, and there can be no quick solution to the problems it creates. However, we would suggest that as post-war immigrant communities come to experience its negative implications themselves – and to share the bitterness of parts of the white working class – a concerted attack on it becomes viable. And the responses of established immigrant groups will be crucial here. It is the needs of the poorest groups that have justified the emphasis on targeted, means-tested benefits. As these groups become better off, more of them will gain from a universalist system. No consensus will be possible unless the welfare state includes some renewal of the expectation that full citizenship should be contingent on conscientious contribution to the common good. Revival of reciprocity is the key.

The logic of give and take is far more compelling within small groups, where people can see who is giving and what they take. In small groups it is infinitely harder for people to ignore their obligations to other people, or the fact that often the best way to help yourself is by helping others. So one way to stem the tide of demoralisation lies in rediscovering the importance of small groups as a source of civic virtues, and giving them some protection. At the heart of this is the family. The culture of individual rights has obscured the value of family ties and local community for many people. The most practical way to resist that culture may lie in strengthening family.

It is significant that one of our strongest findings is of the value of family and community ties in keeping ordinary people in control of their lives. In Bethnal Green those white families who coped best with the challenge of change were precisely the ones where such local ties ran like threads throughout their lives – and especially when incorporating family businesses. Indeed the family firm, a small business which relies heavily on family support and contacts through family and community networks, emerged for us as a working arrangement pre-eminent in enabling ordinary people to resist the corrosive effects of state control, and to bring the force of their private ties legitimately into the public domain. A family business stands steadfast against the twin dangers of state control and moral individualism.

These findings are important because in the East End over the centuries small family enterprises have been vital to the economic survival of the community. They are also the traditional way for minorities to settle here. Much formal local employment has been in large industrial or public concerns – as until recently in the docks. But in most communities – Huguenot and Jewish in the past, Bangladeshi more recently – it has been small family businesses that have eased the accommodation of new migrants, brokered roles for them in the neighbourhood and accumulated the capital which eventually allowed transition into mainstream employment. Whether you choose to regard the movement out from the East End of the businesses which have gone on to become national commercial giants – Tesco is a good example – as a gain (small business becomes big) or loss (departure from the local scene) is beside the point. This is how many newcomers have been able to make their initial contributions to British society, and earned their families' passage to respect. Ironically, given its failure to reflect most changes that have taken place in the area, small businesses still form the backbone of *EastEnders*.

This is relevant to the future of the Bangladeshis, as small businesses, pre-eminently restaurants, may be what stand between many in that community and an uncomfortable slide into the demoralised underclass of the inner-city poor. The underclass does not include many recent migrants because most new arrivals are still part of close family networks. They labour with and in order to support relatives, so even their work as employees possesses some of the same character as small family enterprises. The people who seem most at risk of slipping into underclass dependency in the coming years are those in the second or third generation, who share some of the cultural values and interests of white working-class youth and who may not have much community support to help them. Young Bangladeshis who are not lifted by education into the middle classes, and spurn the opportunities offered by existing businesses within the community, are prime candidates for this fate. Others, of course, may be in line for a worse one: becoming embroiled in a destructive brand of politically motivated religious extremism.

A more general defence against state-dependent forms of citizenship can, of course, be achieved by moving the administration of social supports back to local organisations, and where possible non-state groups.[7] Tariq Modood has described American political scientist Jeff Spinner-Halev's insight into the current liberal dilemma thus:

> While majority cultures are not homogeneous, there is indeed a growing mainstream that cuts across ethnicity and has an inclusive dynamic. This mainstream is individualistic, consumerist, materialist, and hedonistic and is shaped by a globalizing political economy, the media, and commercialized popular culture. This allows it to be pluralistic in terms of accommodating niche markets [and] lifestyle choices ... What it cannot accommodate so easily are minorities who *as groups* reject or are rejected by significant parts of this individualistically diverse mainstream.[8]

As the culture of rights has blossomed, central government has grown with it, around the proclamation that full equality is possible only when services are allocated strictly according to individual need. This argument has been shielded from proper scrutiny by the perception that it is protecting the interests of the most vulnerable. But perhaps the message to give now is that more *collective* rights and social capital are needed, to compensate for the growing concentration of state-managed *individual* social capital such as educational qualifications. Allowing more rights to groups means giving greater priority to individuals' obligations to each other. This is in the interests of incoming minorities just as much as it is of the indigenous white population. When the pursuit of personal rights is taken too far, then we all suffer. And what has happened in the East End over the last few decades illustrates, albeit in an extreme form, problems to which all who live in Britain are to some degree subject.

Appendix

Research Methods and Key Findings*

General ICS Style

To carry out this project we followed the social research techniques developed at the Institute of Community Studies (ICS) from the 1950s. These involve calling on a mixture of approaches in collating information. At the start of a project, facts and figures are gleaned from existing reports which relate to a chosen topic, in order to provide a general picture of what is already known or understood, and to see where there are gaps or contentious issues. Then a randomised sample survey is carried out among the relevant population to establish a reliable, broadly representative set of data concerning this subject. Following that a smaller sub-sample of respondents is interviewed in greater detail, often on more than one occasion. This is done to flesh out the survey findings and to make better sense of them.

This third stage of enquiry is particularly important to ICS researchers, who believe that most people understand their own lives better than any expert can. The job of a social researcher lies in pooling people's accounts in order to elicit the wider patterns of which they form a part. Researchers need to listen very carefully to what respondents have to say, and make an effort to see things through their eyes. Otherwise they will not be able to use the detailed discussions to throw light properly on survey statistics, and may fail to come up with an overall interpretation of the research topic which genuinely encompasses the views – and behaviour – of their subjects.

Clearly, the way in which informants for the more detailed study are picked is very important. Care has to be taken to find cases which both represent the larger sample reasonably and illuminate the key questions under examination. So selection of informants has to fit closely within the framework of survey findings. Often there will also be a need to find some additional, specialised informants (usually people with a very active or leading role within the area or process under study) to fill in gaps which are not covered by those randomly selected. But such respondents then have to be treated differently – that is as sources on particular issues rather than as ordinary members of the population under scrutiny.

---

*A more detailed account of this research project can be found on the Young Foundation website, www.youngfoundation.org.uk.

Progress of this Study

Our aim at the outset of this study was to repeat the 1953 enquiry that had led to *Family and Kinship in East London*. To that end, we planned a population survey in Bethnal Green to follow as far as possible the original questions and methods used in the 1950s. The main difference was that we did not conduct the survey stage ourselves, but contracted the work to a social and market research company, BJM Ltd. We did, however, design the interview questionnaire and participate in the interviewing process. A sample of adults living in wards corresponding to the old borough of Bethnal Green was picked at random from the electoral register in the autumn of 1992, and interviewed over the next few months. A total of 799 interviews were completed with people aged 18 or over, giving information not just for themselves but for all other members of their households too. In all this provided data on 2,565 people living in the 799 households, as well as on a number of categories of relatives living outside respondents' households. Altogether data on around 8,000 people was amassed.

Over the next few years, fifty-one of these respondents with children (thirty-three white and eighteen Bangladeshi) were interviewed more intensively, along the lines of the 'parents' sample in the original Bethnal Green study. In many cases more than one interview was carried out, and in several instances more than one family member was contacted. Much of the interviewing among Bangladeshi respondents was carried out by Bengali-speaking researchers. On top of this, additional informants were recruited among local teachers, youth workers (and club members), council officials and long-standing residents. Further, the scope of the study was extended beyond the old borough boundaries to take in the whole of Tower Hamlets. Because of the importance of understanding as much as possible about the family life of Bangladeshi residents, additional one-to-one interviews were conducted with Bangladeshi informants, mainly young women, over many months. Each of these informants contributed several hours of transcribed interviews to our overall research material.

Key Findings

On all the main demographic characteristics, the 1992 random sample corresponded very closely with 1991 census figures for Bethnal Green (and tolerably well for Tower Hamlets as a whole). The most striking difference to emerge between the 1992 sample and that of 1953 lay in the racial/ethnic composition. In 1953 there were few non-white people in Bethnal Green, and none recorded in the survey, but in 1992 only two-thirds (535) of the respondents described themselves as white, while over one in five (171) had been born in Bangladesh. The rest were divided mainly among Black African, Black Caribbean and other south Asians. Table A.1 gives the details, together with the figures for Tower Hamlets and Inner London taken from the 1991 census data.

Table A.1 **Ethnic origin of all respondents and for Tower Hamlets and Inner London in 1991 by percentage**

Ethnic origin (self-defined)	1992 Bethnal Green survey	1991 census for Tower Hamlets	1991 census for Inner London
White	67.0 (535)	64.4	74.4
Bangladeshi	21.4 (171)	22.9	2.8
Black Caribbean	2.6 (21)	3.6	7.0
Black African	2.8 (22)	2.4	4.4
Pakistani	1.5 (12)	0.7	1.2
Chinese	– (2)	1.1	1.1
Other groups	4.4 (35)	4.7	9.1
No response	– (1)	–	–

Note: 1992 survey respondent numbers in brackets.
Source for census data: *OPCS County Monitor: Inner London*, 1992.

However, the Bangladeshis had an even greater share of the resident population of our survey respondents' households. Quite a number of the white respondents lived alone, especially the elderly, but most Bangladeshis lived in large households (with a high ratio of children). As a result the Bangladeshi households in the survey accounted for 40 per cent of the total household residents against 48 per cent for whites. These findings showed us early on that the study could not simply compare the current white population of the area with that in the 1950s, but would need to focus on the two major communities.

These two communities differed greatly in their demographic structure, as shown in table A.2, which gives the age and sex of household members belonging to them.

Table A.2 **Age and sex of residents of white and Bangladeshi households by percentage**

	Sex		Age				Total number
Ethnic group	Male	Female	0–15	16–35	36–55	56+	
Bangladeshi	52	48	45	33	15	7	1,024
White	51	49	14	34	20	32	1,241

Family Life-stages

These differences between the two sectors are very germane to questions about family life, and we are hoping to produce a further report later which looks at how families in Bethnal Green now compare with those in the 1950s. However, for present purposes the most important thing to note is that the white community consists of two rather different components, in that many of its younger members are newcomers to the area who are following very different lifestyles from the existing white population. To explore this we divided respondents into four 'family life-stage' categories. The first of these (*Dependent*) contains childless adults (aged 18 and upwards) still living with their parents. The next (*Independent childless*) covers those who have left the parental home and are living by themselves, with friends, or with spouses/partners, but do not yet have any children. This category includes some elderly respondents.

The third category is *Parents*, meaning here those respondents of any age who are either co-resident with children (of any age) or who have children legally dependent on them (whether living with them or not). Finally there are *Family elders*. This refers to respondents who have grown-up children (or grandchildren) who are *not* living with them. When white respondents are sorted according to their place of birth, we find the pattern depicted in table A.3.

Table A.3 **Place of birth of white respondents, by family life-stage (by percentage)**

	Place of birth			
Life-stage	Tower Hamlets	Other London	Elsewhere	Total number
Dependent	71	22	7	41
Independent childless	25	21	54	204
Parent	52	27	21	146
Family elder	62	20	18	139
Total number	244	120	166	530[a]

a Full information available only for this number.

These figures show the way in which the population of Tower Hamlets has changed. Among parents and elders more than half of the respondents were born locally, and more than four out of five in London. Of the white elders, 41 per cent were born in Bethnal Green itself, which is approaching the level recorded in *Family and Kinship*. However, among the childless adults not living with parents, the majority are newcomers to the area. Barely a quarter come from within Tower Hamlets, and less from Bethnal Green, and more than half have come in from outside London.

Local Family Network Density

The differences between segments of the white population sharpen when we look at a wider range of kinship ties. White respondents were grouped according to the number of their close relatives living in the borough but outside their own household. We created three levels of local family network density: None (no local relatives), Some (that is, one or two) and Dense (three or more local kin). The distribution of results in table A.4 shows a clear discontinuity between parents and elders on one hand and the younger, non-family newcomers. In the fifties there would not have been this pattern, as even young adult childless people would have been locals, with plenty of siblings, parents and grandparents living nearby.

Table A.4 **Family life-stage vs. local family network density (white respondents; by percentage)**

Life-stage	Local family network density			
	None	*Some*	*Dense*	*Total number*
Childless	83	43	9	245
Parent	10	30	44	146
Family elder	7	27	47	139
Total number	177	198	155	530[a]

a Full information available only for this number.

An important aspect of this distribution is that relatively large numbers of younger people born in the area in the past have moved out – with more than half the children listed by older Bethnal Greeners now living outside London altogether. This departure of young East Enders, coupled with the arrival of young newcomers, means that the white sector of the population is the least engaged in family lifestyles. It is members of minority ethnic groups who contain the family-based element of the local community. Of these, we see from table A.5 that the Bangladeshis are the *most* family-centred sector of the population – with only one in twenty living in a 'non-family' life-stage – and overall the most different from the white residents.

Table A.5 **Life-stage profiles of respondents, by ethnic community group (by percentage, rounded)**

Life-stage	Whites	Other BME[a]	Bangladeshis
Dependent	8	22	18
Non-family	39	15	5
Parent	28	51	75
Elder	26	13	1[b]

a Black and minority ethnic
b Rare among Bangladeshis as grandparents tend to live with their children and grandchildren as part of a three-generation family household.

Racial Hostility

These demographic and family characteristics proved useful when it came to interpreting the pattern of hostility to newcomers. As explained in chapter 9, we divided white respondents into four groups according to the views they expressed relating to the settlement of Bangladeshis. These groupings are quite strongly and consistently associated with the individual and above all family/kinship status of respondents (see table A.6).

Table A.6 Association of racial hostility with personal and family characteristics (by percentage, rounded)

| | Attitude to Bangladeshis | | | |
	Hostile	Mixed	Positive	Indifferent
Overall responses	41	18	11	30
Respondent birthplace				
Bethnal Green	55	16	6	23
Other London	43	21	9	28
Elsewhere	27	16	17	40
Partner birthplace				
Bethnal Green	75	12	4	9
Other London	54	21	4	22
Elsewhere	34	18	14	34
Sex and age				
Male 18–34	25	17	21	37
Male 35–54	38	19	15	28
Male 55+	43	20	7	30
Female 18–34	30	19	11	40
Female 35–54	53	15	9	23
Female 55+	54	18	4	24
Family life-stage				
Childless	23	19	17	41
Parent	55	16	6	22
Family elder	59	18	4	19
Local family network density				
None	19	15	21	46
Some	40	27	7	27
Dense	70	10	3	17

Notes

Introduction: Outside the City Gates

1. Sanders, 1989, p. 91.
2. Gavron, 1995.
3. From an interview in 1995, quoted in Briggs, 2001, p. 7.

Chapter 1: Old Bethnal Green and New

1. Fishman, 1988, p. 144.
2. Palmer, 1989.
3. *Daily Mail*, 11 January 1906, quoted by Husbands, 1982, p. 12.
4. Thornbury, 1873.
5. Samuel, 1981.
6. Quoted in Booth, 1902, p. 181.
7. Husbands, 1982.
8. Young and Willmott, 1957, p. xvii.
9. Briggs, 2001, p. 131.
10. Gross, 2001, p. 132.
11. Platt, 1998.

Chapter 2: Settlement of the Bangladeshis

1. Figures given from the 1981 and 1991 Bangladesh census are from the Bangladesh Bureau of Statistics. Those given for dates 2000 or later are from World Bank/ CIA World Book Data, years 2000–2003.
2. Allen, 1905.
3. Gardner, 1995.

4. Only 11,000 (1 per cent) houses were built using cement and these are almost all in Sylhet town; 30 per cent are built of thin brick with a plaster covering; these are common for the rural Londoni households.
5. Gardner, 1995, p. 94.
6. Jones, 1986.
7. Anwar, 1979.
8. Adams, 1987.
9. Forman, 1989, p. 32.
10. Tinker, 1977, p. 166.
11. Young and Willmott, 1957; see also chapter 8, below.
12. Forman, 1989, p. 188.
13. See Wilson, 1994.
14. Forman, 1989, p. 54.
15. Ibid., p. 197.
16. Hugo Young, 1989, p. 111.
17. Bethnal Green & Stepney Trades Council, 1978; Leech, 1980.

Chapter 3: Spread and Conflict

1. We could not apply our 'family status' categories to census data, for while it contains information about household composition there is little about kinship ties. We therefore used age as an approximation.
2. This also illustrates a growing loss of control by parents: see Malone and Foster, 1994.
3. See also Sampson and Phillips, 1995.
4. Some commentators have felt, however, that 'Banglatown' itself might be too inward-looking. See Barker, 1998a, and Carey, 2004, pp. 29–32, on the reduction of racial incidents in Brick Lane.
5. See also Malone and Foster, 1994; Syal, 1994.
6. Wright, 2000. This is part of a national trend, though.
7. See, for example, Dennis et al., 2000, who argue that, by creating a concept of 'institutional racism' which officers can be deemed guilty of unconsciously, Macpherson has subjected the police to politicised intimidation.
8. When the figures appeared some authorities became suspicious that nationally there had been a 'white backlash' of 'perverse reporting'. See Prasad, 2001a.

Chapter 4: Bangladeshi Life in London

1. Storkey, 1994, pp. 38, 40, 42.
2. Based on 3 per cent anonymised records from 2001 census.
3. Ibid., and Storkey, 1994.
4. 1991 census information taken from Coleman and Salt, 1996, p. 195.
5. One of the unusual households consisted of a man and his son living together. This man's wife was living in Bangladesh but he described himself as married, not separated. In a similar case there was a young woman, living with her small son, whose husband was in Bangladesh; she was married but did not describe her husband as being part of the existing household. Then there were two households of siblings whose parents had died. Finally, one man lived in a flat with eight tenants; a married couple and their six children. His own wife and ten children were living in Bangladesh.
6. Murphy, 1996, p. 224.
7. And the average number of children 5.2. See Phillipson et al., 2000.
8. Berthoud, 1998; Brindle, 1996.
9. An increasingly common sentiment; see Younge, 2000.
10. And may be hostile to citizenship; see Jacobson, 1996.
11. Phillips, 1998.
12. See Buruma, 2002, for example.
13. Images are changing, though. See Bunting et al., 2001; Prasad, 2001b; Ballard, 2002.
14. For a general argument concerning patriarchy as a means of managing men, and the importance of illusions (or 'patriarchal theatre') in this, see Dench, 1996.
15. Islam, 1995.

Chapter 5: The New Individualism

1. Peter Sanders (1989) describes both the family-based systems of housing allocation (pp. 107–8) and the lack of interest in religion (pp. 97–8) in Bethnal Green at the beginning of the twentieth century.
2. See Melanie Phillips, 1999; Dench 1996, 2003b.
3. Young and Willmott, 1957, p. 49.
4. Ibid., p. 76.
5. Ibid., p. 33.
6. Young, 1954, p. 136.
7. Ibid., p. 141.
8. Jamieson, 1998, pp. 43–4.

9. Rathbone, 1924, p. 270.

10. Hansard, House of Commons, 8 March 1945 (second reading of the Family Allowances Act 1945), col. 2279.

11. Ibid., cols. 2325–6.

12. Mumford and Power, 2003.

13. Tower Hamlets Regeneration Strategy, 27 April 2005. Census data showed a figure of 21.8 per cent in 1991 (see Willmott, 1994, p. 32).

14. Young and Willmott, 1957, p. 4.

15. Giddens, 1992, p. 58.

16. Young and Willmott, 1957, p. 53.

Chapter 6: Work and Family

1. Young and Willmott, 1957, p. 95.

2. Ibid., p. 103.

3. For recent information about Indian restaurants in Brick Lane, see Carey, 2004.

4. Adams, 1987, p. 52.

5. Collingham, 2005, p. 230.

6. Adams, 1987, p. 52.

7. Carey, 2004.

8. See also Rhodes and Nabi, 1992.

9. Sweeney, 1993; Kosvinar, 2003.

10. Rates of social mobility and relevant government policy have been discussed extensively, for example recently in Reed and Robinson, 2005.

11. Hall, 2005.

Chapter 7: Education and Segregation

1. Both quotes are from Booth, 1902, p. 204.

2. Report of the Tower Hamlets Contract Services Directorate (date unknown).

3. Sproston and Nazroo, 2002.

4. Figures supplied by the Tower Hamlets Education and Community Service.

5. In 1998, Section 11 support was replaced by EMAG (Ethnic Minority Achievement Grant).

6. 'Attendance at School, 1996-7', in the minutes of Tower Hamlets Education Committee for 12 November 1997.

7. Booth, 1902, p. 223.

8. Mackinlay, 2003.
9. With 'anti-education culture' in particular groups taking the blame for their poor performance: see Sewell, 2002.
10. Young and Willmott, 1957, p. 147.
11. Information from Tower Hamlets Education Service.
12. Modood, 2005, p. 202.
13. Franek and Sinnott, 1994.
14. Although Irish people from the Republic of Ireland are not UK citizens, they are often regarded effectively as such.

Chapter 8: Whose Home?

1. Rose and Deakin, 1969.
2. See, for example, Willmott and Hutchinson, 1992, and Willmott, 1994, also Cattell, 1997.
3. Sanders, 1989, p. 107.
4. Young and Willmott, 1957, p. 23.
5. Ibid., p. 24.
6. Ibid., p. 197.
7. Power, 1999b.
8. Rustin, 1996. On top of this, commercial development in Spitalfields has seen a broader rise in rents: O'Neill, 1990; Monbiot, 1999.
9. Phillips, 1986, and Commission for Racial Equality, 1988.
10. The SDP, which had formed in 1981, amalgamated with the Liberals as the Liberal Democrats in 1988.
11. Bradford, 1984.
12. Bunting, 1993; Chaudhury and Travis, 1993; Chittenden and Syal, 1993; Driscoll, 1993; Pilkington, 1993.
13. The local LibDems were all-round losers, following repudiation by the party at national level after the by-election; White, 1993 and Wintour, 1993.
14. See also Dench 2003a, p. 238.
15. Following a wider revival of provisions for 'Sons and Daughters' in other London boroughs. See, for example, Goodall, 1994.

Chapter 9: Hostility to New Communities

1. Young and Willmott, 1986, p. xi (emphasis added).

2. See Berthoud, 1998, for example, among much research showing the poverty of Bangladeshis relative to other minority ethnic groups.
3. Worsley, 1957.
4. See, for example, the discussion by Chris Husbands (1982, p. 21), which describes anti-immigrant political positions in the East End as 'lacking political sophistication and implying very limited and often confused perception of social structure and a corresponding readiness to apportion blame in inappropriate directions'.
5. Burns, Hambleton and Hoggett, 1994.
6. Ibid., p. 236.
7. Furedi, 2001; see also Black and Prescott, 2000.
8. And indeed in many other studies, e.g. Rothon and Heath, 2003.
9. On such fraternalism, see Dench, 2003a, pp. 182–95.
10. As in, for example, Heath, Rothon and Jarvis, 2002.
11. Although very few responding parents did *not*, in fact, also have some children living locally, or other local kin.

Chapter 10: Promises and Betrayal

1. Young and Willmott, 1956b.
2. Discounting the 'invited' invasion by William of Orange in 1688.
3. Clarke, 1996, p. 200.
4. Young, 1940, pp. 3 and 32.
5. *East London Advertiser*, 9 February 1945.
6. The exchange was reported in the *East London Advertiser*, 9 August 1946.
7. Report in *East London Advertiser*, 6 December 1946. The phrase 'some of the first' presumably refers to the fact that many of the passengers would not be East Londoners.
8. Hennessy, 1992, p. 454.
9. Shils and Young, 1953, p. 77.
10. Shore, 2000.
11. Clarke, 1996, p. 125.
12. Ibid., p. 208.
13. *East London Advertiser*, 1 November 1946.
14. Ibid.
15. Quoted in Hennessy, 1992, p. 163.
16. *East London Advertiser*, 26 July 1946.
17. Forshaw and Abercrombie, 1943, Frontispiece.
18. Yelling, 1989.

19. Forshaw and Abercrombie, 1943, 77.
20. Ibid., pp. 79–83, 117–9.
21. Barnett, 1972.
22. Toynbee, 2001.
23. Dench, 1975, pp. 92–5.
24. Banton, 1955.
25. Foulser, 1960.
26. See also Dench, 1975, pp. 71–2.

Chapter 11: Managing Diversity

1. Barnett, 1972. Peter Hennessy (1992, p. 221) emphasises American concerns about the Cold War when discussing post-war US foreign policy, but agrees that the US was also critical of Britain's colonial policy.
2. Modood, 2005, p. 191.
3. Denham, 2004.
4. This probably a cultural universal (see Mauss, on the Gift). There are, however, specific national forms that attitudes take. See Law et al., 1994, on positive views towards contributory benefits among older Bangladeshis.
5. From an unpublished paper, 'Living on Labour', by Shariful Islam.
6. Burns, Hambleton and Hoggett, 1994, p. 77.
7. Ibid., p. 212.
8. Ibid., p. 217.
9. Ibid., p. 230.
10. Ibid., p. 235.
11. Ibid., p. 237.
12. Young and Willmott, 1986, p. 86.
13. Sawyer, 1998.
14. Burns, Hambleton and Hoggett, 1994, pp. 235, 242.
15. See also Dench, 2003a, p. 238, on 'honorary minorities'.
16. It is not clear from the statistics whether this refers only to people from the Republic of Ireland or includes those from Northern Ireland too.
17. Phillips, 1988.

Conclusion: Reclaiming Social Democracy

1. Presentation given by Ben Page, Market Opinion and Research International, to Commission for Racial Equality conference 'Building an Integrated society', 12 July 2005.
2. One influential part of the public debate was started by Wolfe and Klausen's article in the December 2000 issue of *Prospect* and continued over a number of later issues, most notably in the editor David Goodhart's own widely reported article of February 2004.
3. For example Denham, 2004.
4. Usefully described in the conclusion of Modood, 2005, pp. 201–5.
5. Hall, 2005, p. 155.
6. Dench, 2003a, chapter 3.
7. 'The social democracy of the 21st century must recover the decentrist, participatory strands in its own tradition' (Marquand, 2001). See also Young and Lemos, 1997; Barker, 1998b.
8. Modood, 2005, p. 179, (emphasis in original).

Glossary of Bengali Terms

allua-jallua Fisherman-farmer; used to describe a Sylheti caste, also used colloquially by Sylhetis to describe dysfunctional families.

bari Compound of homes built on one site and often sharing some facilities; usually the families are members of the same patrilineal kinship group.

burkha Head and face covering that also conceals the whole body.

farz A religious obligation for Muslims, for example the obligation to pray five times a day or to give *zakat*.

gushti Patrilineal lineage group.

haji One who has completed *hajj*.

hajj The pilgrimage to Mecca. The obligation to perform *hajj* once in a lifetime is one of the five pillars of Islam.

halal Pure, clean, ethical; in the case of meat, from animals that have been correctly slaughtered.

haram Forbidden or impure.

hijab Covering for a woman's head.

imam Officer in the mosque who leads prayers and devotions.

kare Area of land, just under one-third of an acre.

Khutbah (or *waz*) A religious sermon given by an imam in a mosque (our interpreter used the word *waz*).

kutcha (adj.) Describes housing built with bamboo/straw/mud walls, rather than solid walls.

Londoni British Bangladeshi, but also can be used for migrants living in other parts of the world, so a '*Londoni* family' would be a family with migrant members.

mama Mother's brother.

mullah Learned Muslim man; often a teacher in a mosque.

nabob An important or wealthy European in India in the past (Hindi equivalent is *nawab*).

paan Literally, the leaf of the betel tree; commonly describes such a leaf wrapped around a mixture of tobacco, betel nut, lime paste and other spices which are chewed as a mild stimulant.

ranir jamai Literally, Queen's son-in-law; a man arrived to marry and who has failed to find work.

ranir mehman Literally, Queen's guest; someone living on welfare payments.

salwar-kameez Trouser/long-shirt suit worn by women.

serang Port-based agent used by shipping companies for the hiring of sailors.

Sufi A Muslim adherent of Sufism, the first form of Islam established in south Asia.

taka Unit of Bangladeshi currency.

thana Administrative area in Bangladesh, usually containing many villages and some 200,000 people (Gardner, 1995).

Ummah Worldwide community of Muslims.

waz See *Khutbah*.

zakat One of the five pillars of enlightenment in Islam, the obligatory giving of a set proportion of income (traditionally 2.5 per cent) for charitable purposes.

zat Caste.

Bibliography

Aaronovitch, Sam, and Egan, Sue, 1991, *Change in Spitalfields: A Survey of Residents' Skills and Recommendations for Training*, London, South Bank Polytechnic (Local Economy Policy Unit)

Abbott, Rachel, 2005, *Social Housing Allocations and Family Networks*, London, Young Foundation

Ackroyd, Peter, 2002, *Albion: the Origins of the English Imagination*, London, Chatto & Windus

Adams, Caroline, 1987, *Across Seven Seas and Thirteen Rivers: Life Stories of Pioneer Sylhetti Settlers in Britain*, London, THAP Books

— 1994, *Approaches to Conflict Resolution in Tower Hamlets Schools and Youth Service*, London, Institute of Community Studies

Adams, Caroline, and Salvat, Gilli, 1993, *Them*, London, Docklands Forum Project

Ahmed, Akbar, 2001, 'Veiled truth', *Guardian*, 22 October

Aleinikoff, T. Alexander, and Klusmeyer, Douglas, 2002, *Citizenship Policies for an Age of Migration*, Washington, DC, Carnegie Endowment for International Peace

Ali, Monica, 2003, *Brick Lane*, London, Doubleday

Ali, Rushanara, 1997, 'Race and housing policy in the London Borough of Tower Hamlets', BA dissertation, Oxford University

Allen, B. C., 1905, *Assam District Gazetteer*, Vol. II, *Sylhet*, Calcutta, Caledonian Steam Printing Works

Ambrose, Peter, 2000, *A Drop in the Ocean*, Brighton, University of Brighton (Health and Social Policy Research Centre)

Anwar, Mohammad, 1979, *The Myth of Return*, London, Heinemann

Ballard, Jackie, 2002, 'Another kind of freedom', *Guardian*, 7 January

Ballard, Roger, and Kalra, Virinder Singh, 1994, *The Ethnic Dimension of the 1991 Census*, Manchester, University of Manchester Press

Bangladesh Bureau of Statistics, 1984, *Bangladesh Population Census 1991, District: Sylhet*, Dhaka, Bangladesh Bureau of Statistics

Banton, Michael, 1955, *The Coloured Quarter*, London, Cape

— 1999, 'Reporting on race', *Anthropology Today*, 15 (3), 1–3

Barker, Paul, 1998a, 'London is no place for this ghetto mentality', *Evening Standard*, 3 August

— 1998b, 'It takes more than bricks to build a real community', *Evening Standard*, 29 September

— 1999, 'Moving with the times', *Guardian*, 4 August

Barnett, Correlli, 1972, *The Collapse of British Power*, London, Methuen

— 2000, *The Verdict of Peace*, Basingstoke, Macmillan

— 2001, 'A decade that sold off the future', *Sunday Times*, 5 August

Barrett, Michèle, and McIntosh, Mary, 1982, *The Anti-Social Family*, London, Verso/ New Left Books

Basu, Anuradha, and Altinay, Eser, 2003, *Family and Work in Minority Ethnic Businesses*, Bristol, Policy Press

Beishon, Sharon, Modood, Tariq, and Virdee, Satnam, 1998, *Ethnic Minority Families*, London, Policy Studies Institute

Bermant, Chaim, 1975, *Point of Arrival*, London, Methuen

Berthoud, Richard, 1998, *Incomes of Ethnic Minorities*, Colchester, University of Essex, Institute for Social and Economic Research

Besant, Walter, 1912, *London*, London, Chatto & Windus

Bethnal Green and Stepney Trades Council, 1978, *Blood on the Streets*, London, Bethnal Green and Stepney Trades Council

Birch, J. G., 1931, *Limehouse through Five Centuries*, London, Sheldon Press

Black, Eben, and Prescott, Michael, 2000, 'Labour says the old are racist', *Sunday Times*, 16 April

Booth, Charles, 1902, *Life and Labour of the People in London*, first series, *Poverty*, vol. III, *Blocks of Buildings, Schools and Immigration*, London, Macmillan

Bradford, Ray, 1984, 'House Britons first!', *Bethnal Green Patriot*, supplement

Briggs, Asa, 2001, *Michael Young: Social Entrepreneur*, Basingstoke, Palgrave

Brindle, David, 1996, 'Blacks and Asians still at social disadvantage', *Guardian*, 8 August

Bunting, Madeleine, 1993, 'Island where equality is a loaded word', *Guardian*, 18 September

Bunting, Madeleine, Chrisafis, Angelique, and Soueif, Ahdaf, 2001, 'The other side of the veil', *Guardian Weekend*, 8 December

Burns, Danny, Hambleton, Robin, and Hoggett, Paul, 1994, *The Politics of Decentralisation*, Basingstoke, Macmillan

Buruma, Ian, 2002, 'Why Blunkett is right about curbing arranged marriages – even if it means stepping on extra-sensitive toes', *Guardian*, 12 February

Butler, Tim, and Rustin, Michael (eds), 1996, *Rising in the East? The Regeneration of East London*, London, Lawrence & Wishart

Cabinet Office Performance and Innovation Unit, 2002, *Ethnic Minorities and the Labour Market*, London, The Stationery Office

Carey, Sean, 2004, *Curry Capital: the Restaurant Sector in London's Brick Lane*, London, Institute of Community Studies

Carey, Sean, and Shukur, Abdus, 1985, 'A profile of the Bangladeshi community in east London', *New Community*, 12 (3), 405–17

Cass, Bettina, 1994, 'Citizenship, work and welfare: the dilemma for Australian women', *Social Politics*, 1 (1), 106–24

Cattell, Vicky, 1997, *London's Other River: People, Employment and Poverty in the Lea Valley*, London, Middlesex University, Social Policy Research Centre

Cattell, Vicky, and Evans, Mel, 1999, *Neighbourhood Images in East London*, York, Joseph Rowntree Foundation

Chaudhary, Vivek, and Travis, Alan, 1993, 'Brothers in arms fight for the streets', *Guardian*, 16 October

Chittenden, Maurice, and Syal, Rajeev, 1993, 'Race-attack gangs fuel fears of street wars', *Sunday Times*, 12 September

Choudhury, Yousuf, 1993, *The Roots and Tales of Bangladeshi Settlers*, Birmingham, Sylhet Social History Group

Clark, Laura, 2003, 'Asian pupils pulling ahead of whites in exam success', *Daily Mail*, 21 February

Clarke, Colin, Peach, Ceri, and Vertovec, Steven (eds), 1990, *South Asians Overseas*, Cambridge, Cambridge University Press

Clarke, Peter, 1996, *Hope and Glory: Britain 1900–1990*, London, Allen Lane

Coleman, David, 1982, *Demography of Immigrants and Minority Groups in the United Kingdom*, London, Academic Press

Coleman, David, and Salt, John (eds), 1996, *Ethnicity in the Census*, vol. I, *Demographic Characteristics of the Ethnic Minority Populations*, London, HMSO

Collingham, Lizzie, 2005, *Curry: a Biography*, London, Chatto & Windus

Commission for Racial Equality, 1979, *Brick Lane and Beyond: an Inquiry into Racial Strife and Violence in Tower Hamlets*, London, CRE

— 1988, *Homelessness and Discrimination: Report of a Formal Investigation by the CRE into the Allocation of Housing by the London Borough of Tower Hamlets*, London, CRE

Cooper, Jeremy, and Qureshi, Tarek, 1993, *Through Patterns not Our Own*, London, University of East London

Cornwell, Jocelyn, 1984, *Hard-Earned Lives*, London, Tavistock

Cross, Malcolm, and Keith, Michael, 1993, *Racism, the City and the State*, London, Routledge

Crowther, M. A., 1982, 'Family responsibility and state responsibility in Britain before the welfare state', *Historical Journal*, 25 (1), 131–45

Cullingworth Committee, 1969, *Council Housing: Purpose, Procedures and Priorities*, London, HMSO

Cunningham, John, 1999, 'Oh, what a lovely wharf', *Guardian*, 28 July

Curtis, S. E., and Ogden, P. E., 1986, 'Bangladeshis in London: a challenge to welfare', *Revue Européenne des Migrations Internationales*, 2 (3), 135–50

Davies, Nick, 1998, *Dark Heart: the Shocking Truth about Hidden Britain*, London, Vintage

Dench, Geoff, 1975, *Maltese in London: a Case Study in the Erosion of Ethnic Consciousness*, London, Routledge & Kegan Paul

— 1996, *Transforming Men*, New Brunswick, NJ, Transaction Books

— 2003a, *Minorities in the Open Society*, New Brunswick, NJ, Transaction Books

— 2003b, *Rediscovering Family*, London, Hera

Dench, Geoff, and Ogg, Jim, 2002, *Grandparenting in Britain*, London, Institute of Community Studies

Denham, John, 2004, 'The fairness code', *Prospect*, 99 (June), 28–33

Dennis, Norman, Erdos, George, and al-Shahi, Ahmed, 2000, *Racist Murder and Pressure Group Politics*, London, Institute for the Study of Civil Society

Dhondy, Farrukh, 1976, *East End at Your Feet*, Basingstoke, Macmillan

Donald, James, and Rattansi, Ali, 1992, *Race, Culture and Difference*, London, Sage

Downes, David, 1989, *Crime and the City: Essays in Memory of John Barron Mays*, Basingstoke, Macmillan

Driscoll, Margarette, 1993, 'Hotbed of hate', *Sunday Times*, 19 September

Duffy, Patrick, 1979, *The Employment and Training Needs of the Bengali Community in Tower Hamlets*, London, Commission for Racial Equality/Manpower Services Commission

Eade, John, 1989, *The Politics of Community: the Bangladeshi Community in East London*, Aldershot, Avebury

— 1990a, 'Bangladeshi community organisation and leadership in Tower Hamlets, east London', in Clarke, Peach and Vertovec (eds), 317–30

— 1990b, 'Nationalism and the quest for authenticity: the Bangladeshis in Tower Hamlets', *New Community*, 16 (4), 493–503

Eade, John, Vamplew, Clive, and Peach, Ceri, 1996, 'The Bangladeshis: the encapsulated community', in Ceri Peach (ed.), *Ethnicity in the 1991 Census*, Vol. II, *The Ethnic Minority Populations of Great Britain*, London, HMSO, 150–60

Eade, John, and Zaman, H., 1994, *Voices from Educationally Successful Bangladeshis*, London, Roehampton Institute (Centre for Bangladeshi Studies)

Edsall, Thomas Byrne, and Edsall, Mary D., 1992, *Chain Reaction: the Impact of Race, Rights and Taxes on American Politics*, New York, W. W. Norton

Erens, Bob, 1993, *The Residents of Bethnal Green: their Characteristics and Views*, London, Social and Community Planning Research

Evans, Kathy, 1994, 'Radical time-bomb under British Islam', *Guardian*, 7 February

Faruk, A., and Fenton, M., 1995, *Living in Bethnal Green*, London, South Bank University

Federation of Bangladeshi Youth Organisations, 1984, *Health Report*, London, Health Education Council

Field, Frank, 1998, 'A hand-up or a put-down for the poor?', *New Statesman* 27 November

Fishman, William, 1981, *The Streets of East London*, London, Duckworth

— 1988, *East End 1888*, London, Duckworth

Forman, Charlie, 1989, *Spitalfields: a Battle for Land*, London, Hilary Shipman

Forrest, Ray, and Murie, Alan, 1988, *Selling the Welfare State*, London, Routledge

Forshaw, J. H., and Abercrombie, P., 1943, *County of London Plan*, London, Macmillan

Foster, Janet, 1990, *Villains: Crime and Community in the Inner City*, London, Routledge

Foulser, George, 1960, 'Cablestrasse', *Observer*, 28 August

Franek, Hania, and Sinnott, John, 1994, 'Admissions and transfers to secondary schools', report by Tower Hamlets Education Department

Freedland, Jonathan, 2005, *Jacob's Gift*, London, Hamish Hamilton

Fukuyama, Francis, 1999, *The Great Disruption: Human Nature and the Reconstitution of Social Order*, London, Profile

Furedi, Frank, 2001, 'British racism: a new original sin', *Spiked-online*, www.spiked-online.com/Articles/00000002D092.htm

Gardner, Katy, 1991, *Songs at the River's Edge: Stories from a Bangladeshi Village*, London, Virago

— 1995, *Global Migrants, Local Lives: Travel and Transformation in Rural Bangladesh*, Oxford, Clarendon Press

Gardner, Katy, and Shukur, Abdus, 1994, 'I'm Bengali, I'm Asian, and I'm Living Here: the changing identity of British Bengalis', in Roger Ballard (ed.), *Desh Pardesh: the South Asian Presence in Britain*, London, Hurst, 142–64

Gartner, Lloyd Philip, 1960, *The Jewish Immigrant in England, 1870–1914*, London, Allen & Unwin

Gavron, Kate, 1995, 'Embracing new communities', in Geoff Dench, Tony Flower and Kate Gavron (eds), *Young at Eighty*, Manchester, Carcanet

— 1996, 'Du mariage arrangé au mariage d'amour', *Terrain*, 17 (September), 15–26

— 1997, 'Migrants to citizens: changing orientations among Bangladeshis of Tower Hamlets, London', PhD thesis, London School of Economics

Gershuny, J., Jones, S., and Godwin, M., 1989, *The Allocation of Time within the Household*, London, Unilever Research

Giddens, Anthony, 1990, *Modernity and Self-identity*, Cambridge, Polity Press

— 1992, *The Transformation of Intimacy: Sexuality, Love and Eroticism in Modern Societies*, Cambridge, Polity Press

Gillborn, David, Green, Anthony, and Youdell, Deborah, 1996, *Underachievement among White Secondary School Students in Tower Hamlets*, London, University of London, Institute of Education

Glass, Ruth, 1964, *London: Aspects of Change*, London, MacGibbon & Kee

Goldenberg, Suzanne, 1996, 'Bangladeshi Britons keep lifeline home', *Guardian*, 20 February

Goldthorpe, John, 1995, 'The service class revisited', in T. Butler and M. Savage (eds), *Social Change and the Middle Classes*, London, UCL Press, 220–38

— 2002, 'Globalisation and social class', *West European Politics*, 25 (3), 1–28

Goodall, Chris, 1994, 'Sons and Daughters homes boost: new deal for kids of council tenants', *Islington Gazette*, 5 May

Goodhart, David, 2004, 'Too diverse?', *Prospect*, 95 (February), 30–37

Gordon, Paul and Klug, Francesca, 1985, *British Immigration Control: a Brief Guide*, London, Runnymede Trust

Gross, John, 2001, *A Double Thread: a Childhood in Mile End and Beyond*, London, Chatto & Windus

Hall, Tarquin, 2005, *Salaam Brick Lane: a Year in the New East End*, London, John Murray

Harris, Rosemary, and Robins, David, 1997, 'A death in the ghetto', *Prospect* (July), 48–54

Heath, Anthony, and Payne, Chris, 2000, 'Social mobility', in A. H. Halsey and Josephine Webb (eds), *Twentieth-century British Social Trends*, Basingstoke, Macmillan, 254–78

Heath, Anthony, Rothon, Catherine, and Jarvis, Lindsey, 2002, 'English to the core?', in Alison Park, John Curtice, Katarina Thomson, Lindsey Jarvis and Catherine Bromley (eds), *British Social Attitudes: the 19th Report*, London, Sage, 169–84

Henderson, Jeffrey, and Karn, Valerie, 1987, *Race, Class and State Housing*, Aldershot, Gower

Hennessy, Peter, 1992, *Never Again: Britain 1945–51*, London, Cape

Herbert, Alicia, 1996, *Credit Use and Ethnic Minorities*, London, Policy Studies Institute

Hewett, Gary, and Adams, Mark, 1994, *Tower Hamlets: the Race for Power*, London, Tower Hamlets Homeless Families Campaign

Hill, Stephen, 1977, *The Dockers: Class and Tradition in London*, London, Heinemann Educational

Hiro, Dilip, 1991, *Black British, White British*, London, Grafton

Hobbs, Dick, 1988, *Doing the Business*, Oxford, Clarendon Press

Hobsbawm, Eric, 1997, 'To see the future, look at the past', *Guardian*, 7 June

Holmes, Colin, 1979, *Anti-Semitism in British Society*, London, Edward Arnold

Honeyford, Ray, 1988, *Integration or Disintegration? Towards a Non-racist Society*, London, Claridge Press

House of Commons, Home Affairs Committee, 1987, *Bangladeshis in Britain*, London, HMSO

Husbands, Christopher, 1982, 'East End racism, 1900–1980', *London Journal*, 8 (1), 3–26

Hyndman, S. J., 1990, *Housing and Health amongst British Bengalis in Tower Hamlets*, London, Queen Mary & Westfield College

Iganski, Paul, and Payne, Geoff, 1996, 'Declining racial disadvantage in the British labour market', *Ethnic and Racial Studies*, 19 (1), 113–34

Islam, Shariful, 1995, *A Generation in Limbo*, London, Institute of Community Studies

Islam, Shariful, Croucher, Ray, and O'Farrell, Mary, 1996, *Paan Chewing in Tower Hamlets, London*, London, Tower Hamlets Health Strategy Group

Jacobson, David, 1996, *Rights Across Borders: Immigration and the Decline of Citizenship*, Baltimore, Johns Hopkins University Press

Jamieson, Lynn, 1998, *Intimacy: Personal Relationships in Modern Societies*, Cambridge, Polity Press

Jenkins, Simon, 1998, 'Towering strength of the new East End', *Evening Standard*, 6 March

Johnson, Paul, 1987, *A History of the Jews*, London, Weidenfeld & Nicolson

Jones, Dan, 1986, *Tea and Justice: British Tea Companies and the Tea Workers of Bangladesh*, London, Bangladesh International Action Group

Jones, Trevor, 1993, *Britain's Ethnic Minorities*, London, Policy Studies Institute

Joshi, Heather, 2000, 'Production, reproduction and education: women, children and work in contemporary Britain', Professorial Lecture, London University, Institute of Education, October

Karn, Valerie, and Stafford, Bruce, 1990, *Housing Allocations: Report of a Survey of Local Authorities in England and Wales*, London, Institute of Housing

Kerrigan, Colm, 1982, *A History of Tower Hamlets*, London, London Borough of Tower Hamlets

Kettle, Martin, and Hodges, Lucy, 1982, *Uprising! The Police, the People and the Riots in Britain's Cities*, London, Pan

Kipling, Rudyard, 1998, *Best Short Stories*, London, Wordsworth Editions

Kosvinar, T., 2003, 'The gun gangs of curry mile', *Evening Standard*, 10 February

Kraemer, Sebastian, and Roberts, Jane, 1996, *The Politics of Attachment*, London, Free Association Books

Krywko, J., 1995, *A Workforce to Reflect the Community*, London, Borough of Tower Hamlets Personnel Department

Kyambi, Sarah, 2005, *Beyond Black and White: Mapping New Immigrant Communities*, London, Institute of Public Policy Research

Langley, Charles, 1999, 'A fitting tribute, at last', *Evening Standard*, 6 May

Law, Ian, Karmani, Alyas, Hylton, Carl, and Deacon, Alan, 1994, 'The effect of ethnicity on claiming benefits: evidence from Chinese and Bangladeshi communities', *Benefits*, 9 (January), 7–11

Leech, Kenneth, 1980, *Brick Lane 1978: the Events and their Significance*, Birmingham, AFFOR

Leech, Kenneth, and Amin, Kaushika, 1988, 'A new underclass?', *Poverty*, 70, 11–14

Lemos, Gerard, 2000, *Racial Harassment: Action on the Ground*, London, Lemos & Crane

Local Economy Policy Unit, 1995, *Living in Tower Hamlets*, London, South Bank University

Local Goverment Ombudsman, 1993, *Report on Investigation against London Borough of Tower Hamlets*, London, Local Government Ombudsman Commission for Local Administration in England

London Research Centre, 1970–, *Annual Abstract of Statistics of Greater London*, London, London Research Centre

— 1994, *Housing needs in London*, London, London Planning Advisory Committee

— 1997, *Focus on London*, London, London Research Centre

Mackinlay, Rob, 2003, 'East End's schools are top of the class', *East London Advertiser*, 6 February

Malik, Kenan, 2002, *The Real Value of Diversity*, London, Commission for Racial Equality: www.cre.gov.uk/pubs/connections/conn_02wi_diversity.html

Malone, Andrew, and Foster, Howard, 1994, 'Asian youths rebel against good image', *Sunday Times*, 21 August

Marquand, David, 2001, 'The breath of renewal', *Guardian*, 20 March

Mauss, Marcel, 1990, *The Gift: the form and reason for exchange in archaic societies*, (translation by W. D. Hall), London, Routledge

Modood, Tariq, 1992, *Not Easy being British*, London, Runnymede Trust

— 2003, 'Muslims and the politics of difference', *Political Quarterly*, 74 (1), 100–15; simultaneously published in Sarah Spencer (ed.), *The Politics of Migration*, Oxford, Blackwell

— 2005, *Multicultural Politics: Racism, Ethnicity and Muslims in Britain*, Edinburgh, Edinburgh University Press

Modood, Tariq, Berthoud, Richard, Lakey, Jane, Nazroo, James, Smith, Patten, Virdee, Satnam, and Beishon, Sharon, 1997, *Ethnic Minorities in Britain: Diversity and Disadvantage*, London, Policy Studies Institute

Monbiot, George, 1999, 'Power of the pound fans fires of hate', *Guardian*, 29 April

Morrison, Arthur, 1896, *The Child of the Jago*, London, Methuen

Mumford, Katharine, and Power, Anne, 2003, *East Enders: Family and Community in East London*, Bristol, Policy Press

Murphy, Mike, 1996, 'Household and family structure among ethnic minority groups', in Coleman and Salt (eds), 213–42

Murphy, Orla, 2000, *Findings of an Audit of Organisations Working on Racial Harassment in Tower Hamlets*, London, Tower Hamlets Racial Harassment Consortium

Myers, Norma, 1995, 'The black poor of London: initiatives of eastern seamen in the eighteenth and nineteenth centuries', in Diane Frost (ed.), *Ethnic Labour and British Imperial Trade: a History of Ethnic Seafarers in the UK*, London, Frank Cass, 7–21

Nazroo, James, 1997, *The Health of Britain's Ethnic Minorities*, London, Policy Studies Institute

Neighbourhood Initiatives Foundation, 1996, *Neighbourhood Think Tank Pilot Scheme: Teviot Estate, London E14*, Telford, Neighbourhood Initiatives Foundation

Office for National Statistics, 1996, *Social Focus on Ethnic Minorities*, London, HMSO

Ofsted, 1994, *Educational Support for Minority Ethnic Communities*, London, HMSO

O'Neill, Gilda, 1999, *My East End: a History of Cockney London*, London, Viking

— 2003, *Our Street: East End Life in the Second World War*, London, Viking

O'Neill, Sean, 1990, 'Battle cries in Banglatown', *Guardian*, 5 June

Orwell, George, 1937, *The Road to Wigan Pier*, London, Gollancz

Owen, David, 1992, *Ethnic Minorities in Great Britain*, Coventry, University of Warwick

— 1994, *Ethnic Minority Women and the Labour Market*, Manchester, Equal Opportunities Commission

Palmer, Alan, 1989, *The East End*, London, John Murray

Park, Robert E., and Miller, Herbert A., 1921, *Old World Traits Transplanted*, New York, Harper & Bros.

Parker, Tony, 1983, *The People of Providence*, London, Hutchinson

Peach, Ceri, 1990, 'Estimating the growth of the Bangladeshi population of Great Britain', *New Community*, 16 (4), 481–91

Pepinster, Catherine, 1995, 'Havens may become ghettoes', *Independent on Sunday*, 18 June

Percy, Andrew, 1998, *Ethnicity and Victimisation: Findings from the 1996 British Crime Survey*, London, Home Office Research and Statistics Directorate

Phillips, Deborah, 1986, *What Price Equality? A Report on the Allocation of GLC Housing in Tower Hamlets*, London, GLC

— 1988, 'Race and housing in London's East End: continuity and change', *New Community*, 14 (3), 356–69

Phillips, Melanie, 1998, 'We should shut down the race industry', *Sunday Times*, 20 December

— 1999, 'Treasury cold hearts target the widows', *Sunday Times*, 23 May

— 2001, 'Class revolt', *Sunday Times*, 17 June

— 2002, 'How "equality" is wrecking our schools', *Daily Mail*, 15 July

Phillips, Mike, 1999, 'Ethnicities', *Guardian*, 10 April

Phillipson, Chris, Alhaq, Ermadad, Ullah, Saheed, and Ogg, Jim, 2000, 'Bangladeshi families in Bethnal Green', in Anthony M. Warnes, Lorna Warren and Michael Nolan (eds), *Care Services for Later Life*, London, Jessica Kingsley, 273–90

Phillipson, C., Bernard, M., Phillips, J., and Ogg, J., 2001, *The Family and Community Life of Older People*, London, Routledge

Pilkington, Edward, 1993, 'Bark of the dogs of war', *Guardian*, 16 September

Platt, Jennifer, 1971, *Social Research in Bethnal Green*, London, Macmillan

Platt, Steve, 1998, 'Spirit of '68', *Guardian*, 2 December

Porter, Roy, 1994, *London: a Social History*, London, Hamish Hamilton

Power, Anne, 1987, *Property before People*, London, Allen & Unwin

— 1999a, 'Pool of resources', *Guardian*, 3 February

— 1999b, *Estates on the Edge: the Social Consequences of Mass Housing in Northern Europe*, Basingstoke, Macmillan

Prasad, Raekha, 2001a, 'Whites in "backlash" over race attacks', *Guardian*, 11 May

— 2001b, 'Cover story', *Guardian*, 5 November

Prescott-Clarke, Patricia, Allen, Patrick, and Morrissey, Catrin, 1988, *Queuing for Housing: a Study of Council House Waiting Lists*, London, HMSO

Prescott-Clarke, Patricia, Clemens, Samantha, and Park, Alison, 1994, *Routes into Local Authority Housing*, London, HMSO

Qureshi, Tarek, Berridge, David, and Wenman, Helen, 2000, *Where to Turn? Family Support for South Asian Communities*, London, National Children's Bureau

Ratcliffe, Peter, 1995, ' "Race", housing and the city', in N. Jewson and S. MacGregor (eds), *Transforming Cities: New Spatial Divisions and Social Transformation*, 1995 BSA annual conference volume, London, Routledge, 87–99

Rathbone, Eleanor, 1924, *The Disinherited Family*, London, Edward Arnold

Reed, Jodie, and Robinson, Peter, 2005, 'From social mobility to equal life chances: maintaining the momentum', in Nick Pearce and Will Paxton (eds), *Social Justice: Building a Fairer Britain*, London, Politico's, 282–300

Rhodes, Chris, and Nabi, Nurun, 1992, 'Brick Lane: a village economy in the shadow of the City?', in Leslie Budd and Sam Whimster (eds), *Global Finance and Urban Living*, London, Routledge, 333–52

Rix, Vikki, 1996, 'Industrial decline, economic restructuring and social exclusion in London east, 1980s and 1990s', *Rising East*, 1 (1), 118–40

Robb, J. H., 1954, *Working-class Anti-Semite*, London, Tavistock

Robins, David, 1991, *Family and Community in East London*, London, Institute of Community Studies

— 1992, *Tarnished Vision: Crime and Conflict in the Inner City*, Oxford, Oxford University Press

Rose, E. J. B., and Deakin, Nicholas, 1969, *Colour and Citizenship*, Oxford, Oxford University Press

Rothon, Catherine, and Heath, Anthony, 2003, 'Trends in racial prejudice', in Alison Park, John Curtice, Katarina Thomson, Lindsey Jarvis and Catherine Bromley (eds), *British Social Attitudes: Continuity and Change over Two Decades*, British Social Attitudes series no. 20, London, Sage, 189–214

Rowe, Kathleen Susan, 1995, 'Conflict resolution at the community level: initiatives and strategies in the London Borough of Tower Hamlets', BA dissertation, University of Bradford

Runnymede Trust, 1993, *Neither Unique nor Typical: the Context of Race Relations in the London Borough of Tower Hamlets*, London, Runnymede Trust

Rustin, Mike, 1996, 'Perspectives on east London', in M. Rustin (ed.), *Rising in the East: the Regeneration of East London*, London, Lawrence & Wishart, 1–19

Ryle, Sarah, 1997, 'All this could be yours', *Guardian*, 8 November

Saggar, Shamit, 1991, *Race and Public Policy*, Aldershot, Avebury

— 1999, 'Where the black vote goes', *Guardian*, 25 November

Sampson, Alice, and Phillips, Coretta, 1992, 'Multiple victimisation: racial attacks on an east London estate', Crime Prevention Unit Series Paper 36, London, Home Office

— 1995, 'Reducing repeat racial victimisation on an east London estate', Crime Prevention Unit Series Paper 67, London, Home Office

Samuel, Raphael, 1981, *East End Underworld: Chapters in the Life of Arthur Harding*, London, Routledge

Sanders, Peter, 1989, *The Simple Annals: the History of an Essex and East End family*, Gloucester, Allan Sutton

Sawyer, Patrick, 1998, 'Families in bomb danger have never heard of Blitz', *Evening Standard*, 4 August

Seabrook, Jeremy, 2001, 'The making of a fanatic', *Guardian*, 20 December

— 2003, 'No one asked Blackburn's people what they wanted', *Guardian*, 30 December

Sewell, Tony, 2002, 'The race challenge', *Sunday Times*, 15 December

Shaikh, Muksood, 1995, *Substance Use: a Needs Assessment of the Young Bengali Community in Tower Hamlets*, London, Asian Drugs Project

Shils, Edward, and Young, Michael, 1953, 'The meaning of the coronation', *British Journal of Sociology*, 3 (2), 63–81

Shore, Peter, 2000, 'Traitors to their nation', *Guardian*, 28 November

Short, Eileen, 1998, 'Mother courage', *Guardian*, 2 September

Sinnott, John, 1995, *Living in Tower Hamlets: a Survey of the Attitudes of Secondary School Pupils*, London, Tower Hamlets Education Strategy Group

Sly, Frances, 1995, 'Ethnic groups and the labour market: analyses from the spring 1994 Labour Force Survey', *Employment Gazette*, June, 251–62

Smith, David, and Tomlinson, Sally, 1989, *The School Effect: a Study of Multiracial Comprehensives*, London, Policy Studies Institute

Smith, Teresa, 1989, *Politics of Race and Residence*, Cambridge, Polity Press

Sofer, Anne, Klein, Lesley, and Porter, Judy, 1996, 'Columbia Primary School, Tower Hamlets, London', in National Commission on Education (ed.), *Success against the Odds: Effective Schools in Disadvantaged Areas*, London, Routledge, 91–112

Spencer, A. Benjamin, and Hough, Michael, 2000, *Policing Diversity: Lessons from Lambeth*, London, Home Office Policing and Reducing Crime Unit

Spinner-Halev, Jeff, 2000, *Surviving Diversity: Religion and Democratic Citizenship*, Baltimore, Johns Hopkins University Press

Sproston, Kerry and Nazroo, James (eds.), 2002, *Ethnic Minority Psychiatric Illness Rates in the Community (EMPIRIC) – Quantitative Report*, London: The Stationery Office

Stedman Jones, Gareth, 1971, *Outcast London: a Study in the Relationship between Classes in Victorian Society*, Oxford, Clarendon Press

Steven, Stewart, 1995, 'The betrayed', *Evening Standard*, 9 January

Storkey, Marian, 1994, *London's Ethnic Minorities*, London, London Research Centre

Sweeney, John, 1993, 'East End boys', *Observer Magazine*, 5 December

Syal, Rajeev, 1994, 'The violence that breeds violence', *Sunday Times*, 5 June

Taylor, Diane, 2002, 'Being there', *Guardian*, 6 August

Taylor, Laurie, 2000, 'Relatively successful', *Guardian Society*, 19 July

Thompson, E. P., 1974, *The Making of the English Working Class*, Harmondsworth, Pelican

Thornbury, Walter, 1873, *Old and New London: a Narrative of its History, its People and its Places*, London, Cassell, Peter & Galpin

Tinker, H., 1977, *The Banyan Tree: Overseas Emigrants from India, Pakistan and Bangladesh*, Oxford, Oxford University Press

Tomlinson, Sally, and Hutchinson, Sarah, 1991, *Bangladeshi Parents and Education in Tower Hamlets*, London, Advisory Centre for Education

Tower Hamlets, 1984/5, *Housing Strategy Statement and HIP Bid*, London, London Borough of Tower Hamlets

Tower Hamlets (Education & Community Services), 1995, *An Analysis of the 1995 London Reading Test*, London, London Borough of Tower Hamlets

— 1996, *Ethnic Background of Pupils in Tower Hamlets*, London, London Borough of Tower Hamlets

Tower Hamlets Homeless Families Campaign, 1993, *Tower Hamlets: the Race for Power (Part 1)*, London, THHFC

Toynbee, Polly, 2001, 'Keep God out of class', *Guardian*, 9 November

Travis, Alan, 2001, 'Yawning gulf that spawned inner city riots', *Guardian*, 11 December

Troyna, Barry and Hatcher, Richard, 1992, *Racism in Children's Lives*, London, Routledge

Ward, Robin, and Jenkins, Richard, 1984, *Ethnic Communities in Business: Strategies for Economic Survival*, Cambridge, Cambridge University Press

White, Cynthia L., 1989, *Small Businesses in Spitalfields*, London, City of London Polytechnic (Ethnic Minority Business Development Unit)

White, Michael, 1993, 'What took them so long?', *Guardian*, 18 September

Whyatt, Anna, 1997, 'Thames Gateway London in the millennium', *Rising East*, 1 (1), 38–58

Widgery, David, 1991, *Some Lives*, London, Sinclair-Stevenson

Willmott, Peter, 1966, *Adolescent Boys of East London*, London, Routledge & Kegan Paul

— 1994 (ed.), *Urban Trends II*, London, Policy Studies Institute

Willmott, Peter and Hutchinson, Robert, 1992, *Urban Trends I*, London, Policy Studies Institute

Willmott, Phyllis, 1999, *Bethnal Green Journal, 1954–55*, London, Institute of Community Studies/The Future Foundation

Wilson, Wendy, 1994, 'Local authorities' duties to the homeless', research paper 94/65, London, House of Commons Library, Education and Social Services Section

Wilson, William Julius, 1996, *When Work Disappears: the World of the New Urban Poor*, New York, Knopf

Wintour, Patrick, 1993, 'Tower Hamlets councillors "pandered to racism"', *Guardian*, 17 December

Wolfe, Alan, and Klausen, Jytte, 2000, 'Other people', *Prospect*, 58 (December), 28–33

Worsley, Peter, 1957, *The Trumpet Shall Sound: a Study of Cargo Cults in Melanesia*, London, McGibbon & Kee

Wright, Stephen, 2000, 'Soaring numbers of whites become race crime victims', *Daily Mail*, 13 October

Xavier, Jane, 1997a, *Staff Audit*, London, Borough of Tower Hamlets Equalities and Personnel Department

— 1997b, *Census Research Report*, London, Tower Hamlets Corporate Policy and Equalities Division

Yelling, James Alfred, 1989, 'The Origins of British Redevelopment Areas', *Planning Perspectives*, 3, 282–96

Young, Hugo, 1989, *One of Us: a biography of Margaret Thatcher*, London, Macmillan

Young, Ken, and Connelly, Naomi, 1992, *Policy and Practice in the Multi-racial City*, London, Policy Studies Institute

Young, Michael, 1940, *London under Bombing*, London, Political and Economic Planning

— 1948, *Small Man, Big World: a Discussion of Socialist Democracy*, London, Labour Party Research Department

— 1954, 'The planners and the planned: the family', *Journal of Town Planning Institute*, 40 (6), 134–42

— 1958, *The Rise of the Meritocracy*, London, Thames & Hudson

Young, Michael, and Lemos, Gerard, 1997, 'Roots of revival', *Guardian*, 19 March

Young, Michael, and Willmott, Peter, 1956a, 'Social grading by manual workers', *British Journal of Sociology*, 7 (4), 337–45

— 1956b, 'Jobs and social standing', *Guardian*, 29 December

— 1957, *Family and Kinship in East London*, London, Routledge & Kegan Paul

— 1973, *The Symmetrical Family*, London, Routledge & Kegan Paul

— 1986, *Family and Kinship in East London*, revised edn, Harmondsworth, Penguin

Younge, Gary, 1999, 'Britain bites the hand that feeds it', *Guardian*, 11 August

— 2000, 'Asians fly the flag for traditional family values', *Guardian*, 18 December

Zijderveld, Anton, 1999, *The Waning of the Welfare State*, New Brunswick, NJ, Transaction Books

Index